INVISIBLE
COUNTRY

The Charles and Joy Staples South West Region Publications Fund was established in 1984 on the basis of a generous donation to The University of Western Australia by Charles and Joy Staples.

The purpose of the Fund is to highlight all aspects of the South West region of Western Australia, a geographical area much loved by Charles and Joy Staples, so as to assist the people of the South West region and those in government and private organisations concerned with South West projects to appreciate the needs and possibilities of the region in the widest possible historical perspective.

The fund is administered by a committee whose aims are to make possible the publication by UWA Publishing, of research and writing in any discipline relevant to the South West region.

Charles and Joy Staples South West Region Publications Fund titles

1987
A Tribute to the Group Settlers
Philip E. M. Blond

1992
For Their Own Good: Aborigines and government in the southwest of Western Australia, 1900–1940   Anna Haebich

1993
Portraits of the South West   B. K. de Garis
A Guide to Sources for the History of South Western Australia   compiled by Ronald Richards

1994
Jardee: The Mill That Cheated Time
Doreen Owens

1995
Dearest Isabella: Life and Letters of Isabella Ferguson, 1819–1910   Prue Joske
Blacklegs: The Scottish Colliery Strike of 1911
Bill Latter

1997
Barefoot in the Creek: A Group Settlement Childhood in Margaret River   L. C. Burton
Ritualist on a Tricycle: Frederick Goldsmith, Church, Nationalism and Society in Western Australia   Colin Holden
Western Australia as it is Today, 1906. Leopoldo Zunini, Royal Consul of Italy. Edited and translated by Richard Bosworth and Margot Melia

2003
Contested Country: a history of the Northcliffe area, Western Australia   Patricia Crawford and Ian Crawford

2002
The South West from Dawn till Dusk
Rob Olver

2004
Orchard and Mill: The Story of Bill Lee, South-West Pioneer   Lyn Adams

2005
Richard Spencer: Napoleonic War Naval Hero and Australian Pioneer   Gwen Chessell

2006
A Story to Tell   Laurel Nannup (reprinted 2012)

2008
Alexander Collie: Colonial Surgeon, Naturalist and Explorer   Gwen Chessell
The Zealous Conservator: A Life of Charles Lane Poole   John Dargavel

2009
It's Still in our Heart This is Our Country: The Single Noongar Claim History   John Host and Chris Owen
Shaking Hands on the Fringe: Negotiating the Aboriginal World at King George's Sound   Tiffany Shellam

2011
Manang and *Noongar Mambara Bakitj*
Kim Scott and Wirlomin Noongar Language and Stories Project
Guy Grey-Smith: Life Force   Andrew Gaynor

2013
Dwoort Baal Kaat and *Yira Boornak Nyininy*
Kim Scott and Wirlomin Noongar Language and Stories Project

2014
A Boy's Short Life: The Story Of Warren Braedon/Louis Johnson   Anna Haebich and Steve Mickler
Plant Life on the Sandplains: A Global Biodiversity Hotspot   Hans Lambers
Fire and Hearth (revised facsimile edition) Sylvia Hallam
The Lake's Apprentice   Annamaria Weldon

2015
Running Out: Water in Western Australia Ruth Morgan
A Journey Travelled: Aboriginal-European Relations At Albany And Surrounding Regions From First Colonial Contact To 1926 Murray Arnold
The Southwest: Australia's Biodiversity Hotspot Victoria Laurie

INVISIBLE COUNTRY

SOUTH-WEST AUSTRALIA: UNDERSTANDING A LANDSCAPE

BILL BUNBURY

First published in 2015 by
UWA Publishing
Crawley, Western Australia 6009
www.uwap.uwa.edu.au

UWAP is an imprint of UWA Publishing
a division of The University of Western Australia

THE UNIVERSITY OF
WESTERN
AUSTRALIA

National Library of Australia
Cataloguing-in-Publication entry:
    Bunbury, Bill, 1940– author.
    Invisible country: Southwest Australia: understanding a landscape /
    Bill Bunbury.
    ISBN: 9781742586250 (paperback)
    Includes bibliographical references and index.
    Environmental management—Western Australia.
    Environmental protection—Western Australia—Citizen participation.
    Western Australia, Southwest—History.
    333.7099412

Typeset in Bembo by Lasertype
Printed by Lightning Source

CONTENTS

Invisible Country is dedicated to the memory, the achievements and the generous contribution, the late and greatly missed historian, Geoffrey Bolton made to this book and many others. His own pioneering work, vividly expressed in *A Fine Country To Starve In*, a Social History of the Great Depression of the 1930s, in WA and his more recent *Environmental History, Spoils and Spoilers*, Australians make their environment, are just two works I could cite. Geoffrey Bolton has been an inspiration to many who seek to learn from the past and especially those who see the vital connection between land and people.

Bill Bunbury

FOREWORD

Often our gaze is so captured by the exotic, the distant, the dramatic, the global images that swirl through our world that we fail to see what's right under our noses. At a time when these universal images threaten to obliterate our sense of the particular, valuing and telling stories about our place may be more important than ever. When it seems that the uniformity – and superficial glitz - of international popular culture is imperilling the grounded local, Bill Bunbury adjusts our line of sight so that we can begin to really see the effect we've had on the land where we live: the salinity in the wheatbelt paddocks and towns, the disappearing native mammals; the dieback attacking our peerless Banksia (and so much else); and how we diminish our own lives by degrading our environment in this way. In exploring the general bewilderment of the early European arrivals to our shores, he exposes our continuing, collective failure to learn from past mistakes and lays bare the pain we inflict in the process.

Using diaries and official documents, local histories and interviews, Bill puts his broadcaster's documentary skills to good effect, inviting us to wonder at what still remains of our unique and fragile wildlife, while questioning the mind sets that have wrought so much devastation. He does not hector or preach, but rather asks us to look dispassionately at the folly of behaving as if we had no choice in how we relate to our natural world. Through his informants, many of whom have witnessed the steady and inexorable despoliation of our forests and woodlands and waterways, he invites us to explore what we can do to live fruitfully in a warming, drying world where the old certainties are being overturned. He asks us to remember and learn from the

Aboriginal people who were here before us and from the few, farsighted settlers who were able to discard their blinkers; and to celebrate those today who see what is and what needs to be done. People like Keith Bradby driving the restoration of vegetation and habitat in the inspiring Gondwana Link Project; like Nyungar leader, Eugene Eades who runs a centre at Nowanup to re-trace and re-connect with the old trails and dreaming tracks throughout the Stirling Ranges and the Porongorups.

While reading *Invisible Country*, I was reminded of my own family history, which is typical of so many of those who found themselves exiled, one way or another, in this unexpected land. Many of these voices are unrecorded and – perhaps unremarkable. Several were convicts, and they came without apparent prospects and probably without much hope either; they were extruded from their homes, miserable though they may have been. For the most part these weren't people who had either the time or the education to allow them to reflect publicly on their changed circumstances. They came with no understanding of the aboriginal people or the place – and appeared blind to both; clearing and controlling the land; eking out a living in conditions which were utterly unlike anything they had encountered before. Many of them were city dwellers to begin with, plucked from the slums of London and Dublin and Liverpool with few of the skills to farm the new land, which they could neither read nor understand.

In her essay on the Irish of Toodyay (my people), Rica Erickson traced the lives of some of these newcomers: she showed them working for the local "squires", as my great great grandfather William Murphy did; as teamsters, cutting and selling sandalwood - the poor man's gold- until there was almost none left; capturing and selling the wild horses, which had already become very numerous; building roads and fences and shepherding sheep; in time acquiring their own lands through the system of special occupation leases; subduing the land and all its living things.

As Bill Bunbury so effectively documents, these habits die hard and appear, time and again, in official pronouncements and policy – and always in the guise of "progress", a form of idolatry still practiced with pure faith, despite mounting evidence that the god has feet of clay. Not only do we need to stop worshipping false gods, we also need a more profound social commentary on what has been lost; of the absences which populate our lives; the tracks we leave over the centuries, the mysterious and weathered scripts of our passing. The additions and subtractions most of are blind to without the eyes of writers and story tellers like Bill Bunbury.

It may seem strange that it should need to be said, but whether we are aware of it or not, we *are* deeply connected to and influenced by our environment; indeed, it is clear that our well-being depends on the quality of that relationship. Too often we – and our leaders - appear to take literally the biblical injunction that we should enjoy "dominion over all the earth", adopting an exploitative separateness from our places that renders us blind to the destructive power of our actions to alter our environment and fray the links that bind us to the past.

But we do not simply *exist* in a physical environment, we also derive meaning and succour from it. And these meanings are not just individual ones but part of a shared fabric. Reading and understanding these detailed, local meanings is imperative if we are to avert some of the looming catastrophes of our globalised world. We have a profound need for connection with the natural world and cherished places. Jacobs has argued that such attachment to place is a deep human trait:

> People do not simply look out over a landscape and say 'this belongs to me'. They say, 'I belong to this'. Concern for familiar topography, for the places one knows, is not about the loss of a commodity, but about the loss of identity. People belong in the world: it gives them a home (p. 109).[1]

Our relationships with the places we know and in which we live are not abstract, but intimate and intricate. As these places change, so do we. Even though we may only dimly apprehend the deeper human loss which ensues from the destruction of our environment, the effects are, nonetheless, real and lasting. This alone is reason to be grateful that Bill Bunbury has taken on the task of rendering our invisible country visible.

Professor Carmen Lawrence
Chair, Australian Heritage Council

---

1   Jacobs, M. (1995). Sustainability and community: Environment, economic rationalism and sense of place. *Australian Planner*, 32, 2, 109-15.

Northam

Avon

Mundaring

PERTH

Fremantle

Helena River

Beverley

BROOKTON HWY

Brookton

INDIAN OCEAN

GREAT

Pinjarra

Dwellingup

ALBANY

SOUTHERN

SOUTH

Bunbury

Geographe Bay

SEE ENLARGEMENT (BELOW)

Katanning

Pingrup

Ravensthorpe

HWY

Quindalup

Busselton

WESTERN

VASSE

Cowaramup

BUSSEL

Blackwood

River

Gnowangerup

Jerramungup

Ongerup

Nowanup

Fitzgerald River National Park

Fitzgerald River

Hamelin Bay

Karridale

HWY

Dingup

Donnelly River

Warren River

Lake Jasper

Stirling Range National Park

Augusta

Pemberton

HWY

Frankland River

Kalgan River

COAST

Northcliffe

Mount Barker

D'entrecasteaux National Park

Denmark

Walpole

Nornalup

Albany

SOUTH

King George Sound

Princess Royal Harbour

0   N   100 km

Scale

Rabbit proof fence

WESTERN AUSTRALIA

Burekup

Arthur River

Wagin

Dumbelyung Lake

Bunbury

Picton

Collie

GREAT

Cobinine River

Geographe Bay

BUSSEL HWY

Boyanup

Arthur River

ALBANY

SOUTHERN

Wonnerup Estuary

SOUTH

Donnybrook

Towerinning Lake

Beaufort

Busselton

WESTERN

Carrolup River

Ewlyamartup

Capel River

Ludlow River

Katanning

Vasse

Yoganup

VASSE

Blackwood

Kojonup

HWY

Margaret River

Nannup

Bridgetown

HWY

Beaufort River

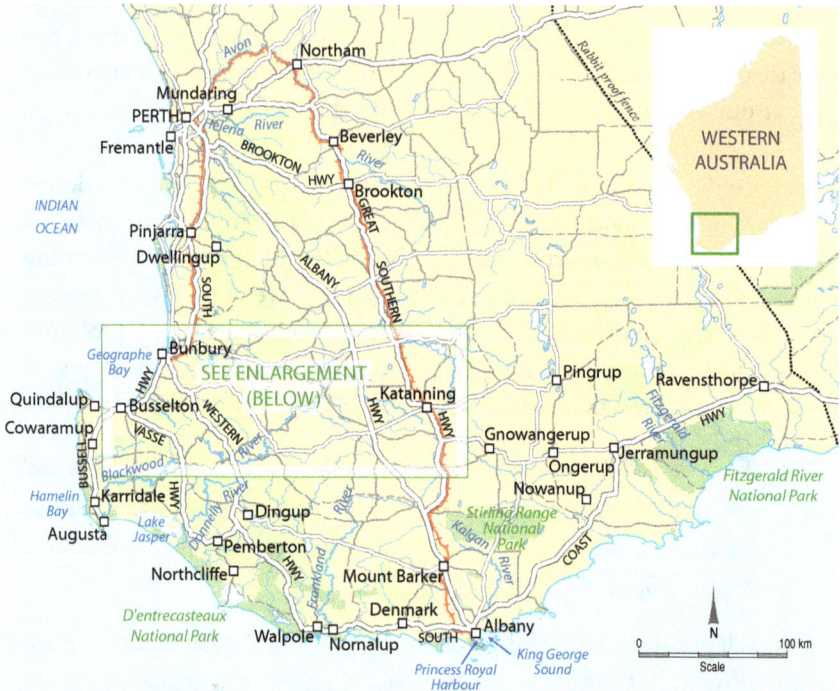

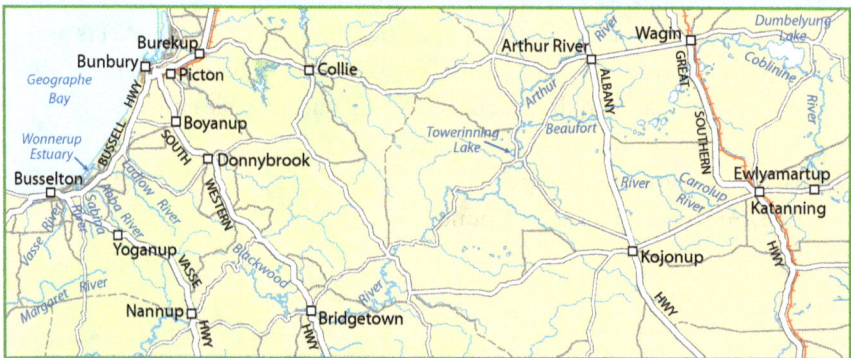

South-west Western Australia

Introduction

It struck me some time ago that when Europeans first settled in Western Australia, the land, particularly in the south-west, had withheld many of its secrets from these early nineteenth-century occupiers.

There were broad rivers, wide plains and tall forests, all of which, to European eyes, suggested promising sites for settlement. The land was also home to long-term inhabitants. Their presence, however, as writer and actor Phil Thomson reminded me several years ago, was

not mentioned in the immigration brochures.

To many new settlers these, the First Australians, were a puzzle. They seemed healthy. They moved freely through country which they knew intimately. Yet for Europeans, their lifestyle showed few familiar signs of a recognisable culture. There were no permanent dwellings, no bricks and mortar, no temples and no wheeled transport. In short, the locals' culture was not apparent to the newcomers. What few realised then was that Aboriginal people and the land they lived in were indistinguishable. Failure to read the people made it hard to read the country. Both were potentially invisible.

And yet, as a few thoughtful outsiders, like Western Australian early colonial lawyer, landed proprietor and diarist George Fletcher Moore learned in the 1830s, the original inhabitants had useful things to say to the European newcomers – if they would listen.

This book details just four case studies of environmental change which have occurred since European settlement: developments that affected the rivers, forests and coastal plains of south-western Australia. These four 'stories' are book-ended by an examination of the historical perspective in which these changes have occurred and a final chapter which looks at different perceptions of a changed environment and the society it supports.

All of these major changes have occurred since the late 1820s, when the first Europeans arrived in the south-west. They tell a tale of lessons learned about an ancient country with unique and incredibly diverse ecosystems. We are still learning the secrets of this land, country that still challenges us as Wadjellas (whitefellers) to think in new ways about the home we have adopted.

But whether we have adapted to a new country remains for the moment unanswered. For the first Australians no such question existed. The land had adopted them.

In the course of compiling this book I have been made increasingly aware of two issues: the complexity of our natural world and the strong connections people, whether Aboriginal or non-Aboriginal, have to the place they call home. The south-west is a place with many ecological stories that can be shared if we wish to hear them.

In that context the Indigenous people have a powerful sense that the land owns people, not the other way around. But I have detected that more-recent arrivals have also developed a growing sense of place and identification with land.

I have talked with farmers who feel an obligation to the country that gives them a living and on which they live, and others, like foresters, tourist operators and ecologists, who find beauty in and express reverence for the piece of earth on which they stand.

For some readers these chapters may seem more like 'verbal documentaries' than conventional text. The style derives from my experience as a radio feature producer but it is an approach that I have also applied to my work as a writer. I have often found that conversations with those closely involved with an issue offer lively and direct comment and can make the issue discussed come alive for a listener or reader.

If the content of this book indicates that there are more questions than answers then I hope that this suggests that we are able to recognise ecological complexity when we meet it. I hope that we can then find it easier to talk these issues through in the community and find how to understand and care for a land that we are all lucky to live in.

It is probably useful to remember that we don't live on land, we live in it.

Bill Bunbury

Chapter 1

More than a single walk

I do not remember since leaving England, having passed a more dull, uninteresting time. The country viewed from an eminence, appears a woody plain, with here and there rounded and partly bare hills of granite protruding...Everywhere we found the soil sandy & very poor; it either supported a coarse vegetation of thin, low brushwood and wiry grass, or a forest of stunted trees...The general bright green color of the brushwood & other plants, viewed from a distance, seems to bespeak fertility. A single walk, however, will dispel such an illusion. And he who thinks like me, he will never wish to walk again in so uninviting a country.[1]

Charles Darwin's 'single walk' traversing the country around the small settlement of Albany in March 1836 might have been just a little short to give the author of *On the Origin of Species* a full understanding of the landscape of south-western Australia. It needed a much longer journey.

We now know with reasonable certainty that our universe (we're not sure whether there are any others) started, or rather exploded into life, with a Big Bang 13.7 billion years ago. But whoever or whatever triggered that first moment in what we humans call time, also set off a seemingly endless chain of cosmic and ultimately geological evolutions. And our planet, in itself a casualty or by-product of supernovae collapses, took shape aeons later and evolved to the point where life was eventually possible.

Three hundred million years ago one large supercontinent dominated the earth's surface: Pangaea. The name, taken from Greek, means 'entire earth'. This 'mother of terrestrial landmasses' included the Americas, Eurasia, India and Antarctica. Then, a hundred million years later, Pangea began to break up, re-forming into separate chunks of terra firma that are still vaguely recognisable today. A new Pangea sub-division, Gondwanaland, included *Terra Australis*, which was still attached to both India and the Antarctic, and was in itself an archipelago of large islands.[2]

Thirty-three million years ago our continent finally became one island and began to develop the features we still recognise: notably aridity and insularity and, as it drifted south from the equator, the Antipodean land mass became cooler.

Landscape east of Albany

As Professor Stephen Hopper recounts this ecological narrative, vast ice sheets then covered much of today's Australia, to a depth of five kilometres, flattening the landscape with consequences for the much-later arrival of mankind and, even more recently still, European humans.[3]

Parts of this now-distinct continent, notably the south-west of Western Australia, then lacked mountains and, consequently, many rivers. As rain from the oceans fell across flat land it distributed small amounts of sea-borne salt which built up over time. With few waterways there were not many natural drains to dilute or carry that salt back to the sea. Lakes and underground reservoirs stored gradually increasing quantities of salt. This salt might have largely stayed there but for the arrival of new settlers with European intentions for land use.

Today salinity in our wheat-growing country already presents problems and, while salt is a long-term element of our environmental inheritance, land-clearing practices have, quite literally, brought it to the surface.

But what of the land itself, created from such ancient cosmic evolution? What could it support? Crushed for aeons by ice, the soil of much of south-western Australia is deeply weathered and nutrient deficient. However, some remarkable plants have survived long-term climate variation. They have continued to evolve and adapt as separate land masses formed and conditions changed. As Stephen Hopper describes that process: 'In this region of Western Australia flora evolved to match its own habitat. Plants conserved their resources via long-lived root-stocks, leaves and seeds'.[4]

Much of this unique flora had survived what could have marked the end of life on earth 65 million years ago. That was when an enormous asteroid fell onto the Yucatán Peninsula in what is now Mexico, creating an enormous crater and much more besides. Massive dust clouds, thrown up by the impact, caused major climate change. Clouds blocked out the sun, creating extremely cold conditions, followed in turn by extreme heating, as greenhouse gases in the earth's atmosphere then raised land temperatures to life-killing levels.[5]

Much of the animal and plant life that had evolved over previous aeons disappeared at this time. Dinosaurs and many other animal and plant species became extinct. However fossil records show that some of the unique plant life of this region not only existed before Yucatán but went on adapting and hence surviving.[6] In the Australian context, the arrival of Aboriginal people at least 40,000 years ago marked the first human impact on this continent.

Any long-term changes Aboriginal people made to the environment are hard to pinpoint, given the considerable length of their tenure, but we do know that they acquired, and still hold, an immense wealth of knowledge about the land, its flora and fauna and its life-giving waters. In a paper prepared in 2005, the Department of Water cited the importance of water to the Nyungar people of the south-west. The study found that:

> The Aboriginal people of the south west (known collectively as the Nyungar people) base much of their culture, identity and spirituality on their close association with groundwater. The Nyungars share these associations with Aboriginal groups throughout the Australian continent. Naturally, access to healthy freshwater sources was central to the survival of the Aboriginal people since they first arrived in Australia, and it has been argued that Aboriginal people are now so closely connected with groundwater in all its forms, that the long-term health of their culture depends on its maintenance.[7]

While rivers and streams remained relatively unaffected by European occupation until the early twentieth century, large-scale land clearing in Western Australia commenced with nineteenth-century European settlement, and this made a greater environmental impact than the strategic forest management practised by the First Australians. Today, fortunately, there is growing recognition that while much of the original vegetation has been lost, we can still preserve part of this ancient and impressive heritage.

There is much to cherish. South-western Australia is known for having some of the most distinctive flora in the world, and the coast and hinterland between Albany and Esperance (Fitzgerald River, Ravensthorpe) is now internationally recognised as a bio-diversity hotspot.[8]

However, it has taken us a long time to appreciate the unique and characteristic qualities of the ground we tread, farm, mine, play or build on. The English settlers who arrived in the Swan River colony in 1829 came into a country and met a people they did not understand. They also failed to recognise Aboriginal land-management practices. That in itself is understandable. The newcomers' perceptions of land were inevitably shaped by the landscapes of Europe, especially Britain, by then largely deforested and given over to an agricultural system centuries ago. The soils of Europe were younger, with a rich nutritional base which lent itself easily to both arable and animal farming.

Here in Australia the long-term tenants had lived by other means. They held a largely metaphysical sense of land where creation stories provided a kind of ecological and spiritual guidebook to country. For Nyungar people, the main inhabitants of south-western Australia, as for other indigenous Australians, landscape is a sustaining force, not just in terms of immediate need for food and shelter. It is also a vital presence in their lives. Anthropologist W. E. H. Stanner understood this well.

No English words are good enough to give a sense of the links between an Aboriginal group and its homeland. Our word 'home', warm and suggestive though it is, does not match the Aboriginal word that may mean 'camp', 'hearth', 'country', 'everlasting home', 'totem place', 'life source', 'spirit centre' and much else all in one. Our word 'land' is too spare and meagre. We can now scarcely use it except with economic overtones unless we happen to be poets.[9]

In many ways the Aboriginal interpretation of the origin of land and its inhabitants parallels the biblical creation account in Genesis. Their creation stories speak of huge movements of earth and water, enriched through images of serpents and other creatures which create the landscape. But Aboriginal people also see an unbreakable unity in the elements that make up a landscape.

As with the land, Aboriginal people conceptualise water sources such as rivers, lakes and wetlands to have derived from the Dreaming, a time when the world attained its present shape...Water is described as the living element that both creates and defines the shape and character of the country and gives it sacredness and identity.[10]

It is no accident that many Nyungar names in the south-west end in the suffix '-up': Gnowangerup, Kojonup, Boyanup, Cowaramup, Burekup etc. 'Up' means 'place of'[11], but a good place to live preferably includes water. Proximity to water meant not only a means of quenching thirst but also the capacity to catch animals for food, as edible creatures would also be drawn to the same life-giving streams.

Craig McVee, Chair of the Kojonup Aboriginal Corporation, explains the relationship.

Wherever there's a natural water resource, Aboriginal people have a real affection for it. It creates life from the waterhole, with the supply of water to animals and plants so it really supported the Aboriginal way of life.

Tradition has it that Aboriginal people didn't actually camp on the water site. They camped away from the water sites to allow hunting to happen. This allowed the animals to come to the water to drink. But of course when the European settlers arrived they set up camp right on top of the waterholes and so the Aboriginal people had to find other places to hunt.[12]

The sense of water as life-giving also embraced a deeply felt sense of the sacred and the practical. Anthropologist Kado Muir once explained this neatly in describing the function of gnamma holes, the ingenious stone-capped mini-reservoirs of water for dry times. As he saw it, the practice of 'purification', cleaning a gnamma hole, was not only an act of reverence and gratitude for the blessing of water, it was also essentially a hygienic act, 'if water was to remain safe to drink'.[13]

Gnamma hole

It seems that we have taken a long time to accept that blessing. A hundred and fifty years on from European occupation of the Swan River Colony, the then Public Works Department decided to improve the flow of the Avon River through the Northam region, east of the Darling Escarpment. Farmers in the area had complained about annual flooding, but at the same time they also benefited from the large pools that the winter rains created, both for recreation and for watering their livestock.

Unfortunately the engineering work changed the Avon from a slowly flowing, but naturally dammed, water-course into a fast-flowing drain. Annoying natural obstacles like logs and trees which occupied islands mid-stream or overhung river banks were often removed to allow for faster drainage. The river's natural inhabitants – herons, ducks and pelicans – lost their habitats and food sources. River banks eroded as water flowed faster and fish populations declined sharply, and the Avon became more salty as a result of riparian clearing.

Some of the damage is now being repaired by government and other agencies, but the Avon River story exemplifies how long it has taken us to recognise and come to terms with our continent. A local Nyungar elder, Fred Collard, told me that in his childhood in the 1940s

> *The water was lovely and clear and we used to dive from the top to the bottom to see who could reach the sand at the bottom. And we couldn't reach it. It must have been over twenty feet deep. Now it's only three to four feet deep. And you can't see the bottom any more.*[14]

Much of the Indigenous way of life was invisible to Europeans when they first encountered Aboriginal people. Outwardly there were few signs of what Westerners understood to represent 'civilisation'. They saw no recognisable permanent dwellings or temples and no wheeled transport. There was no evidence of horticulture, forestry, animal husbandry or tilling of fields, in the sense that Europeans understood these practices.

And while the newcomers found Aboriginal culture invisible, perhaps they also saw the land as needing taming, cultivating and rendering acceptable to their sense of country. We get a sense of their own cultural inheritance from a Biblical injunction in the Book of Isaiah, affirming that land is there for humanity to modify and subdue. That sense is strong in George Frederick Handel's magnificent eighteenth-century oratorio *Messiah*, which took its words from the Authorised Version of the Bible: 'Every valley shall be exalted, and every mountain and hill shall be made low: the crooked shall be made straight, and the rough places plain'.[15]

While this view of nature goes back a long way, in the European eighteenth century it was certainly still going strongly. This was, after all, the great age of landscape gardening: horticulture on a scale greater than backyards and including the clearing of large tracts of land and dredging for new waterways. It coincided with the expansive character of the British agrarian revolution which changed farming practices, replacing smallholdings with broadacre farms.

It was also difficult then, and still is, for many Europeans, to comprehend a spirituality that values land not as real estate but as a source of bounty, which in turn demands care of the country. When Austrian diplomat and botanist Baron Charles von Hugel visited the Swan River Colony shortly after its establishment, he lamented the poverty, as he saw it, of the Nyungar diet and lifestyle.

> Nature has been very niggardly in the matter of providing a livelihood for the Aborigines. There are no indigenous cereals, no fruit except a small berry, pleasant to taste but so minute that it would seem to have been created as a bad joke. There are no milk-producing animals and no domesticated animals except dogs, who consume part of their food supply. There are no wool-producing animals, no vegetables, and no tubers except for 'Dioscorrhoea' [sic] (yams).[16]

Western Australian soil itself seemed incomprehensible. It certainly puzzled Von Hugel.

> As in so many respects New Holland is just the opposite to Europe and in fact to the rest of the world. The vegetation of the sandy coastal country and that of the deep soil of the hinterland are utterly different from each other. The sand is completely covered with a wide variety of luxuriant plants through which it is often difficult to make one's way, while, except for widely scattered large trees, the deep soil country carries hardly any vegetation, or, at most, only small insignificant plants.[17]

Earlier still, Matthew Flinders, during his circumnavigation of the continent, had formed a similar impression when he explored the Albany hinterland in late December 1801.

> The country through which we passed in this excursion has but little to recommend it. The stony hills of the south coast were indeed covered with shrubs but there was rarely any depth of soil and no wood.
>
> The soil of the hills is very barren, except near the sea coast, generally covered with wood, and that of the plains at the head of Princess Royal Harbour has been described as shallow and incapable of cultivation.[18]

European occupation would involve cultural, agricultural and inevitably environmental implications, even if they were not recognised at the time. As historian Patricia Crawford has commented:

> *When in 1826 the British established a settlement at Albany...they believed that property in land depended on cultivation...They argued that those who walked over the land, hunting and gathering, had no right of possession...Unoccupied land, according to British ideas, was to be rendered fruitful.*[19]

Interestingly, that earliest English settlement in Western Australia at Albany in 1826 was not typical of later occupations. King George Sound was initially established as a garrison to counteract potential rival French ambitions. Under Captain Collet Barker's command, soldiers were instructed to develop and maintain good relations with the locals.

Barker's record of that time, his *King George Sound Journal*, is filled with accounts of contact with the original inhabitants and, while he is critical of some of their customs, such as reprisal killings, he shows curiosity about their way of life, language and custom. The journal reveals no discussion of land ownership between Barker and Mokare, a local leader, from whom he learnt much about their way of life. Barker's task at Albany was not to prepare the region for future agricultural development. That would come hard on the heels of his departure. However, his final entry in his *King George Sound Journal* suggests a certain ambivalence about that prospect.

> *Those who conceive that there is no independence except in the accumulation of money will mistake the meaning of the word as it is here used. N. S. Wales is not the country to realise a fortune, either by farming or grazing — at least those who do make fortunes by such pursuits must possess advantages not attainable by everyone and be gifted with acuteness and a spirit of enterprise which are more often found among merchants than farmers. The settler will, in most cases, have a little*

money and it will or ought to be his happiness that he will have little occasion for it; he will be ready in the desirable situation contemplated by the poet: 'Happy the man whose wish and care. A few paternal acres bound.'[20]

Are we hearing a warning here about modest ambitions for a new land or is Barker, very much in the sense of the eighteenth-century Age of Enlightenment, simply re-imaging an English rural idyll?

But whatever its rationale, the Barker garrison tenure (1828–31) was also a period of exploration and investigation of new country. In December 1829, Dr Thomas Wilson accompanied an expedition to map the country west of Albany. He describes the appearance of Rivetts Creek near the later site of St Werburgh's farm, not far from Mt Barker.

> *...we observed that its banks were covered with luxuriant grass, sprinkled with yellow buttercups, which put us in mind of home...The alluvial soil, however, extends no great distance; but gently swelling lightly wooded adjacent hills are well adapted for sheep-walks.*[21]

Apart from the evident floral reminder of 'home', this passage carries the European sense of seeing a new landscape as an entity which its new tenants hope to redesign. Sheep, it is hoped, may safely graze in newer pastures.

New pasture meant less forest. That loss was foreshadowed early in the life of the Swan River Colony. In 1830 Captain Thomas Bannister set out on an expedition to survey the potential of land as far south-east as King George Sound (Albany). He kept notes of his progress.

> *From the 23rd of December to the 5th January, we pursued a S E direction for 80 or 90 miles of actual distances, though in many tracts a country which surpassed our most sanguine expectations, a very great proportion of this tract was land of the first description fit for the plough, sheep or cattle. The beauty of the scenery in many places near to and distant from the rivers which we crossed, is equal to any I have seen in the*

most cultivated timbered country in those parts of Europe where I have happened to have passed through.

The character of the country generally is undulating with here and there moderately high hills, some of them crowned with rocks...but there are broad, flat lands and valleys, the former of which...not unfrequently [sic] extended several miles, even in some places to a distance far beyond our power to ascertain...When I consider that the rivers, five of which we crossed not to mention the numerous water courses, some of which still had water in pools in them, traversed the country from East to West...I cannot but think that the Colony must possess a considerable quantity of fertile land in this part of its territory.[22]

Bannister's ensuing report to Governor Sir James Stirling, *A Splendid Vision*, reiterated that optimism.

I think that there is a body of available land with certain extensive tracts of the richest description fit for the plough, sheep or cattle or indeed any cultivation of the interior commencing about 25 or 30 miles north of King George's Sound, which, under the judicious system of colonization the main roads being made in the first instance by forced labour, would in the course of a few years become inhabited by thousands of industrious men sent out by their families in England, Scotland and Ireland or brought out by individuals bettering their own condition.[23]

Eighty years later an 'industrious man' was singled out for praise at Moodiarrup, a settlement between the Blackwood and Beaufort rivers.

Mr Hull has only been on his selection two years and has already 80 acres under wheat and oats...and he is fast clearing more of his land. He had in use an ordinary ship's winch, with which he was doing marvellous work, pulling down small and medium-sized trees and afterwards hauling them into piles for burning. It appeared to me almost incredible that one man could handle the class of timber which he was dealing with.[24]

Historians Ian and Patricia Crawford have reminded us of a seemingly long-forgotten royal warning. In seventeenth-century

England, the Scottish King James I complained about his new domain that, 'If woods be suffered to be felled, as daily they are, there will be none left'.[25]

Does this suggest that an English heritage predisposed new settlers to tree removal? Land clearing began almost as soon as the settlers arrived and took up farmland, initially in the river valleys that ran behind and through the Darling Ranges. Early clearance was gradual and relatively small scale. It was slow, axe-driven work, unaided initially by mechanical assistance, but its effects were widespread. As the nineteenth century wore on, there were warnings. Botanist Ferdinand Von Mueller noted in 1879:

> But as nowhere, not even in the most extensive woodlands, can the supply of timber from natural forests be considered inexhaustible, a rational, far seeing provision for the maintenance (if not the enrichment) of its forest treasure is needful for West Australia, however indiminishable [sic] these may appear to be at present.[26]

A century later Rhoda Glover's history of the Plantagenet Shire (1979) reveals change to those 'extensive woodlands'.

> This vast seemingly endless plain was described by the explorers Collie, Clint and Dale in 1831 and 1832. Eventually, 116 years later this plain carried twenty-five farms, each 2,400 acres, with 1,000 acres cleared, for future-selected soldier–settler owners. Its history of experiment, hope and success is a record of achievement, governmental and personal.[27]

As farmland expanded forests fell, aided frequently by the new railways which then carried away agricultural produce. Rail lines linked settlements but they also helped to expand them. Wherever the steel lines ran, farms grew and woodlands shrank. In railway construction, the use of timber sleepers, and the hunger for locomotive fuel, the new steam-power, also consumed forests.

The 1889 completion of the Beverley to Albany railway line alone required a massive quantity of timber for sleepers. The logging company Millars was granted a licence to cut 50,000 acres of forest between the Deep and Frankland rivers in the far south of the State; a region where trees grew to the water's edge and hence, once felled, offered the prospect of easy transport.

Almost forty years earlier (1st May 1850), the Colonial newspaper *The Enquirer* had already noted the proximity of trees to the shores of the Nornalup Inlet.

> *If only the trees could be felled and taken across the bar in flat-bottomed boats of 150–200 tons, it would be possible to supply the Government dockyards in England and for the colony to attain a degree of importance in the eyes of the Home Government which it never before possessed.*[28]

Later investigation probably kept the inlet in a more natural state, suggesting that at the mouth of the inlet there was not enough clear water draught to lift such flat-bottomed boats, especially laden with felled karri.[29]

Towards the end of Western Australia's first European century, there was belated recognition that continuous clearing and parting with a valuable primary source was, in the long run, not in the colony's best interests.

Perhaps the first to voice that concern publicly was John Ednie Brown, the Scots-born inaugural Western Australian Conservator of Forests. In 1895 he was asked to write a *Report on the Forests of Western Australia* and a year later was appointed as their Protector. His 1896 report emphasised that:

> *The loss to the state in the absolute destruction of the forest is a matter of grave responsibility to those who carry it out or even countenance it in any way…Forests are the natural regulator of climate and, therefore, it is man's duty to see that no action of his, in regard to these, leads to any disarrangements of nature's balance…I claim therefore that the forest reserve question should not always be dominated by that of the popular cry, 'the settlement of the land'.*[30]

Brown attempted to limit the loss of trees to agriculture and the growing timber industry. He was fighting an uphill battle. Already by 1896 nearly five hundred thousand acres (over two hundred thousand hectares) of timber concessions had been granted in the south-west of WA. Timber company Millars held huge leases in the south-west and its practices then were scarcely sustainable. In some ways early forest exploitation resembled mining rather than silviculture. A visit to Denmark, WA, by the Scottish Agricultural Commission in 1910 describes the state of the district five years after Millars had abandoned tree cutting.

> *Denmark is largely a place of abandoned wooden houses in all stages of decay. The devastated forest still retains enough of giant trunks erect and recumbent to tell of its wealth of timber before the axe and the fire wrought its ruin.*[31]

Denmark's picturesque appearance today is perhaps a tribute to the resilience of the karri tree despite earlier virtual quarrying. But at the end of the nineteenth century the south-west region was almost certainly facing a similar prospect of massive clearing, a practice that had already begun to change the landscape of the Great Southern and the central and northern wheatbelt.

Picturesque Denmark WA today.

When the Western Australian government set up the Forests Department in 1918, this amounted to a recognition that unlimited clearing for farms threatened the long-term survival of the forest itself. Huge tracts of land had already been cleared and burnt in the more lightly forested wheatbelt alone, and the south-west now risked the same fate.

Timber exporters had been at work on the west coast for many years. M. C. Davies had worked in eastern Australia as a supplier of wood for the Adelaide to Melbourne railway. Given the scarcity of suitable sleeper material along the proposed route, he then sought timber from the remote and sparsely populated jarrah and karri country of south-western WA. By 1875 Davies had established timber mills at Collie. Two years later he set up a large new mill at Karridale, north of Augusta.

Western Australian hardwood was now finding its way to England and France. Exported by sea from Hamelin Bay and Flinders Bay, the timber became railway sleepers, paving blocks and even garden fences for wealthy English families in the Home Counties. Much was cut from the superb stands of karri along the Leeuwin Ridge. By 1890 Davies was shipping away over 30 per cent of Western Australia's timber exports.

New jarrah fence in Caterham, Surrey,
near London, c. 1901.

At that time timber cutting meant clearing large areas of trees and burning the remaining stumps. One remarkable survival from this practice is a superb stand of regenerated karri at Boranup, north of Hamelin Bay.

The story goes that after a fierce burn in autumn and a generous deposit of ash, good rainfall encouraged seed growth and an entire valley regenerated. However, it has taken more than a hundred years for this forest to reach something close to its original stature and magnificence.

One hundred year karri regrowth, Boranup.

In Western Australia in the late nineteenth century strong commercial imperatives still dominated forestry thinking. The demand for timber itself was a major shaping factor. Hardwood was in demand for housing and bridge-building, and in the Eastern Goldfields the Kalgoorlie Woodlines were already supplying huge quantities of timber for pit props and fuel to be used in the rapidly expanding gold industry.

When Charles Lane Poole, a distinguished forester and early conservationist, came from England in 1916 to become Conservator of Forests in Western Australia, he, like his predecessor Ednie Brown, argued for 'a publicity campaign in Western Australia, the object of which would be to form a strong public opinion regarding the proper management and utilisation of the forest heritage of the State...I consider that, by a publicity campaign, the democracy will realise the wealth that the forests represent'.[32]

Charles Lane Poole, WA Conservator of Forests, 1916–21.

While Lane Poole wrote the bill for the new *Forests Act 1918* in the hope that it would ensure forest survival through restraint and regeneration, he later resigned because the then State Government was determined to extend Millars' logging permits and thus threaten forest sustainability. He had hoped people would develop 'a forest conscience'.

More than sixty years later, long-time Manjimup resident Olive Robinson movingly demonstrated that she had acquired 'a forest conscience' but also that she had the intuition that in 1983 Western Australia still hadn't yet fully acquired one. She told me what karri trees meant to her personally: 'I feel that there's something unique, something majestic about them. I feel they are not really appreciated as they should be'.[33] That comment alone suggested an apt title for an early ABC Radio National feature I made on life in the south-west forests: *Something Unique, Something Majestic.*[34]

Karri on a south-west road.

Olive's description was echoed by another timber-town resident, Kathleen Ffoulkes, describing the felling of long-lived trees: 'You feel that it's a living thing that's gone. You felt something was dying every time you saw a tree fall.'[35]

The vital relationship between water, agricultural land and original woodland is a key to understanding the story of land change in Australia, and particularly in Western Australia given its vast landmass and original woodland cover. In *Contested Country*, the Crawfords describe the large-scale removal of native forest in the Northcliffe area in the 1920s. It was just one more major intrusion into the original landscape and was conceived as part of a post–World War I farm-creation scheme, known as Group Settlement.

Group Settlement was heavily backed by WA's then premier, and later governor, Sir James Mitchell. His idea was to encourage migrants from the British Isles and Australian city dwellers to try their luck at farming. A common incentive for both was unemployment here and in England. Some would-be farmers were displaced soldiers back from the trenches of Europe's 'war to end all wars'.

In Mitchell's view WA needed a proper dairy industry because milk and other dairy products were mainly imported from Victoria. His nickname 'Moo Cow Mitchell' is testimony to Mitchell's commitment to establishing small-scale farms throughout the south-west. Wherever the giant karri grew, he argued, good pasture could thrive, if, of course, you first took out the trees. Few at the time realised that the rich-looking brown loam, while it nourished karri, was not capable of creating lush English meadows.

If the professional agricultural scientists lacked that knowledge, the settlers and their families, now enticed from Britain to create farms of their own, were even less likely to understand the nature of the land they'd been allocated. Their task was simple but literally back-breaking. They were under orders to turn 'forest into field'. Some questioned that instruction.

Don Syme, son of a Group Settler, told the Crawfords of his father's reluctance to remove a small group of three or four trees as they were 'too good to destroy'.[36] Don was overruled by the foreman and the offending trees were duly felled. His son was both witness and executioner.

> *Dad called me over and told me to ring-bark these beautiful creations, which I did, and in so doing, destroyed, in a few minutes, what the Master Creator had taken four or five hundred years to perfect.*[37]

Laura Mumford felt that the Group Settlers seemed driven, always under pressure. She and her husband were in a good position to observe. They had settled in Denmark several years before the onrush of Group Settlement and saw the newcomers arrive.

> *Everybody was wanting to make something of themselves. They were going so quickly. And farming isn't a thing you can rush. My husband used to say, 'They're going mad. They're going too fast'.*[38]

The offspring of Group Settlers, with childhood time on their hands, were delighted with the country that was now their home. In Denmark, Peggy Cross recalls that in the one-teacher school she attended, her teacher drew his pupils' attention to the beauty of the bush environment in which they lived. Each Friday he took nature study classes in the country itself, with long walks to the ocean, studying the coastal wildflowers as they went.

> *We used to have a wheel that was made up every month, as the wildflowers came out. We used to bring them to school and we were allowed to draw on this wheel the month and the date as to when that flower came out. And we had a complete twelve months' record. As a matter of fact I'd love to have that record now of all the wildflowers and orchids that we used to find. It gave us a lot of incentive to look for the flowers so that we could bring them along to draw them on this calendar wheel.*[39]

But for their parents there was little time to contemplate nature. Their work was hard and unremitting and for many set in a strange and unforgiving environment. Historian Geoffrey

Bolton observed, at least for adults, a sense of alienation: 'Many of the settlers, the women especially, found the bush overpowering – surrounded by tall trees, very different from the cleared fields of England'.[40]

In the 1980s, and with the reflections of a lifetime among them, many settlers began to question the massive removal of trees. Jack Ricketts, a long time Denmark resident, felt that clearing of the karri forest along the south coast hills:

> ...was wasteful and the timber was not put to any good use, just ring-barked or burnt. There was millions of dollars' worth of timber just ruined through farming. I think it should never have been used for farming but kept as forest.[41]

A reminder of what much of that forest might still look like, but for Group Settlement, comes from William Nairne Clark in 1841. He was then exploring the south coast for its agricultural potential. As he reached the Frankland River:

Cross cut sawing – early twentieth century.

26

I saw many blue and white gum trees of enormous growth; one had the immense diameter of no less than 14 feet or 42 feet in circumference. If I had not seen this tree with my own eyes I would not have believed the fact.[42]

Clearing so much timber in the 1920s proved a pyrrhic victory for many Group Settlers. The work was hard and exhausting and many of the blocks carved from the bush were too small, often less than a hundred hectares (247 acres), to be viable for dairy grazing. Their cattle frequently died from wasting diseases due to the lack of vital minerals in the original forest soil. The south-west dairy industry only began to show rewards after the addition of trace elements. Hard lessons from a land seemingly hard to read.

Another interesting description of this richly timbered coastal region in the 1920s comes from an American visitor, Ernest H. Wilson, Assistant Director of the Arnold Arboretum at Harvard University, when he visited the Nornalup district.

You have got everything there, wonderful forest scenery, mountain ranges, seascapes, boating, fishing. It is one of the most beautiful sights I ever saw in all my life…It would be a great shame to parcel the land out for dairying country as had been done with the forest land at Denmark.[43]

Group Settlement home near Denmark.

27

Much of the area described by Wilson was saved from agriculture, as it happened, by the same Sir James Mitchell who promoted Group Settlement and agricultural development so strongly elsewhere. Gary Muir, who now runs a tourist boat on the Walpole Inlet, described a significant Mitchell visit.

> In 1910 he brought his ministerial team to approve developments of these places. Imagine these guys turning up and saying 'Look at the great resources down here. We have got this amazing timber. Imagine being able to use the Walpole waterways for transport'.
>
> But the situation changed when the French settler Pierre Boulanger (Bellanger), living on the Frankland River at Nornalup, hosted the party. He took them to some of the beautiful places, like the monastery landing where the mist had risen and formed a ceiling over the karri trees and the waters were still like a mirror and while they had been looking to exploit the natural resources of the area, suddenly they could see it in a quite different light. James Mitchell never forgot how moved he was by this expedition. In the following year, 1911, he said 'Why don't we reserve the waters as well as the forests and protect these reserves? And that was done.[44]

However, as his view of forests versus field showed, Mitchell was seldom swayed by the beauty of trees and had little concept of the fragility of the soil or the richness of the environment.

But we are all still learning about the real potential of the country we live in and how to look after it. Early clearing had been undertaken largely to establish agriculture, but it has taken us longer to see forests as a natural resource and not just as a commodity or an impediment to development.

When major clearing first took place, 'clear felling', as we term it today, was the favoured method of timber extraction. It was partly influenced by technology, or lack of it. Bullock or horse teams which carted away the felled trees could not easily get at a single tree. If, however, cutters could fell an entire block, they could drag the logs to a landing for removal from the forest. Even so, much timber lay where it fell.

Ted Pickersgill, who died in 1999 aged 94, worked in the south-west forests just after World War I. He recalled enormous wastage of jarrah and karri timber in the Pemberton district. He also talked about the destruction. 'When the cutters worked the timber they left fallen logs everywhere just lying to waste. They were just left there. The wastage would make you weep.'[45]

Arboreal management wasn't always under the eye of the Forests Department. It was often, *de facto*, in the hands of farmers. Twenty years or so after the Group Settlement Scheme, pressure to clear land in the south of the state continued.

Originally, farmland in the South Stirling region north-east of Albany was seen as good sheep-grazing country and requiring minimal clearing. But by the 1940s and early 1950s sheep were eating out the native grasses, and as farmers increased the size of their flocks, they expressed a need for bigger pastures. In 1948 one of the largest land development schemes then undertaken in Western Australia, the South Stirling Land Settlement, was launched. The plan was to develop 24,000 hectares of lightly timbered plain country north-east of Albany between the Kalgan River and the Stirling Ranges, and east and south to Manypeaks.

Rhoda Glover, in her *History of the Plantagenet Shire*, describes clearing in the Woogenellup district, west of the Kalgan River.

The comparatively open parkland type of country was the first to be cleared. The large trees were ringbarked by chopping a groove around the trunk at convenient axe height. This cut off the sap supply and allowed the tree to die. The area would then be left for twelve months or so. Leaves, twigs, bark etc would fall from the trees and the whole area would become something of a tinder box. On a suitable summer day, after taking due precautions against burning neighbours out, the area was set alight.

Burning-off operations in those days were fraught with danger. Logs burned for several days after the fire and, should strong winds prevail, the risk of sparks lighting up adjacent land was always present.[46]

Clearing land, while it allowed grass to grow, did not always create better pasture. An anecdote from the other side of the continent might be helpful here. An early twentieth-century dairy farmer in the Hunter River district kept a farm diary, which his grandson found and inspected. His grandfather had kept meticulous records of his milk yield from the well-treed and shady pasture that his cows grazed. Later, his son, keen to have more pasture, felled the trees to gain more room for grass. His records revealed a decline in milk quantity. The grandson, in turn, when he inherited the farm, replanted shade-giving trees and his milk yield went back up to a level close to his grandfather's records. He had understood what his grandfather had noticed, that where trees shaded pasture, there was more morning dew and hence more moist grass.

Over-clearing the country of native vegetation has also brought other problems. Trees and shrubs hold down water tables and prevent that ancient legacy, salt, rising to the surface. Twentieth-century engineering and technology drew public attention to the problem. Salinity affecting our rivers was possibly first noticed by Chief Engineer C. Y. O'Connor during the construction of the Mundaring Weir to hold back the Helena River. Initial land clearing for the dam site in 1898 had caused salinity as the Helena Valley lost tree cover. O'Connor promptly initiated large-scale pine planting on the banks of the surrounding valley to hold down the water table and prevent the weir going salty.[47]

Further inland, in West Arthur, John Bird noted that:

> Clearing of the original jarrah and wandoo forest, for farming in the low rainfall areas of the catchment, caused groundwater levels to rise, bringing up the salt contamination. Unfortunately, the further step of controlling clearing on private land was not considered necessary. So with the advent of bulldozers in the 1950s and 1960s land clearing accelerated and the inflow of salinity into the waterways increased with it.[48]

In more recent times reforestation in this region has attempted to correct the worst effects of salt contamination. But paradoxically, salinity, in our suddenly drier climate, as hydrologist Keith Barrett and others have suggested, has slowed as less water now rises to bring up salt.[49]

In the south-west of Australia we now face considerable ecological challenges. Phytophthora Dieback (formerly known as jarrah dieback), or, to name it more accurately, the pathogen *Phytophthora cinnamomi*, is responsible for the death or decline of many forest trees and shrubs. At the same time salinity in open country, as a consequence of early land-clearing practices, is causing loss of agricultural land, and introduced weeds have changed the dynamics of originally pristine areas.

Animal life has also been affected by our arrival. Broad-scale farming in some areas has resulted in loss of habitat for native animals. The numbat, Western Australia's animal emblem, is now a rare sight. Carnaby's black cockatoo, which once darkened the skies, is now a threatened species. Loss of habitat and invasion of its nests by European bees has reduced its numbers. Survivors form a rather elderly population which reduces the likelihood of reproduction; while the malleefowl, a flightless bird which once occupied woodland areas across much of the south-west, is also now in need of protection. In chapter three we will look at what steps some people are taking to improve their survival prospects.

It is easy for city dwellers to see environmental change as 'over the hills and far away'. But for a comment on the way the environment within the Perth Metropolitan Area has changed, it is hard to go past personal observations like those of author Bill Lines, describing the onset of winter rains as a child in Gosnells in the early 1960s, then a semi-rural settlement south of the city.

> *At eight years old, I still believed I lived in a largely natural world, a world of predictable and cyclical change. I grew up familiar with the uncleared sandy plains of Gosnells, which supported a mosaic of vegetation dominated by woodlands of the common she-oak (Casuarina fraseriana) and banksia trees...*
>
> *In the bush, life absorbed the violent changes and clearing of space caused by heavy rains, floods, winds, and droughts. Life even assimilated the violence of fire. For a very long time Australian species had evolved to absorb precisely this form and magnitude of violence.*[50]

Perth has now largely absorbed both the native bush and the citrus orchards of communities like Gosnells, and with that absorption, much of the physical evidence of the natural world available to an eight-year-old Bill Lines. Testimonies like his are invaluable as memory checks. Take his description of the coming of rain as he remembers it.

> *Rain began when westerly winds replaced the hot dry easterlies of summer. One day each April a grey band of cloud appeared on the western horizon, thickened, and spread until the sky was completely overcast. Wind stirred, and the cloud cover lowered and formed a dark dense canopy...*
>
> *The drizzle thickened, the dampness became cascades of droplets, and the rain steadied into a rhythmic pattering on bush and earth until the swales and plains of Gosnells were enveloped in the strokes of falling rain. Rain fell throughout the night. At dawn it was still raining and rain fell throughout the day...rain fell again, with successive days of drizzle, showers and hours of steadily falling rain. The water soaked through the earth and the sandy soil became saturated.*[51]

Reading a description like that in the second decade of the twenty-first century evokes, for older people at least, a memory of how rain used to fall in south-western Western Australia; a time when, as one forester described it, 'the rain fell in lumps'.[52]

It is now beyond doubt that the south-west has suffered a considerable decline in rainfall from the mid-1970s onwards, and that factor has increasingly affected both the urban and the natural environment. Rainfall decline alone has sounded one of several alarm signals, but have we been listening and looking?

This book explores that question and many others.

Chapter 2

'Two rivers, two plains'

This is one way to describe two discrete regions of south-west Australia – the coastal plain between Bunbury and Busselton, where engineering and increasing settlement have changed the physical environment, and the relatively unchanged country surrounding the Donnelly River, east and south of Busselton.

Europeans did not explore much of what is now called the D'Entrecasteaux National Park, which takes in the lower Donnelly River area, until the latter part of the nineteenth century. However, we do get an earlier glimpse of how the Busselton coastal plain looked to some of its first new Australians. Take this description of the Busselton plain by botanist Georgiana Molloy in a letter to Captain Mangles in England in August 1840.

> The other day, when in search for Nuytsia I had most delightful success. We went for a very nice ride in a south easterly direction, following a small tributary stream to the Vasse. The banks were thickly studded with Banksia, Acacia [sic] and the She-oak; the ground was adorned with the crimson flower of Kennedy, but not so profusely as it will be a week or two hence.

> *All at once, after going through an interminable plain of Jacksonia, we came upon an open plain of many acres in extent, scarcely a tree on it and those that grew there were large and fine, I discovered a plant I have been almost panting for, a very small neat white blossom, on a furze looking bush...*
>
> *As the shades of night were commencing, we reluctantly turned homewards, when other agrements [sic] met my eye — what but a grove of* Nuytsia floribunda!¹

Writing in his journal only a year later, in 1841, newly arrived clergyman the Reverend John Ramsden Wollaston gives quite another picture of the coastal plain.

> *I had always entertained a wish to see a country in a state of primitive nature...but the impression on my mind has been very different to what I anticipated. Nothing can be more depressing than the loneliness of the bush away from any settlement...I have been almost tempted to shed tears at the desolateness of the scene, had I not called to mind the ubiquity of the God of Nature, who can make a wilderness like Eden and a desert like the Garden of the Lord and cause 'joy and gladness' to be found therein, thanksgiving and the voice of melody. Before, however, this happy time can come, the moral wilderness of the world must be broken up and cultivated.²*

In 1841 Georgiana Molloy was not quite such a newcomer to south-western Australia as John Wollaston. With her husband, John Molloy, she had set out for Australia in 1829 and the couple settled in Augusta in 1830, then a very lonely corner of the continent.

Nine years later they moved north to Fairlawn, a property on the Vasse River near Busselton. By this time Georgiana had become a pioneer botanist, sending floral specimens from Augusta to England and delighting in the distinctive flora of her adopted country. It may have helped that she had lived in the beautiful, wild regions of south-west Scotland and north-west England.

In 1841 John Wollaston had taken up residence in Picton, now a suburb of Bunbury. In his new home he also became a smallholder with an interest in farming, derived from his family's association with the long-established farmers of rural East Anglia.

Perhaps the key to these very different perceptions of landscape lies in Wollaston's last sentence: 'Before, however, this happy time can come, the moral wilderness of the world must be broken up and cultivated'.

The association of 'moral' with 'wilderness' and the ensuing word 'cultivated' gives us Wollaston's message; and not just his alone. While Georgiana Molloy, perhaps with more leisure, and certainty plenty of sensitivity, could come to terms with the landscape and learn to value the country for its distinctiveness, most settlers saw the land as in need of taming.

To be fair, Wollaston does acknowledge the beauty of some of the south-west vegetation, notably the peppermint tree, but he cannot resist commenting on the physical neatness of that tree, suggestive of a European sensibility of how nature should present itself. It is easy with hindsight to be critical of such views but probably rather unfair when one acknowledges the situation these

A neat native WA peppermint tree

European settlers faced in the early nineteenth century and their long-inherited sense of not only how land should look, but also how and what it should provide.

As a part-time farmer himself, Wollaston acknowledges that European expectations of Australian soil had been misleading.

> *Harvest has commenced with good promise and plenty of water may be had by sinking wells. Such extreme aridity does not at all suit the eye of an Englishman. How I should relish and enjoy a green lawn before my windows. I am told that Ogle who published on Western Australia, never was in the country himself but compiled his book merely from Sir James Stirling's Statistical Account, for interested purposes no doubt, to enhance the price of land. It contains positive falsehoods.[3]*

Wollaston was almost certainly correct, as Nathaniel Ogle, while a Fellow of the Royal Geographical Society, had never visited Australia.[4] Ogle had indeed painted a glowing picture of the Busselton hinterland.

> *The rivers that flow into the Vasse inlet are very small, their banks, however, are rich in pasture and upon them are situated the most promising farms, producing butter, cheese and potatoes, for which articles there is always great demand. Horses are bred with much success in this district; sheep have not yet been introduced but goats on one farm are becoming numerous, kept merely for the carcass. By these farms…it is probable that the western downs may be turned to account at a time of year when vegetation is most luxuriant, the close of the winter.[5]*

Whatever the expectations and the reality, the important lesson from early attempts to handle a new and unfamiliar landscape is to understand the unforeseen consequences.

My father, James Bunbury, was born in 1901 at Cattle Chosen, just across the Vasse River from the Molloy family's home at Fairlawn. He recalled swimming in the river as a child, not a practice anyone would contemplate in the twenty-first century. The Vasse, as it reaches Busselton, is now a health hazard for any swimmer.

So what happened to the Bunbury-Busselton coastal plain and its rivers after 1841? There are several inter-connected factors. Writing in 1841, Wollaston offers a view of how the country looked then and how it might benefit from 'cultivation'.

> *The soil of this country varies in a remarkable manner; sand, however, greatly predominating, and I do not think there is, taking the country throughout, one acre in twenty, although they may naturally produce scanty herbage for sheep and goats, worth cultivation. On the flats, the borders of estuaries and rivers, where alluvial soil has collected for ages and there are few, if any, trees of large size, the earth will produce spontaneously heavy crops of grain. There is much excellent land too on the borders of rivers, but requiring great labour and expense to bring into cultivation, being heavily timbered.*[6]

Cultivation for agriculture was only one prospect in the minds of other early south-west settlers. Busselton, with its sheltered anchorage in Geographe Bay, became a major port for the export of the unique hardwoods jarrah and karri. Timber cutters cleared the coastal plain of many of its remaining trees from the 1830s onwards.

Western Australian hardwoods were finding their way to South Australia and still further afield, to India and to England. Tuart trees, long dominant on the coastal plain around Busselton, were also cut and sold to the then island of Ceylon.[7]

But from the beginning of European settlement, farming inevitably also began to demand a reduction in tree cover, particularly along that same coastal plain. With a cautionary note about over-clearing, Wollaston describes the process in his own backyard:

> *We find it remarkably luxuriant here and prolific, so that we shall have, this harvest, nine acres of wheat. When I speak of clearing it must be understood that all the great trees are not removed; more will be by degrees but some must always remain. To give as good a notion as I can, upon paper, of the trees and stumps in our cornfield, the following is*

the shape of our first enclosure, containing with the gully or water course,
which runs, semi-circular through it, about 10 acres; the bottom of the
gully, when cleared, can be cultivated in summer and the banks would do
for a vineyard. When it is considered that this has been the result of our
own labour…we have great reason to be thankful.

In the place of a thick and gloomy wilderness, in which, when I first
came, I remember wandering about without knowing where I was and
almost shedding tears at the apparent task of subduing such a labyrinth,
there is now to be seen a beautiful green level of corn, an inexpressible
relief to the eye and no less so the mind. This in the course of two years.[8]

John Garrett Bussell, who had been one of the first settlers
at Augusta, along with Georgiana Molloy and her husband,
moved from the densely wooded settlement 'Adelphi' on the
Blackwood River in the mid-1830s. He took his family north to
the Vasse, later named the Busselton district. Inexpressible relief
was probably uppermost in his mind when the family made the
move north.

The country as we advanced improved rapidly; the ground on which we
trod was a vivid green, unsullied with burnt sticks and blackened grass
trees. Not that it was covered with a decided turf, but the vegetation
seemed more succulent than woody, and the plants, growing to about the
same height presented to the eye a smooth surface…Though the flowers
were perhaps not the same that characterise an English meadow, they
were not the less beautiful in appearance, varied in form and brilliant
in colour. Grass was in plenty and the clover? [sic] I have noticed above
with its bright scarlet and yellow flower, the daisy, the buttercup and the
purple marigold…

Half a mile brought us to a small river, deep and so slow that I could
hardly ascertain the existence of a current. I concluded it to be, as it
afterwards proved, the Vasse. The sound of rushing waters proclaimed
a rapid near. Walking therefore a short distance up the stream we found
what we sought, a passage over…Wide waving lawns were sloping down
to the water's edge. Trees thick and entangled were stooping over the
banks…About a hundred or two hundred yards on the other side we

Vasse River near its source, 2015.

obtained a sight of the sea, bearing N.W. The country here was so clear that a farmer could hardly grudge the fine spreading trees of red and white gum and peppermint the small portions of ground that they occupied only to ornament.[9]

Ever the critical clergyman, John Wollaston held a different 'grudge'. His was about the way some of his neighbours farmed in the 1840s.

Farming has been carried on here after a very slovenly, rambling manner; here a piece and there a piece, according as the soil promised best, and there were fewest trees, but a small quantity of land near home, well and annually cultivated, will yield great and better crops than this lazy method.[10]

It is doubtful that Wollaston had the Bussells in mind, farming their property 'Cattle Chosen', since he knew them well. But Edward Shann, in his history of 'Cattle Chosen' originally published in 1926, offers an explanation for the 'rambling manner'.

The age-long prevalence of dry seasons has stopped the accumulation of humus and the formation of rich soils, save in moist valleys. The woody foliage has dried and been burnt, incessantly by the black fellows' fires, lit to drive the game. The skilled farmers amongst the early settlers soon noted the consequent prevalence of earths without humus and the scattered occurrence of true soils. The humus necessary to profitable cultivation, in the days before scientific manuring, was to be found only on alluvial flats, in swamp lands and in pockets among the hills.

It is unfair, therefore to think of the pioneer settlers as ignorant of the land's powers because they settled it so sparsely. In the then state of agriculture the scattering was ordained by the soil.[11]

The hinterland's hills provide a defining backdrop to the Busselton coastal plain, providing numerous sources of flowing water. Backed to the east by the Darling Range and to the south by the Whicher Range, the Capel River, the Abba, the Sabina, the Ludlow, the Vasse and many smaller brooks. All feed the level ground as they flow towards the sea. And not only running rivers, as John Wollaston described them more than 150 years ago.

I was much struck with the view from the summit of the sea hills. Looking inwards from these heights you immediately descend into a flat swampy valley, beyond which the country again rises. The view of the impassable and extensive swamps, interspersed with lagoons, is very solemn.[12]

Not a view we would recognise today. Those 'impassable and extensive swamps' have largely been drained. But for early settlers they were a constant reminder of just how much water fell across the plain.

A tremendous quantity of rain has fallen — with much thunder and lightning and violent gales. Altogether last night the weather was the worst we have yet experienced in this country. The waters are out to a greater extent than last year. All the low grounds of our garden are flooded. One part is quite isolated. We can only get at our vegetables by rafting over the gully on some planks.[13]

In August 1862, John Garrett Bussell's wife, Charlotte, wrote to her sister in law, Fanny Bussell, then in England, to complain about too much rain.

We were suddenly surprised by a flood through the colony — such has never been witnessed before. All communication with Perth was at an end for about a month. The road was covered with water. The last journey the poor postman made upon it before the flood was at its height, nearly cost him his life.[14]

Flooding, inevitable in such a level and well-watered plain, would persist, but tree clearing, whether for export or agriculture, increased in volume as time went on. There were now fewer tuarts, marri and jarrah trees to absorb winter rain and hold down the water table.

In his history of Busselton, Rodger Jennings comments that drainage was one of the biggest problems facing local farmers in the early twentieth century.

Indeed, the district was first settled because of its swampy nature, thus providing an adequate water supply for agriculture and grazing pursuits. By this time it was realised however, that big quantities of valuable land were available if the streams and swamps were brought under control.[15]

In December 1910, the local newspaper, the *South-Western News*, was urging swift action to address the problems being experienced by local farmers.

It is beyond question that a large area of land exists in that part of the District [Quindalup and Lennox, now known as Jindong] suitable for the culture of root and fodder crops and under favourable conditions capable of carrying large numbers of dairy cattle and other stock. Under present conditions it is useless and lying idle through being covered with water for several months of the year...

The topographical features of the area under review are peculiar in that the brooks and streams from higher ground inland have no defined outlet to the sea, but all empty into a lagoon or swamp which runs parallel to the sea coast for many miles and which again has no definite banks or proper outlet but when filled by heavy rains spreads over the adjoining lands in all directions.

This imprisoned flood then has to find its way slowly to the sea through devious and quite inadequate openings. The position is further complicated by the fact of this huge swamp being only a few feet above sea level and subject at times to tidal influence.[16]

There were now two imperatives: the need to control flooding, while at the same time making more land available for agricultural use. Edward Shann, writing in 1926, saw this as part of a far longer cultural pattern.

In Western Australia the long war between men and trees has hardly begun. The land is in the Roman era, speaking comparatively. The pioneers, in effect, were like raiders on the Saxon Shore, in haste to make good their footing by the capture of a clearing that would give them instant returns. They tried the jarrah and the karri forest and, failing, were forced to seek out the open limestone lands, where the tuarts grew, or the coastal-alluvial areas.[17]

Back in 1907, the inheritors of the 'Saxon Shore' had begun their attempt to 'tame', and thus make more use of, these coastal alluvial areas.

Some months ago the Public Works Department, to overcome the ever-recurring trouble experienced in keeping the mouth of the Wonnerup Estuary open, decided to place two weirs at the Lockville. The ultimate object of the weirs was understood to be keeping out altogether the sea water and so, in time, freshening the flats along the inlet so that they would be rendered fit for cultivation and at the same time keeping the tops of the weirs just at the river high mark to allow the surplus waters at the time of heavy rains out to sea.[18]

Drainage was now uppermost in the minds of many settlers in their now-altered landscape. However the state government's 'present scheme' for draining the Busselton flood plain took several more years to even begin to take effect. By that time there were more famers on the coastal plain. The introduction of what became known as the Group Settlement Scheme in the early 1920s swelled the local rural population, as it did elsewhere in the south-west.

Under this scheme, would-be farmers, largely from Britain, often former servicemen from World War I, were encouraged by both the British and the Western Australian governments to become dairy farmers. The State at that time lacked a dairy industry and the cool conditions of the south-west looked like an ideal area in which to establish one.

But more farms meant more clearing. Sid Slee, whose father emigrated to Busselton from England in 1925, recalls a boyhood where:

> I cut my teeth on an axe and a mattock. We spent a lot of time with just the horse and the slinging harness on the back. And that's how we cleared the land, Dad and I, before the bulldozers came.[19]

When he was not exploring newly built drains in his home-made canoe, it seemed to Sid that more drains were urgently needed. He recalls that when he and his father were clearing their land in the late 1920s, the paddocks still: 'got flooded and the grass wouldn't grow properly because it was too wet. A lot of farms were virtually cut off with water not getting away'.[20]

Major drainage work finally started in 1926, ten years after the *South-Western News* had urged the urgent completion of a major drainage project.

The main problem facing water engineers was the number of rivers which flowed through the region and the way in which several of them were vitally intertwined. T. A. D. Phelan points this out in his 1968 *Survey of the Busselton District Drainage Scheme*.

> *The Wonnerup Estuary is the feature into which all rivers flow and it is here that the drainage problem is critical. The Sabina flows into the*

Vasse which in winter overflows with the water of the Wonnerup Estuary. The Abba river flows into the flood plain of the estuary during winter and into the Vasse direct in drier months; while the Ludlow River has been directly diverted by a drain into the Wonnerup.[21]

Phelan's study also noted that it was necessary to provide for year-long productivity.

Prior to the start of the twentieth century, the land being used rurally was inundated each winter due to the relative winter rainfall from April through to August and also because of the poor drainage pattern of the area. Accordingly a great deal of the land was useless, which would not have been so if a drainage scheme could have been evolved for the area.[22]

The size of the area to be drained and the demands of different localities meant that the scheme proceeded slowly and in phases. Work to remove surface water from the Abba and Sabina rivers, and associated projects including the installation of floodgates and drains at various sites, took until 1924.[23]

As Phelan explained, this scheme in itself could not solve the entire drainage problem, and a major plan was laid down in 1926.

The chief characteristic of the area was a large expanse of swamp land half a mile from the sea on the Vasse-Wonnerup Estuary. To overcome this it was decided to attempt to carry the whole of the water drained from the uplands across the estuary at a high level and to provide outlets accessible to the sea, thus leaving purely local drainage gravitating to the estuary to be carried to the sea through low level outlets protected from inflows of salt water by flood gates…Success would be due to the fact that upland water would not be allowed to flow into the estuary swamps.[24]

The 1926 scheme was not completed until 1932 and, during the Great Depression of the early 1930s, it gave employment to the 'susso' (sustenance) generation: men who dug the long drains at Busselton and Vasse and elsewhere in the south-west.[25]

In fact, the Busselton district drainage project continued into the 1950s and the 1960s. Phelan concluded his 1968 survey by commenting that that while some criticism had been made of its economic viability:

> *Certainly without the system, the district would be economically sterile regarding agriculture which would have quite a strong effect on the state economy. Consequently the economic feasibility of drainage extensions must be considered but still today this district is certainly unique in regard to its drainage problem, and what the future holds in the field of drainage will be a point of interest for many people.*[26]

When Coralie Tarbotton, now a Busselton City Councillor, and her husband began farming in the district in 1976, the benefits of the drainage scheme were apparent. 'If we hadn't had drainage, the land would have been very wet and probably not manageable, particularly in the wet season: June, July, August'.[27]

But as annual rainfall has decreased, that situation has changed.

> *Today it is very different. Our place is very dry. When we first came... we used to park our car on the main road past our gate, Doyle Road, and walk in gum boots two hundred and fifty metres up to our house. Now we have a beautiful dry gravel driveway.*[28]

Phelan, writing in 1968, expressed uncertainly as to what the future might hold for the Busselton Drainage Scheme. In the twenty-first century that future has now arrived. Today those same drains now carry away not just excess water, but at times also heavy algal blooms – another excess resulting from many years of phosphate fertiliser from farms seeping into both rivers and drains.

Kath Lynch, District Manager Geographe Capes area for the Department of Water, outlines the current situation on the coastal plain.

> *Where we have high agricultural intensity in our south-west catchments like the Busselton plain, we have added difficulties, in that we now have a heavily cleared catchment where a lot of the native vegetation has already gone. And we have a heavily drained catchment. And while*

drains are very good at taking water off land, they are also good at quickly taking nutrients into our rivers. Our sandy soils have a very low phosphorus-binding capacity so a certain percentage of fertiliser that is applied to the soils leaches off quite quickly, whereas with heavy clay soils that would not happen.[29]

So has the drainage system turned out to be part of the current problem? Kath Lynch looks back at the pre-drainage era for some of the answers.

We are no longer getting the flushing of those sediments and nutrients that we had many years ago before the modification of the river system. The Busselton River System is a very flat system. In the past a lot more water flowed naturally into that area. A good flow helps to keep the bar open and the water going through. And that removes the sediments.

So in those big flow years more of the sediments and nutrients would have dropped out naturally. But both land clearing and drainage have substantially increased sediment loads. At the same time agriculture has also increased nutrient load. Given that this was always a 'flat' system, sediments would previously have been trapped naturally in the estuary but would have then been flushed out during higher flows. We no longer get those higher flows due to a drying climate and river diversions.[30]

The effect of excessive nutrients in an estuarine system is explained in the *Vasse Wonnerup Wetlands and Geographe Bay Water Quality Improvement Plan*, published by the Department of Water in March 2010.

The Vasse Wonnerup Wetlands and the catchment waterways have experienced severe water quality problems for many years. These problems have included regular blooms of toxic algae, sudden mass fish deaths, reduced recreational opportunities and unpleasant odours resulting from the decomposition of algae and exposure of anoxic sediments. Limited flushing opportunities arising from the installation of floodgates at the mouth of the estuaries [are] likely to have increased the susceptibility of this system to nutrients. Thousands of waterbirds have continued to use the Vasse Wonnerup Wetlands each year, despite severe nutrient enrichment, but there is concern that further increases in nutrient loads may alter the waterbirds' food sources. Managing the levels of nutrients that enter the wetlands from catchment sources will not only minimise risks to waterbirds, but also help to mitigate nuisance water quality problems in the area.[31]

So, given the severity of the nutrient problem, what do farmers and other fertiliser-users need to know and now do?

Damien Postma, Chief Executive Officer at South West Catchments Council, has worked with many of them in recent years.

Truthfully, better information is all they need. Better information about what they should put on their paddocks and 'when and where'. We work very hard to do whole-of-farm soil mapping so that farmers understand literally, paddock by paddock what is needed to help them calibrate their fertiliser spreaders so they know what they are applying and to understand the chemistry involved.

Ibis on the Vasse Estuary.

The traditional response from primary producers has been 'We're not getting that growth, so let's put on more phosphorus'. But often it is the pH that is wrong; for example, a really low pH in acidic soil can stop phosphorus being available to the plant. Farmers don't need more phosphorus. The land might just be acidic. What they need is some way of improving their soil, such as adding lime or introducing practices which change the chemistry of the soil.[32]

Vic Rodwell, farming on the coastal plain near Boyanup, has worked to change the chemistry of his soil. He draws on family experience.

Before my time, within this Bunbury-Busselton coastal plain, this area was traditionally a very wet, waterlogged area. I assume that's why they put the drains in. Then my Dad grew maize crops on dry land years ago. Those were stories that I grew up with.

The drains have brought both good and bad. Ultimately they have dried out the country and allowed it to be more productive. The negative side is that, due to poor farming practice, a lot of the nutrients end up getting into the estuaries more quickly and affecting conditions downstream.[33]

As he admits, those long-standing practices die hard.

Up to ten years ago it was common practice to put your phosphorus on, in large amounts, in the dry, February–March, because the Department of Agriculture and tradition said that was what you had to do. But certain soils hold phosphorus in different ways and if you had a very wet start the phosphorus would move. A lot of this country is quite sandy so its phosphorus retention index is low and a lot moves.[34]

Vic also looks back to the way expanding agricultural areas has affected vegetation. He notes particularly the effects of nineteenth- and twentieth-century land clearing.

If the trees have gone, the understory has gone and the ability to retain water through the natural process of nature has gone. I think the trees going and then putting in the drains just compounded the problem.[35]

As a farmer himself, and with his father's experience behind him, Vic naturally wanted to improve agricultural production but to also learn more about soil science.

We started to realise that there was more phosphorus within our dairy systems than we needed. So ten years ago I became part of the Greener Pastures project: mainly a nitrogen-based research program. Working with that project alerted me to the actual amount of phosphorus needed within a dairy system to maintain high levels of production. So from that period onward, we soil test every paddock, every year. The cost of testing is miniscule compared to the benefits.

We have stopped applying phosphorus in many areas of our systems to the point where in this last year we have actually got areas of the farm that have become phosphorus limited.

So now we are having to apply phosphorus again. But the important thing is to understand where you need phosphorus, what you need and how much you need.[36]

The problems raised by excessive nutrients don't stop at the farm gate. They affect the entire region in terms of recreation and health, both human and environmental. In that context, Kath Lynch suggests, urban dwellers (and she includes herself), have to share responsibility.

While townsite gardeners obviously use less fertiliser than the farming community, the nutrients it creates can still find their way into the waterways that surround Busselton and also into the Geographe Bay; where it could affect sea-grass and fish stocks.

Increasing urban development and nutrients from new urban areas threaten Geographe Bay and there is a risk of things getting worse. So when we, as a Department, look at a proposal for an urban development site, we require water-sensitive urban design principles and practices to reduce nutrient runoff as an important feature for any new suburbs. We want to make them better than the suburbs we live in now.

A lot of the progressive thinking and work has been done with the developers and their consultants. We aim for 'Bay Friendly' gardens with low nutrients and low water requirements, but still beautiful gardens.[37]

The Vasse River is seen as one of Busselton's distinctive aesthetic assets. It threads through the town and slowly broadens into an estuary before it reaches the sea.

In April 2014 I talked with Allan Pastega, Program Manager (Catchment Science and Investigations) at the Department of Water, and with Senior Hydrographer Darren Orr. We met at the Vasse Floodgates just before the river empties into Geographe Bay and thence the Indian Ocean. Looking upstream from the floodgates the river both looked and smelt bad. Large lumps of putrid algae, the result of phosphates in the water, detached themselves as they drifted towards the gates and, almost magnetically, re-attached themselves to large blackish green and scummy deposits. The stench was overpowering.

Allan and Darren regularly monitor this 'end of summer' situation as the local community has concerns about algal bloom and fish kills that happen here at the floodgates. There are houses nearby, and the local people want more information as to why this is happening.

> Our job is to try and predict when the next one might happen and put some management in place to deal with that like opening the flood gates and trying to flush some of the bad water out.[38]

Allan and Darren had just rowed ashore from their inspection of four yellow buoys, placed strategically in the river, upstream of the floodgates. They had been put there in response to community concern and the potential for more algae blooms in late summer and early autumn.

> The buoys are powered by solar panels. They give us real-time data that goes onto the internet so they are logging every two minutes 24 hours a day. Upstream, where there is a fish kill, is where it happens worst. So we've got one buoy there. It measures dissolved oxygen temperature, salinity, and we can look at those and, hopefully, give some sort of warning that an event may be about to occur and the floodgates can be opened or closed, depending on what is needed.[39]

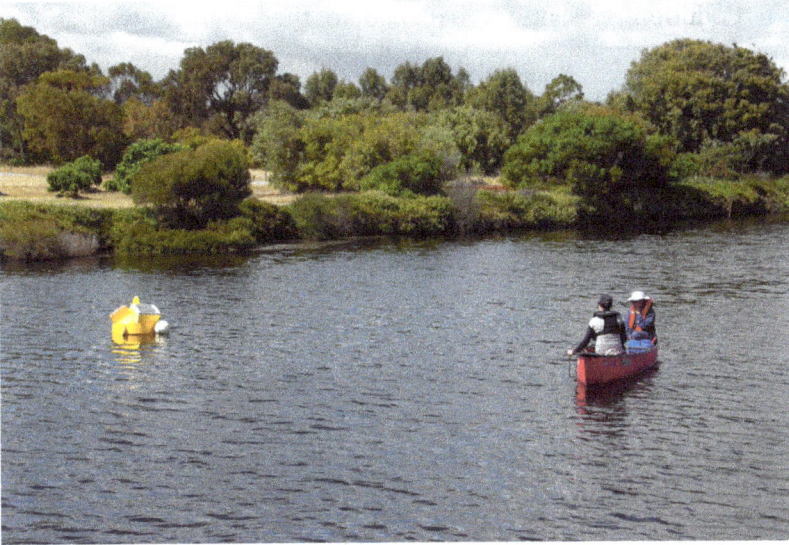

Yellow buoys on the Vasse Estuary.

In the future, it seems likely that the region will receive more rain in summer. Kath Lynch is concerned that if this happens:

There is a risk that fish kills may become more frequent even if the system is at status quo. By late summer the system is at a really bad point, and the river is really saline. If you get any rainfall then it puts a cap of fresh water on top of the saline water. It's called stratification and prevents oxygen exchange. If the river was still fresh at that time of year, it would dilute the effect, but because the river is saline by then and then hyper-saline, you end up with stratification. I think if we get increased summer rainfall, we may expect more fish kills.[40]

As Kath Lynch explained, water pollution throughout the Vasse–Wonnerup estuary is also due to topography.

The catchment doesn't flush well. Areas like the Vasse–Wonnerup wetlands are very flat, varying about a metre between the coast and many kilometres inland. So when water from the catchment, carrying nutrients and sediments, gets into these big broad bodies of water, the sediment just falls out.[41]

Pollution presents a challenge to the town as well as the wetlands. Busselton City Councillor Coralie Tarbotton describes the current urban situation.

> The challenge is that the Vasse River has been diverted into a drain. We allow the water to come down the river during the wet season, when the water level is at its highest. But we don't allow the initial rains to stay in the Vasse because we feel that they contain a lot of fertiliser. That water goes down the drain and out into the bay.[42]

Inevitably the construction of the drain has affected the Vasse River. Its flow is lower for part of the year and some fertiliser still finds its way into the estuary beyond the town limits. So can the Vasse be returned to its original cleaner condition? Coralie Tarbotton does not think this is possible.

> There are probably many people who would like to see the Vasse River returned to its former state. But you can't. Urban development has spread around the fringes of the town and the risk of flooding remains. There is only a very slight difference between having good water and lovely wetlands and some areas being flooded.[43]

Algae infestation in a Busselton diversion drain, summer 2015.

As Kath Lynch points out, the riverbed itself is now heavily affected by decades of acquired contaminants.

> *There are nutrients in the groundwater that are still moving and nutrients in our streams. So even if we stop applying any nutrients, there are still probably ten years of available nutrients coming through the system.*
>
> *And in the lower Vasse River, the nutrients in the sediments could probably keep that system affected by blue-green algae for fifty years. So we have to look at a long-term reduction of nutrients and not putting more nutrients into new developments.*[44]

So would dredging the Vasse help the situation?

> *Yes, once we have reduced the nutrients from the catchment, removal of sediment will be a good idea. It has been trialled by Geo-Catch and the City of Busselton. There are a couple of problems. Dredging is really difficult to do. The material is so fine and silty and nutrients are still coming in, every time it rains. It is also a very costly exercise. Future decisions to dredge the river will need to be made on a cost–benefit basis. Over recent years we have put our efforts into reducing the nutrients from the catchment area. But there is no quick fix or cheap fix.*[45]
>
> *In many ways the Vasse is and has been central, not just to the geography of Busselton, but also to a sense of place; especially for older residents. The people who get most unhappy about the river are the older generation and I think it is because they have seen it deteriorate. They recall a time when there were paddle-boats on the Vasse every year for the Festival Queen. I think people who have been here for less time don't see the change as much. But the people who get really upset about the Vasse River are the people who enjoyed recreation on the river and remember something wonderful and now see this terrible system. They've seen real change.*[46]

Time, diligence and patience seem to be key factors in this environmental context.

> *It will be a long time before the Vasse looks good. The problem is that it doesn't take a lot of phosphorus to create an algal boom. We have seen*

Vasse River at Busselton, 2015.

reductions in phosphorus that look exciting but visually you can't see a
scrap of difference because in the river system, the phosphorus needs to
decrease by 70 per cent for an algal bloom not to occur.[47]

So where does the community now stand in relation to the
environmental problems facing both town and country? As a
Busselton City Councillor, Coralie Tarbotton sees the task as a
very-long-term effort.

A lot of research has been done but distilling what comes from the research
and then interpreting it into an activity requires quite a lot of time and
effort. Are we making progress? Yes and no. We are looking at how we
can all work together to improve the water quality, the wetlands, how we
are managing the drainage and how we could manage it better.

An important consideration is that if we make an alteration in one
situation we have to think about possible repercussions at another site. So
we have to continually research to do it better.[48]

Furthermore, not all the problems flow from the hinterland:

The rural fertiliser contribution is quite significant but also the town's industrial areas don't have infill sewerage. These are some of the areas where we are working to get the government support. And behind all these is funding and unfortunately there is not as much funding available as there could be. Everyone wants improvements but it all can't be done at once. A lot of environmental community groups volunteer, groups who are just fantastic in supporting the different agencies in what they do.[49]

While in the past, the priority was draining the rural land for agriculture, this practice is giving way to:

...looking at ways and means of retaining the water. Not necessarily where it used to pool. But in the new residential developments we've put in swales, areas that are set aside and ponds that capture the water but naturally dry out as the season dries out. They don't build on that area in the subdivision.[50]

As Kath Lynch observed, the major problem for both Busselton and its hinterland still comes down to the state of the water, whether in town or on the land. But the risk also eventually applies to the sea if polluted water flows into Geographe Bay and poses a threat to the seagrass.

To help Geographe Bay you have to work on the entire catchment. If you only work on the lower Vasse, you are only intervening halfway down the system. You have do dredging, changing the hydraulics, spending a lot of money on an engineering solution. We also need to treat the broader catchment and spend money on protecting Geographe Bay. While most people right now see only the river problem, we need to work on both the bay and the river.

Unfortunately by the time the bay shows signs of distress and people say we should concentrate on that, it might be too late because once you lose your seagrass beds you are in real trouble. They affect the health of the entire bay.[51]

Station Gully, looking north to Geographe Bay.

Whether salt or fresh, water, in Kath Lynch's view, remains the key to the health of field, town and sea.

> *It has taken over a hundred years to reduce water quality to the low level where it is now. It is probably going to take us ten, twenty years to get back to anywhere near where community expectations lie.*[52]

And back on cleared land, dairy farmer Vic Rodwell looks at where some of the problems began.

> *We are probably the creators of our own problems. Back when there were lots of little dairies and everyone milked fifty cows and made a living, there were no issues with the environmental impact because fifty cows weren't in the yard long enough to cause too many issues.*
>
> *But to stay viable we had to intensify – again intensifying the level of nutrients being brought onto one site. With the cost price squeeze a lot of people are looking at being more intensive. But we really need to stop and look at how we farm on the coastal plain. And if the environmental pressures keep coming maybe we need to do things differently. That is one of our biggest challenges.*[53]

While people living in Busselton and on its surrounding coastal plain wrestle with environmental changes dictated by the demands of European-style agriculture, the Donnelly River and the associated Warren River wetlands, on the south coast, have been less affected by 'progress', although there has been human intervention in the area.

The Donnelly River, in its lower reaches, near the timber town of Pemberton, is navigable by canoe or launch as it winds its way through what is now dense woodland. Peter Casonato takes tourists on a boat journey out to the Southern Ocean. This is the only way to reach the sea at this point. There are no roads, not even any four-wheel-drive tracks.

> *The Donnelly is one of the most pristine rivers around. It keeps that way because the river is very short; only about 150 kilometres in length. Its catchment area is only 1,600 square kilometres. By comparison the Blackwood River is 22,000 square kilometres.*
>
> *Only approximately 14 per cent of the catchment is cleared farmland. This is mostly in the upper reaches and quite low-intensive farming so it, the river, doesn't have salinity problems. There is no fertiliser run off because farming impact is minimal. The remaining 86 per cent of land in the catchment area is either state forest or national park so there are few introduced species.*[54]

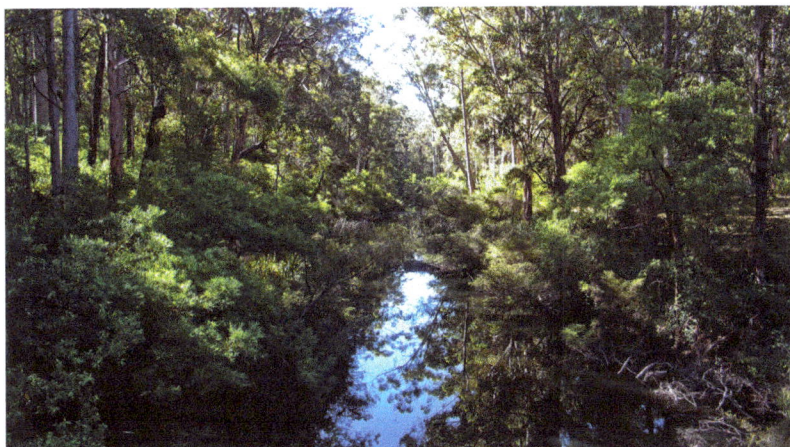

Upper Donnelly River from One Tree Bridge.

Today, most of the area around the lower Donnelly River is either state forest or national park. While in the past the area has been influenced by human activity, those interventions have had fewer negative impacts.

The landscape around these wetlands and down to the south coast, as it existed when European settlers arrived in the mid-nineteenth century, was the result of centuries of deliberate land management practices by the First Australians.

Roger Underwood, the former General Manager of WA's then Department of Conservation and Land Management (CALM), relates that when the nineteenth-century settlers began to establish farms along the Blackwood River Valley, they were told by the local Aboriginal people about '...a vast area of grassland to the south along the coast. They went down and they explored and they found this beautiful savannah woodland with scattered trees and grass'.[55]

Roger suggests that the Nyungar people deliberately kept the country in this state to provide good summer hunting grounds.

> *The Aboriginals used to burn the country whenever it would burn. They would burn it in small patches so the animals would come in and get fresh shoots and so the Aboriginals would have a smaller ground to hunt them on instead of large areas. Then later on, when the stockmen started going down there, most of the stockmen were Aboriginals in the really early days. The white people used to burn the country the same way as the Aboriginals had done so that their cows had fresh food as well.*[56]

So where are the cows now? Looking at the densely wooded land bordering the Donnelly River today, it is hard to believe that this whole area provided rich summer pasture for cattle. Bill Ipsen's family, originally from (Scandinavian) Denmark, were farmers and cattle drovers in this country for over one hundred years. When they, and other families like the Muirs and the Scotts, first took up farming around Bridgetown and Manjimup, they found that, while their cattle did very well to start with, after a time they would lose condition. So, as Bill Ipsen tells the story, one of the newcomers consulted the people who understood the country.

> Thomas Giblett talked to the local Aboriginals and they suggested that the settlers should take the cattle down to the south coast, where there were a lot of low shrubby plants and a lot of native grasses. So they took their cattle down there and they did all right for a while and then they started to lose condition there and so they took them back up inland.

What the settlers didn't know then was that both the inland and the coastal pastures lacked minerals that grazing cattle needed: cobalt, copper and selenium. However, rotating the stock between the two areas allowed the cattle to remain in good condition all year. As Bill Ipsen recalls:

> That is why they started shifting them backwards and forwards. A number of settler families obtained large leases over this coastal country and brought their cattle down in summer. Those who didn't use that method faded away.[57]

The presence of cattle can lead to the introduction of exotic plants, their seeds often carried in the cows' stomachs, but as Peter Casonato points out:

> Fortunately these cattle spent a few days in the bush before they arrived here. That way it cleaned out their systems, So we didn't get a large number of introduced seeds into the area.[58]

So, even after over a hundred years of intermittent cattle grazing on the lower Donnelly River area, the long-term impact of cattle on this environment has been, as Roger Underwood sees it:

> Very minor as it turned out. I used to think that the impact of the cattle was important. But what was actually going on was that the cattle were eating the grass, which was an annual crop [and] used to come up every year. It had previously been eaten by kangaroos anyway. And it was really that the cattle substituted as herbivores for the huge flocks of kangaroos that used to be there.[59]

Bill Ipsen himself first drove cattle into the area in 1949 when he was fourteen and continued to do so until the early 1980s. At first it was still open country and easy to ride through.

> In my time when you got to the coast you could not even bash your knees on a bush. But now in the last fifty years it has got that thick that it is impossible to get through. It was grassland under big peppermints. There were a lot of big peppermint trees. There are a few little patches of them today.[60]

Bill remembers that his parents and grandparents also recalled the open nature of this country.

> When they drove the cattle from Dingup to the Donnelly they could ride through there any way they wanted to, so they would ride down through the bush, drive the milk cows down there and drive them back and they would have bullock carts and all that sort of thing to shift their supplies off. So that meant that the bush was fairly open and all my grandparents and my associated family all talk about how open the bush was.

But, adds Bill, that country today is very different. 'Now you can't even get through it with a bulldozer'. The peppermints are thicker because of the burning.

> But this is a different type of burn, because early settlers burned the area regularly and they burned it slowly. Then they closed all burning down, in the early 1920s, when the Forest Department said 'no more burning'. So they found it very difficult to burn without getting caught. So the bush got a little bit harder to burn and it wouldn't burn until it got a very hot fire. Once you got a very hot fire, especially with peppermints, they have a bulb root system. They would burn off hot and at ground level and, where at one time you had only one peppy coming up, you would now have ten peppies coming up which doubles your density. And then you would not burn it for another ten or fifteen years and the next hot fire would be twice as hot because of the extra density of bush. It would be twice as hot and there'd be twice as many plants to burn.[61]

As time went on, there were also fewer cattle trampling the undergrowth.

> *As the farmers got more fertilisers and more knowledge of how to handle mineral deficiencies, they used the coast less and less because they were growing more grass at home. So the cattle numbers dropped off, which meant the bush wasn't burned so often and the stock weren't walking through it making tracks and pads, so it gradually got neglected by the cattle men.*[62]

Cattle droving finally came to an end in the early 1980s and the whole area was gazetted as a national park. Roger Underwood remembers how the area was 'saved' from the threat of 'development' for agriculture and mining.

> *A lot of that coastal area had in fact originally been surveyed as farms back at the time of Group Settlement in the 1920s. The farms had never been taken up and they were still Crown Land but all the surveys were there. Someone had the idea they would have all this land alienated to private property, develop intensive farming and build an abattoir at Broke Inlet.*
>
> *Also at that time that land was pegged for sand mining. So we, in the then Forests Department, came up with the idea of a South Coast National Park. Over a period of several years the proposal was discussed around the place. But it was not popular with the people who still had the cattle leases. There was a public meeting at Manjimup at which I was asked to speak to describe what we were proposing. I remember being booed off the stage by all those people opposed to the idea. But eventually, after the formation of CALM in the mid-1980s, the atmosphere was just right and the new park was created.*[63]

While the establishment of the national park was not popular with the cattlemen, it did limit human intervention. Some, like Bill Ipsen, suggest that this has been to the detriment of the environment.

> *We used to have a lot of wildflowers because they had light and air underneath the big trees. You could pick orchids and other wildflowers*

wherever you went. Since they stopped burning, except for the hot fires, it got so thick that it smothered all your little plants. So without keeping the country reasonably open and reasonably lightly burned, you are losing a lot of your native heritage. To get it back to normal you would have to virtually clear it and then let it come back naturally without getting it too thick again. Otherwise you are going to have the same problem.[64]

This of course begs the question of what is 'normal'. Discussing the flora, the wildflowers, of the region, botanist Neville Marchant, makes this point.

One thing we have to remember is that if the Aboriginal people have been here for forty, fifty, sixty or even seventy thousand years, that is nothing really in the long-term time-frame. WA and the south-west have been isolated from eastern Australia for 50 million years; a long time in isolation and you are looking at five, six or seven million years for the evolution of lots of our species. So the species evolved without that controlled burning effect of the Aboriginal people.[65]

The hydrology of the Donnelly River has also evolved over those millions of years and it has some unique characteristics. Peter Casonato frequently explains to visitors on his boat trip why this river is unusual.

Our river, like most rivers, will close over at its mouth during the year. It is affected by a sandbar which is common to most rivers. But while most rivers close over once and open up once in a year, this one doesn't. It will break through up to two dozen times in a spring, summer and autumn.

One interesting aspect is that we have eighteen kilometres of river that carries a depth of two metres. We have an extremely small catchment but in the middle of summer we could go ten kilometres further upstream from here and detect zero water flow.[66]

So where does the water come from?

It now appears that the Donnelly River is fed from below, by the Yarragadee aquifer, the extensive freshwater aquifer lying beneath the Bunbury Trough and the Scott Coastal Plain.

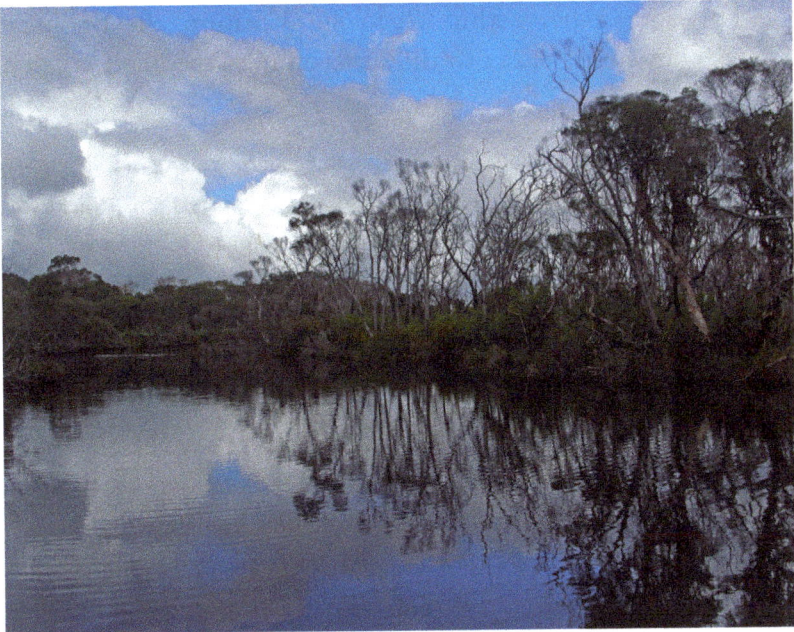

Mid-stream Donnelly River.

As geologist and environmentalist Peter Lane explains, the Yarragadee is an extraordinary aquifer.

> The formation is about 160 million years old and yet the water it contains is less than 40,000 years old. A lot of the water is very recent because it is recharged from just last winter. So the amount of water-flow into the aquifer, and renewed annually, is quite substantial.[67]

The Donnelly River is not the only body of water in this part of south-west WA substantially influenced by the Yarragadee.

> Lake Jasper, the largest fresh water lake in WA, lies to the west of the Donnelly River. It too is recharged annually by discharge water from the Yarragadee aquifer and the overlying Leederville formation. And it has been estimated that it takes about seven months for that water to go through the lake and then it is eventually discharged into the Southern Ocean.[68]

This aquifer lies within a geological feature, the Bunbury Trough, but comes closer to the surface under the Scott Coastal Plain.

The Yarragadee is quite shallow in the western part of the Bunbury Trough. As you go east towards Nannup it goes down to a depth of about 1,600 metres and then shallows again south towards the mouth of the Donnelly River where it is only a couple of hundred metres deep.[69]

So there is a close connection between the Donnelly River and the Yarragadee.

The river actually cuts into the Yarragadee. The Yarragadee is disguised there by superficial sediments such as sand-hills and limestone but the river reflects the water level in the aquifer. If the Yarragadee is drawn on too heavily or doesn't get enough recharge from rainfall, the river level will fall. And this is largely because there is very little flow down the Darling Scarp in the main catchment of the river in summer.[70]

As tourist-boat operator Peter Casonato understands only too well, once the level of the river rises sufficiently as a result of water received from the Yarragadee, it will break out at the sandbar and drop rapidly.

Of course the river level can vary by a couple of metres or more through this constant closing over and opening up. Importantly, this constant flooding and drying out supports the Warren River wetlands that need this temporary but not long-term inundation.[71]

But what if more water is taken from the Yarragadee in summer? How would this affect the Donnelly River and those wetlands? Peter Casonato has some concerns.

Because the catchment is so pristine, a lot of work is being done to try to keep it that way. And obviously rainfall variations are likely to affect the water quality. But I believe the big key factor here will be the taking of water from the Yarragadee. This is one of the most worrying aspects because we just don't know exactly what the transfer rates are.[72]

The Donnelly River, although it has fared much better than the Vasse-Wonnerup system in terms of human intervention, could still become hostage to the requirements of a thirsty capital city, three hundred kilometres to the north. Perth is always looking for more water for a growing population and increased industry. Taking water from the Yarragadee, an enormous and ancient deep aquifer, currently storing about 1,000 cubic kilometres of water (compared with about 20 cubic kilometres in Perth's Gnangara Mound), is an attractive proposition for a thirsty city. Already this aquifer, as Peter Casonato notes, is important in helping to meet other regional water requirements.

> We take water from the ground to feed into our water supply. Our major aquifers are the Leederville and Yarragadee aquifers. Our groundwater system remains vital to meeting our water needs and makes up about 40 per cent of our total supply. To ensure the sustainability of our groundwater, we are investing in a new expanded deep groundwater network. By 2022, around half of Perth's water drinking water will come from secure deep groundwater sources[73].

The Water Corporation's plans for the future also include 'replenishing our deep aquifers with recycled water through a new groundwater replenishment scheme'.[74] Currently the commitment is to use Yarragadee water to supplement the Bridgetown Regional Water Supply and to expand this service progressively to other south-west towns.[75]

However, Peter Casonato remains concerned about the effect on the Donnelly River of taking water from this aquifer.

> We believe that they have now started increasing the volume of water they take from the Yarragadee. And during this last summer, for the first time, for two separate one-week periods, I detected that the river did not rise. Normally the river rises on a daily basis when the bar is closed, even in summer.[76]

Shaun Whittaker, who works with Peter Casonato, thinks that the total effect and value of the Yarragadee aquifer is poorly understood and that people have often grasped only part of the story.

We have people on our Donnelly River boat trips who assert that there is a thousand years of water supply there for Perth's needs. And, sure, if you look at the entire volume that is probably correct.[77]

For both Shaun and Peter, the size of the aquifer is irrelevant because in the rivers and wetlands of the southern coastal fringe, the ecological value of the Yarragadee lies within that shallow part which comes near to the surface in this area and which is responsible for those important fluctuations in the river level throughout the year.

That miniscule percentage that appears near the surface of the entire volume is the important part for us, here on the Donnelly River. That percentage can be lost so very quickly and that is the bit that is important for this environment. That is the bit that people living in and appreciating this environment and the diversity that we have here, want to retain for the future.[78]

Peter Lane thinks that, fortunately, government attitudes to taking water from the Yarragadee aquifer have changed in the last couple of years.

They are looking very carefully at conserving that water. There is always a balance between taking water and some damage to the environment and I believe they have recognised more recently that the weight has moved too far toward environmental damage, if they keep taking water. I think the application in 2007 from the Water Corporation to take more water each year, the investigation of that application and the public outcry, really made them realise how vulnerable the area is, how delicate that balance is.[79]

Obviously public opinion is important. Shaun is also heartened by the fact that people in the city are becoming more aware that water supplies are finite.

I think there is an awareness that aquifers are not an everlasting supply. Perth people are seeing that their backyard bores now have to go deeper and deeper and the lake systems in the Perth area are now drying up as a result of pumping and lowering the water table of the aquifer.[80]

At the same time, the demands of the state's ever-increasing population for a reliable and adequate water supply will remain. So the future may still be uncertain for the Donnelly River, with its unique beauty and character.

And from Coralie Tarbotton in Busselton, living and farming in a coastal environment which Europeans have been modifying for well over a hundred years, a thought about waterways and human intervention.

One of the big things for me is the inter-connection of life. If the waterways are not functioning I am unhappy. And once you begin to learn about what happens when you do one thing, you realise it has a repercussion somewhere else.[81]

Donnelly River reflections.

Chapter 3

'We've cleared the paddock'

The 'cleared paddock' was vast. It took in country from west of the Stirling Range across to the edge of the South West Land Division west of Esperance; but for Keith Bradby, from Albany-based Gondwana Link, it was once part of a single integral ecological zone, inseparable from adjacent landscapes.

> *What I understand now more and more is that I'm not looking at, or talking about, three separate landscapes, I'm talking about one landscape. It's not broken up, or at least it wasn't broken up until we arrived.*[1]

'We' means Europeans and 'arrival' was relatively recent. For almost a hundred and twenty years after the establishment of the Swan River Colony, while the new settlers in this part of the country did some mining and grazed sheep, much of this southern region of Western Australia remained thriving bushland, a biodiversity storehouse of both plants and animals. But that would change. In 1948, the state government, in the spirit of post-war recovery, urged men already on the land and new farmers, often ex-soldiers, to take up and cultivate much of

A broken landscape.

this uncleared land. By the 1960s, the government was looking to put 'a million acres a year under the plough'.

Between 1948 and 1969 that boast was generally realised. Five years into this massive land clearing, in 1953, a War Service Land Settlement project began at Jerramungup, a place of upstanding Yates trees[2], with more land in the area being made available from 1959, for 'new land' farmers, as they became known, under a Conditional Purchase (CP) Scheme. Conditional Purchase terms obliged farmers to clear one third of the land before they could freehold their property. It was an incentive to keep cutting, clearing and burning.

When Keith Bradby came from Victoria in 1976 to start a new life in Western Australia, that clearing was still going ahead apace. But for him the landscape that had survived was a revelation.

> I immediately sensed the immensity of the south-west. I saw the banksia shrub lands as a floral fairyland. I saw my first honey possums and this strange new country started to resonate with me.[3]

Keith's initial occupation as an apiarist in the Ravensthorpe region made him strongly aware of the distinctive local flora and deepened his botanical knowledge.

I eventually realised I was living in some form of 'inland Galapagos' with islands of soils surrounded by a 'sea' made up of other soil islands, all supporting different plant species and providing different wildlife habitats.[4]

At the same time, wildlife, whether fauna or flora, was rapidly disappearing under the plough as the 'new land' farmers cleared more and more bush. For an apiarist on a steep learning curve, the bush spoke back.

You're out in it all the time and to me that is captivating and, being on your own in the bush, you start looking around for like-minded souls; some of the farmers and people like zoologist Andy Chapman. You learnt from them more than you needed to successfully bee-keep.[5]

Andy Chapman, who arrived in Ravensthorpe in 1979, had previously carried out biological surveys with the Western Australian Museum. In his fieldwork he had witnessed contrasting conditions in the Kimberley and the Western Australian wheatbelt, two regions, in his own words representing 'the least and most disturbed WA environments'.[6]

For Andy, the most evident change when he came to the southern coast country was loss of connectivity. Clearing the landscape had not only caused a decline in both plants and animals. It had also left behind so-called reserves that were, in effect, isolated islands of native vegetation.[7]

Even before the land was cleared, plants and animals would have existed in an archipelago of different landforms and soil types. Nevertheless there was a degree of continuity to allow the maintenance of biological processes. And that allowed animals to move through the landscape. Even if a certain patch of it wasn't to their liking they could keep going and find one that was.[8]

A significant case study of loss, in Andy's view, was the recent decline, and in some places disappearance, of small perching birds. Andy found that surveys that he and others had carried out in the 1970s contrasted sharply with work undertaken twenty years later by other scientists: 'By then certain species of birds had literally fallen off the perch'.[9]

A major factor in the disappearance of these birds was their inability, unlike larger birds, to fly over distance and find new homes if threatened by land clearance or feral animal intrusion.

The problem was not just a matter of fuel capacity, i.e. their ability to fly far. As small birds they were particularly vulnerable to predators if they ventured outside the cover provided by the bush. They were accustomed to existing inside very specific but connected habitats. So isolation created by a broken landscape made it difficult for them to re-colonise areas where, for example, local populations of their species had been wiped out in bushfires.

While the small perching bird story is a tale of inability to adapt in a rapidly changing landscape, another ecological case study from the same region suggests both continuity and adaptability.

In undertaking a master's degree at Murdoch University, Andy Chapman also pursued a study of a small freshwater fish, the spotted minnow, which lives in creeks and rivers right across the 'new land' farming area. The concern then was that, while this fish was fairly well distributed, it could suffer from degradation of river banks, through land clearing. Any loss of shade trees could affect water temperature and hence the survival of the fish in warmer water. Salinity was also changing water composition.

But historically what was known about this small fish? Reaching from his bookshelf for one of his favourite sources, *On The Origin of Species*, Andy Chapman made an interesting discovery.

> *It is a very ancient fish and it has a link with Charles Darwin, because he collected the type specimen of the spotted minnow in 1832 during the voyage of the Beagle, in Tierra del Fuego. Later, in New Zealand, he again collected the same species but...possibly he was unaware that he already had it in the bag.*[10]

Andy commented that, as in his own experience, 'in fieldwork you don't always know what you've got until you get home'.[11]

But the story continues.

From New Zealand, Darwin went to Tasmania and he collected the same fish again. Anyway when he got back to the UK he employed Dr Gunther, a fish biologist, to look at his material. Gunther pointed out to him that he had in fact collected the same species from three different countries. And in On the Origin of Species *Darwin makes a lovely claim: 'Here is a wonderful case. It indicates that in a different time and a different climatic regime these species probably had a common origin on an Antarctic continent'. And this is something like fifty years before the theory of continental drift had even raised its head.*

In 1859, when On The Origin of Species *was published, it showed that Darwin had foreshadowed continental drift and the idea that a lot of the southern continents have an element of commonality and a common origin.*[12]

While, in one way, this is an ecological narrative about continuity, its sequel is about long-term adaptation, as Andy Chapman suggests:

Darwin was only half right about commonality because elsewhere, where this fish also lives, it has a marine larval phase. Its larvae go out to sea where they get caught up in the West Wind Drift, a current driven by the Roaring Forties. New Zealand researchers have now found these larvae and small juveniles seven hundred kilometres out to sea from the nearest land. So clearly they have a potential to disperse in ocean currents in recent times.

But in Western Australia the south coast rivers are, for most of the time, barred from the sea. They break out only in floods and that's not often. Some rivers in which this fish lives are permanently barred from the sea. They haven't seen the sea for something like six or seven thousand years. Yet the fish manage to forsake their marine larval stage in the sea. They have developed a different strategy. They swim upstream and spawn. These fish may have been originally programmed to migrate but if that doesn't work for them they will try another way.[13]

If there's an ecological moral to these two tales of the bird and the fish, it is perhaps that the spotted minnow had more than a few thousand years to adapt for its survival. Small perching birds in south-western WA had no such luxury in the last half of the twentieth century when new farmers came to clear their land.

Peter Luscombe is the son of a 'new land' farmer. As a teenager he worked on his family farm and began to look at alternative ways of valuing the bush. He came to recognise the ecological cost of broad-acre farming. Peter began to collect seeds of native plants and, in 1970, at only twenty years of age and still living on the family farm, he started his own business collecting and selling native seeds. Eventually Peter bought his own land to produce native seed, and now runs a 900 hectare conservation farming project at Woogenellup, 90 kilometres north of Albany.

> In the late 1960s everybody was just developing what was called then virgin land, which was also a biodiverse ecosystem. The effect was devastating as far as the natural landscape went. It involved a 90 per cent change in species and systems and basically the natural systems broke down. Right at the onset, it just didn't quite feel right, ploughing in biodiversity. Sometimes, on a tractor, you were trying to avoid some species because it just looked too good to plough in. There was a pretty strong feeling right from the beginning, that it didn't quite feel the project could be justified for what it produced.[14]

While some farmers did hold concerns about the wholesale land clearing, they may not have always realised that 'ploughing in biodiversity' was an irreversible operation, as conservation biologist Professor Stephen Hopper explains.

> If you strip the plant cover away it won't bounce back of its own accord. You have to physically replant seeds or plants and sometimes the flora comes back. But some of it never will, unless we move it back into the landscape.[15]

Professor Hopper, formerly Director of the Royal Botanic Gardens, Kew, in the United Kingdom, is currently Foundation Professor of Plant Conservation Biology at the University of Western Australia.

The south-west is quite a different scenario from most farming lands on the planet. For example, in the United Kingdom, if you walk off a farm, within a year you've got oak seedlings in the middle of the paddock and within ten years you've got a woodland, or a thicket, and within twenty years you've got a proper forest without any human intervention.[16]

Furthermore, when all this human intervention first occurred, the concept of biodiversity was not immediately recognised or valued. It took time for the very special nature of this area to become more widely appreciated. Michael Soule, who is recognised as the father of conservation biology and was a member of the Wild Country Science Council, visited the region in 2006 and observed, 'It's mind boggling for a biologist to be here. This is one of the most extraordinary places in the world'.[17]

Mind boggling the country might have been in its natural state, but it was not necessarily good when cleared for farming. In the 1950s and 60s some farmers, like Sylvia Leighton's family, learned hard lessons about farming in this fragile environment. They saw their pastures increasingly:

...overstocked and blowing away in dust storms in summer. Sometimes fires would come through, leaving the paddocks looking incredibly bare. A lot of the remnant bush that we had left in paddocks was just dying off.[18]

A state government that did not realise the value of this biodiverse environment gave little guidance to the new settlers about how to manage it as farm land.

The government provided very little information. So nobody had any idea of the fragility of the soils. We weren't advised that you had to de-stock in summer and provide supplementary feed. That knowledge came as we learnt from our mistakes, when we saw our sheep starving during summer. So after the district had been cleared for eight or nine years, suddenly we recognised that over-stocked paddocks were causing summer dust storms and we had to change the way we farmed.[19]

Sand blow, Jerramungup.

Clearing also meant burning. Annie Brandenburg, another daughter of 'new land' farmers, witnessed the side effects.

Picking mallee roots every May school holiday, we were thinking about the little animals, the dunnarts that we used to see scurrying around, trying to run for cover under the mallee roots and us knowing that they were going to get burnt to smithereens by the end of the day.[20]

Peter Luscombe observed that even if they survived, those animals were not likely to return.

These fires, especially on fragmented bushland, expelled a lot of wildlife from these little areas and they weren't able to re-colonise very quickly, because these areas were isolated. So there was a complete breakdown of wildlife and we ended up with just the more common species across the landscape.[21]

If fauna and flora were rapidly affected by clearing, an analysis of south-west soils provides a parallel story about land from which people were trying to make a living. Stephen Hopper describes a Kings Park Botanic Gardens study carried out on a banksia woodland just north of Perth, which revealed:

> ...*that the top five centimetres of soil contains 90 per cent of the seed of plants and all the associated helpful fungi and micro fauna that keep the flora community ticking over. And if you go down another five centimetres you've got all of 95 per cent of all that action.*[22]

Keith Bradby, living and working at Ravensthorpe towards the end of the 'million acres' scheme, became aware daily of mixed fortunes. Some farmers had prospered, but for others the fragility of the now-cleared land and the conditions under which they worked were imposing a heavy social as well as environmental cost.

> *Some had done well, but others were going broke and were living in appalling conditions. They were still living in the ends of sheds and saying, 'Well, we've cleared the paddock and we're trying to live in the middle of it and it's a pretty unpleasant place to live'.*[23]

Sylvia Leighton, who later worked with WA's Department of Parks and Wildlife, lived in 'new land' country as child.

> *Everybody was in the same boat. We all lived in these tin sheds. We were all burning bush, ploughing, raking up roots, and everyday life for me as a child was really just going out with the family with the tractor and trailer and just picking up mallee roots all day long, and then being covered in charcoal and dirt. And every other child that I mixed with was living the same life. We were all clearing land together.*[24]

For Keith Bradby, then an onlooker, the effect of such a lifestyle was only too apparent.

> *I think the social conditions and the big bare paddock and the fact that it was deteriorating before our eyes were the primary concerns, and then in 1980, 1981 and 1982 we got three dry years with big wind-blow, which they'd already had in 1976, and that had powerful effects on both men and women.*

I was the token 'greenie' at a few Field Days and I still remember Ted Rowley, the Department of Agriculture representative at Jerramungup, putting up one of their horrifying aerial photos of massive wind erosion and you could see a homestead and sheep yards that were full of sand. And he said, 'Right, so you're all worried about the loss of production going on here. Let's talk about the family living in that shed there. And let's look at the fact that to get to the school bus they've got to get over these sand dunes that have blown over the track.[25]

In August 2009, landscape architect and ecologist Simon Smale, then Greening Australia's Gondwana Link Program Manager, showed me some of that legacy. We looked out from the crumbling verandah of a deserted farmhouse, fifty or so kilometres east of Albany. The neglected sheds, the gaping holes in the homestead roof and a bare windswept paddock all spoke of final despair. The farm had died and the family that had tried to keep it going had eventually gone too. In a way the bare paddock reflected their stoicism; perhaps persisting on the land when things were going badly wrong.

Abandoned farm.

As Simon commented:

Well it certainly gives a new meaning to the term 'resilience'. I think the resilience of some of the occupants, the inhabitants of this landscape, is really quite extraordinary.[26]

Fluctuating crop prices, dust storms due to vegetation removal, bush fires, salinity and soil degradation nonetheless took their toll. Walk-offs and suicides among farmers were not uncommon. And it got worse, as Keith Bradby recalls.

I saw that era when whole paddocks were drifting, when roads were getting covered in drift sand, when some of the areas that had started off with more than fifty settlers were down to five or ten, and a lot of those people had left painfully.

In the south coast region we saw the serious beginnings of salinity, of swathes of dead saline flats, hovering above precious national park areas and so on. And you saw what had been, biologically, a very full landscape, become a very empty landscape. Even now, if you drive through farms you've got only half a dozen plant species left.

And you've barely got half a dozen farmers left, because each farmer would be looking at between three to five thousand hectares to make a living, and that means travelling a long way between different homesteads. So you've gone from a very full landscape to one that's very empty and getting emptier.[27]

As late as 1979, even after the 1976 drought, the state government planned to open up another three million hectares of this southern region for farming. Stephen Hopper was then a member of a government committee offering advice on the planned expansion.

There was still the big push to go further beyond existing farmland. Three million hectares were being considered. The area under consideration included country north of the Fitzgerald River and extended right around the rabbit-proof fence, past Forrestania and into what's now called the Great Western Woodlands.

One of my quiet achievements was to be part of the small inter-departmental group that put a lid on land release for agriculture in those areas. People were dreaming. It was based on a 'one good year in ten' model. As long as you got that year it might be economic. 'It's useless land so why don't we give it a try'. That was the prevailing attitude.[28]

Salinity was the quiet sleeper in the early years of the 'new land' clearing. However, as David Pannell, Professor of Agriculture at the University of Western Australia, points out:

Salinity was always going to increase following any significant amount of clearing. But if decision-makers had factored the impact of salinity on agricultural productivity into their clearing decisions, I think that clearing would still have occurred in most cases because if they cleared 90 per cent of the land and subsequently lost 10 per cent to salinity, they would still have 80 per cent in production. That's rational from a farmer's perspective, but not from a broad community perspective. It misses the impact of salinity on rivers and wetlands, which has been very severe.

Ideally, we would have retained large vegetation buffers around the main rivers and wetlands. But at that time biodiversity and nature conservation were not priorities. Reading documents from those times, it's as if there was nothing there before we cleared away that 'nothing' to allow farming.[29]

'Nothing' was potentially those three million hectares and that pushed Keith Bradby and others into action.

When a local farmer, who'd befriended and helped us enormously, started knocking down another eight hundred acres of his lovely woodland I thought, 'Is that what this phrase "new land" is all about?' And when the acceleration of land clearing was announced, nothing added up for me. For whatever reason I was not caught up in the culture of the time. We're talking about thirty years ago and an inherent and deeply ingrained culture. These people had lived with twenty or thirty years of staggering 'million acre' clearing – 'clear it all, develop the west' rhetoric. It was deeply ingrained and had hardly been challenged.[30]

By now Keith Bradby and a few like-minded activists were doing a lot of door-knocking, seeking wider support for the protection of biodiversity. Initially help was hard to find. Conservationists in Australia, including those in WA, were focusing on two urgent current issues, the wet forests and saving the Franklin River in Tasmania. They had less time for a significant, but yet unrecognised, issue. However by 1982 the importance of preventing more land clearing in this biodiverse region of Western Australia was gaining recognition from a few conservation groups, particularly those in the Eastern States.

Keith felt that, paradoxically, Western Australians themselves were too close, and too accepting of land clearing, to really appreciate what was at stake. They were perhaps still too influenced by the 'develop at all costs' thinking. But those mindsets were slowly beginning to change. Keith gives credit here to the rise of Landcare as a movement and particularly to the part that women played at its outset.

> *I think the women shone because that gave them their opening and a lot of the early tree planting was done by women. Later men dominated the official Landcare Movement. They formed nearly all the committees but the sympathy, support and empathy came very much from the women in the community.*[31]

From the 1970s onwards, land use practices were diversifying and climate was changing. Keith Bradby remembers a turning point in his own awareness.

> *Geoff Moseley, from the Australian Conservation Foundation, got me to go to a conference at Broken Hill in 1982 where a CSIRO guy was talking about dry country farming. He presented a paper about the impact of the greenhouse effect and made predictions about what would happen in south-west Australia. And I've watched those predictions unfold ever since. But for nearly everyone else there it was a total non-issue, it didn't exist, it was totally irrelevant.*[32]

The predictions were for a drying climate in the traditional winter rainfall belt and an increase in extreme events, including extreme rainfall events. Keith later met a farmer at Koorda who had been at a different conference.

> *But he'd heard the same CSIRO guy in the same year and the same presentation. He still had the CSIRO paper pinned to his notice-board and he'd bought a farm out from Roma in Queensland to learn how to farm in a summer rainfall belt because he figured it was coming. So, you know, the odd person listened.*[33]

The 'odd person' was also doing something too. Not that there was anything odd about looking out for a remarkable bird now facing a loss of habitat. Susanne Dennings, from a farming family, grew up in the Ongerup district and then spent many years elsewhere. She returned to live at Ongerup only to find that the malleefowl, common enough in her childhood, was now a threatened species. 'On the way to school we always used to see the mallee hen run across in front of us, but of course that doesn't happen anymore'.[34] Partly, as she freely admitted, because farming practices had reduced mallee-hen habitat.

> *In the bush, it was all about progress in those days, burning and clearing, and some of the fires that got away burnt huge swathes of remnant vegetation. I remember my mother's concern about what was being lost; her feeling for all the animals that were affected.*[35]

Susanne's mother, Kaye Vaux, perhaps best describes what had already been lost, in a poem she wrote, *The 1980 Nightmare*.

An inland sea of green
Rose and fell in deep and shallow
Tides of colour
Sand plains rippled in splendour,
Brilliant as coral reefs
Beneath it all the SOIL
Sap and heartbeats ever reaching out

To hold it firmly
Guarding its fragility, struggling to mend
Its scars after flood
Bursting forth after fire
Rending it with reverence
Man had a dream in the 1950s
The bush flattened on its back
Tanned in the sun
Frightened fauna searched for shelter
Sap hissed in tongues of flame
Tiny creatures lost their souls
In great mushrooms of smoke – higher
Than heaven
The sea of green now deadly black
Panted clouds of ash on every breeze
Machines tore across the SOIL
Grain poured from golden seas
Which stretched on and on into the distance
Treeless
Soft pads of the bush no longer caressed
The SOIL
Hard feet, hurrying feet, more and more
Feet, hungry mouths
Bigger and bigger wheels of wealth
Bruised and broke the SOIL
Sobbing after rain it ran and ran
Leaving salty scabs
And dead trees, leaning against
Rainless skies
Feverishly the SOIL
Gathered in great clouds
Escaping from the turmoil
And the wind wailed
A requiem through the darkness
Wake Up![36]

Hoping to arrest even further decline, Susanne Dennings and friends set up the Malleefowl Preservation Group (MPG) in 1992.

The malleefowl was actually the Nyungar Aboriginal emblem for the Gnowangerup shire. The word Gnowangerup translates as 'The place of the mallee hen'. We didn't know how many there were left. We started out on a block just up from here, went out in the bush on the back of a ute, and went from there.[37]

The MPG was largely made up of farmers: people busy enough just making a living from the land, let alone worrying about species conservation. Nevertheless, as Susanne put it:

There is another aspect and that is the heart and the soul and it is a rewarding feeling for a lot of farmers to go out and see the malleefowl scratching around in the bush or out in the paddock. It's another aspect of their sense of belonging. And I find that with the volunteers I work

Malleefowl with Susanne Denning.

with, that sense of achieving something that means something to them personally. It's a long-term benefit for everybody, including the farmers.[38]

So how successful has this 'rescue operation' been after almost twenty years?

It is really hard to gauge population trends because the species is such a long-living bird and the Malleefowl Preservation Group has been conducting population monitoring since 1993 and has now established over 12,000 hectares of monitoring sites across Western Australia. Of course the seasonal conditions impact heavily on breeding activity each year. For example you may not have any breeding pairs in one particular area for two or three years. But then when a good season arrives we might have two or three active mounds.

So it's a long-term process to truly gauge population trends. However, if we're going on sightings, then that's also difficult to gauge because of raised community awareness and more people reporting sightings. But in most areas they seem to be holding their own. We can only hope that our long-term monitoring will show that the breeding population is also holding its own.[39]

Nevertheless, risks remain for this emblematic bird.

Starvation is a problem. We believe that less than 2 per cent of chicks survive. That depends very much on seasonal conditions. However the malleefowl is a long living bird so their mortality rate has probably always been high but we've tipped the balance with introduced predators and land clearing.[40]

A key factor in malleefowl protection has been ensuring a survival habitat through bush corridors.

The corridor links are critical, particularly in the agricultural areas. We've created a series of wildlife corridors totalling 63 kilometres through farming properties where farmers have donated their land along paddock boundaries that we've fenced off and re-vegetated. This was particularly important for malleefowl because the chicks need to migrate, disperse as soon as they emerge from the mound. Being a ground-dwelling species, they require vegetation cover to disperse safely.

Initially our corridors were narrow but now we've gone out to fifty metres wide, re-vegetated with local plants. We also understand the impact of soil erosion and weed infestation from sand blowing in from adjacent paddocks. Corridors must be broad enough to support a variety of species. The wider the better.[41]

Landscapes everywhere are obviously interconnected, but equally they will vary. Each lake or patch of woodland is subject to external influences: the state of the adjacent land; the proximity or the presence of invasive animals or plants; rainfall variation, often modified by changes in vegetation (e.g. land clearing); and many other factors. This argument inevitably bears on the size and hence degree of usefulness of habitat corridors.

This is particularly important in the landscape of south-western Australia, where biodiversity is both complex and highly variable. This makes it impossible to generalise about the char-acteristics of 'fragmented landscapes'. One may contain a certain suite of remnant flora, and others, similarly described and not far away, may contain a completely different suite.

In this context, Keith Bradby came to believe that the value of the early Landcare plantings had been over-estimated.

Right through the eighties and nineties we just kept understanding more about the richness of the bush down here and the impossibility of restoring a semblance of it by just planting a few of the trees that once grew there.[42]

Keith was also questioning the relevance of thin 'corridor' plantings. In the late 1980s he had attended a conference on this topic in Busselton where a speaker from Ballarat described the free movement of koalas across a landscape. Those comments widened his view of corridors and the scale at which they could best operate.

If the role of corridors is to restore the integrity of the Australian landscape and to promote resilience in our landscapes, health in our ecosystems and the survival of rare species, then this involves much more than providing narrow laneways for fauna to scuttle along under cover of darkness from one oasis to another.[43]

Land corridors.

Before Keith developed his views on corridor planting, Kaye Vaux and other local people were championing another project: a proposal to create a national park in the Fitzgerald River area, south of Jerramungup. Establishing a national park in the middle of an expanding agricultural region was a project which faced many obstacles.

In addition to agricultural development, the area was also potentially in line for mineral exploitation. Miners and casual prospectors had been trying their luck in the Ravensthorpe and Fitzgerald districts since the 1860s. Mineral sands, manganese, copper, spongolite and low-grade coal (lignite) were all to be found in what was then only the 'Fitzgerald Reserve'. But it was the possibility of a coal supply that determined the fate of the region. Would this biodiverse area become a park or a mine?

WA's newly established (1971) Environmental Protection Authority, through its Environment Protection Council, examined an application to mine low-grade coal in the central Fitzgerald Valley. A report after a 1972 inspection described the vegetation of the Fitzgerald River valley as: 'Not visually impressive. It appears chiefly to consist of mallee eucalypts similar to those found in many places in WA'.[44]

In itself this was a surprising comment, given much earlier recognition of the considerable biodiversity of this region. In fact, in late 1846, Toodyay amateur botanist, James Drummond had travelled through this area, 'finding many new plants at every place'[45], and on reaching Cape Riche he had commented in a letter to Sir William Hooker, Director of the Kew Botanical Gardens in England, 'Cape Riche will in time come to be a spot celebrated in the Botany of Western Australia'.[46]

Community opinion about the proposal to establish a national park was divided. Adjacent shires could see the potential for mining in terms of jobs, increased population and alternative employment, particularly for some farmers already undergoing hardship.

On the other side of the fence, conservationists and other farmers who were also beginning to count themselves as conservationists mounted a campaign against mining. At Ongerup an environmental movement, mainly composed of farmers, had already sprung up. Soon nearly eight hundred signatures were collected for a petition to oppose mining. The possibility of a national park, even symbolically, seemed for many people to be a significant step, which would help to redress the effects of previous practice.

Government departments were now drawn into the process. In 1970, scientists from the University of Western Australia, the staff from the Western Australian Herbarium, the Western Australian Museum and the then Department of Fisheries and Fauna all made field trips to assess both plant and animal life. In fact, Herbarium employees had been working in the reserve since 1957 and had collected over two thousand specimen plants, including finding a rare and potentially endangered species.

It was an interesting time. The environmental movement was beginning, if tentatively and with some apprehension, to challenge the old certainties of rip, tear, burn and bust. In 1973, after much hard work by local campaigners, the State Government under Premier John Tonkin upgraded the former 'C'-Class Reserve to the status of national park, and the Fitzgerald National Park came into being. Results from drilling that year had already suggested that any coal mine would be unviable. The likely yield, both in quantity and quality, was not worth pursuing.

A further initiative was the creation of the Fitzgerald Biosphere Reserve in 1978. This was in response to a request for nominations from Australia by UNESCO, which had identified and supported similar zones in many other countries. Biosphere reserves are ecologically significant regions that promote sustainability and conservation by engaging all community stakeholders. Recognised by UNESCO, they support research, share the resulting knowledge broadly and inform policy-makers. Biosphere reserves address one of the most challenging issues we face today: how to maintain the health of the natural systems while meeting needs of communities.[47]

However, the Government's nomination was for the national park only. Members of the local community later activated the biosphere reserve concept, which was then applied to both the park and the broader surrounding landscape. The Fitzgerald Biosphere included the national park and a surrounding 'zone of co-operation'. Landcare and conservation groups involved hoped that farmers and others would learn to work more in harmony with their natural environment. The Fitzgerald Biosphere was described by Dr Bern Von Drost in 1989 as 'the most important Mediterranean ecosystem reserve in the world', not only for its rich biodiversity, but for the way the community interacts with the environment and how they are all working to ensure long-term sustainability.[48]

The creation of such a zone extended conventional notions of farming to seeing land in terms of eco-management. Farmers were now living alongside country no longer 'locked up' as a reserve but under the care and consideration of the community.

Ecologist Angela Sanders came to work for what is now the Department of Parks and Wildlife in the early 1990s, when the national park was under the care of this agency. As she sees it, the biosphere is about 'people interacting with wild places in a sustainable way, and in a way that's one of the reasons why it hasn't been as successful as it might have been'.[49]

UNESCO is currently reviewing the status of biospheres worldwide and has raised questions about the effectiveness of the Fitzgerald Biosphere Reserve. In other developed countries, such as Canada and France, biospheres have developed a strong focus on research, involving local farmers and placing emphasis on supporting traditional farming methods as well as preserving the cultural landscape.

The Fitzgerald Biosphere Reserve presents a different picture from these biospheres, with less interaction between the locals and the natural landscape. Keith Bradby suggests that, in fact, most of the local inhabitants have retained their existing farming practices and have remained unaffected by the biosphere listing.

In Angela Sanders' view, the Fitzgerald Biosphere also presents a different picture from those in developing countries where interaction between the local people and the natural land-scape seems to occur naturally.

> The surrounding farmers are not actually harvesting anything from the bush. The kangaroos and the wallabies are seen as vermin. So it's quite a different concept to biospheres in developing countries where they use the resources of their core areas and have a much more intimate connection with their environment.[50]

Nonetheless, there have been local benefits. Some farmers have also worked hard to bring both the national park and the biosphere into existence and have been major players in Landcare and conservation projects. Author and conservationist the late Professor George Seddon became closely involved with the biosphere project. But he also saw its surrounding envelope, the zone of co-operation, as a social as well as an environmental asset.

There are two things that are really striking. One is that it is an extra-ordinarily enterprising community. It is a pioneering community. People have had hard times. They've had to cooperate and they have to be smart to survive...they're a very innovative community and they absolutely have to be. The other point is that in this area the Fitzgerald River National Park is the only thing of international interest. Ugly little town, raw agricultural landscape, superb natural environment. The community knows that. Now they want to find long-term, not short-term, ways in which we can learn from the natural environment to improve our behaviour in a place where we have to make a living.[51]

There was something in it for the locals. The biosphere offered case studies of landscape stability through hydrological work to improve water control and hence resistance to salinity. Tree planting along creek lines also played a major role here. Important lessons were still being absorbed. Some of the complexities facing this 'live better in land' project arose from assumptions about the nature of ecosystems and their place within a landscape.

For Keith Bradby, support for the Fitzgerald Biosphere Reserve led him to think further about connectivity and eventually to found Gondwana Link.

The footy team mentality of 'Our team's got to win!' has never been part of me. So we were looking for how to work together. But it was when I was sitting with the Fitzgerald Biosphere Project Committee and somehow we'd got hold of some of the first satellite roll-out photomaps that we could see that Fitzgerald was still joined to Ravensthorpe and through to the inland. We were looking at an undivided landscape.[52]

For Keith, the creation of the Fitzgerald Biosphere had illustrated the value of creating a large enough 'oasis' to be effective. He sees it as an example of:

...both a remnant and a corridor. As a remnant it conserves a representative slice of the ecosystems and species of Western Australia's south coast, focused on an area of exceptionally high plant species richness.[53]

Fitzgerald River National Park.

A far cry from French explorer D'Entrecasteaux's 1792 observation when sailing along the coast of this area.

> It is not surprising that Nuyts has not provided any details of this sterile land, the aspect of which is so uniform that even the most fertile imagination would have nothing to say about it. Not the slightest sign of vegetation was seen on the part we had passed alongside that day.[54]

Pieter Nuyts, the seventeenth-century Dutch explorer and diplomat, had been, it would seem, similarly unimpressed by an area later deemed worthy of special environmental protection.

The establishment of the Fitzgerald Biosphere Reserve, while not totally successful, became, in itself, a step towards the establishment of Gondwana Link: a coalition of environmental movements committed to connecting both landscapes and human aspirations for land. Gondwana Link is a collaborative effort aimed restoring ecological connectivity across south-western Australia, protecting and restoring biodiverse bushland and building a link eastward across the continent. In Keith's view, Gondwana Link is one sequel to those earlier efforts to 'stitch the health back into divided places'.[55]

Today Keith senses a change in appreciation of this unique landscape. In his view the early focus of the conventional environmental movement was very recreationally minded, very aesthetically focused and strongly forest focused. But now:

> *I think increasingly people are opening their eyes to what will become the iconic value of this really tough, incredibly diverse and weird heathland and mallee and salmon gum and gimlet country. But, early on we used to grumble that the conservation movement only cared about what we called the four W's: whales, wilderness, waterfalls and w(r)ainforest.*[56]

Early door-knocking, or rather gate-opening, had brought Keith into increasing contact with a significant number of farmers well aware of ecological decline and who wanted to do something about it. One was Kingsley Vaux, Kay Vaux's son and brother of Susanne Dennings. A farmer at Pingrup, Kingsley is also concerned about environmental deterioration.

> *I've always been in touch with the land, but when I came home from school in Perth I noticed changes, and later when I took over on the farm, I had a bit more of an eagle eye on the land and where our dollar came from. So I was taking more notice.*[57]

Kingsley has the remains of a lake on his property. It has sadly shrunk since his childhood days on the family farm.

> *We used to have a boat and cruise around here with the Nyungar kids. There were about ten or twelve of us sometimes out here, building our own rafts and chasing the ducks. If it was within my power I'd be trying to fix it, but I don't really know how to do it. The rest of the land around is still in reasonable good health, but when you get floods, a lot of water runs down here and leaches a bit of the salt out of the surrounding land and then of course the salt's left behind, and when it dries out, you see white crystals on the mud there.*[58]

Kingsley has, however, had considerable success in replanting trees and shrubs in some of those salty patches.

> *We had planted a lupin crop. But the lupins failed and we realised the land was going salt. It was bare. Nothing would grow on it. We then*

planted a prostrate wattle called Acacia redolens *and within four years we had blue wrens nesting in the wattle. That was a real buzz for me to see something come from nothing and also something rare, well rare for us.*[59]

Later he planted sandalwood trees. Again, to his surprise, he was able to harvest these two years in a row.

If we hadn't done anything we'd have lost it to salt. Now, it's a great place to come in the summer time here in the green shade.[60]

Other local people, like seed collector Peter Luscombe, also became interested in alternatives to conventional farming, especially if they suggested another income source. He found it in uncleared bush.

Someone said to me once, 'money doesn't grow on trees'. Well I was able to prove them wrong. I started collecting native seed and found a market for native seed for various uses. My business grew from there, and that really allowed the possibility of getting into re-vegetation work and growing local seed mixes for re-vegetation.[61]

Peter's customers now include mining companies seeking to repair disturbed land and local shires who want to replant road verges. Simon Smale, now Gondwana Link Landscape Manager for Bush Heritage Australia, finds satisfaction in work where groves of trees have replaced bare paddocks and the bush has begun to come back around them.

One of the most wonderful things about the ecological restoration is the extent to which the healing of country is a healing mechanism for people as well. It's an extraordinarily satisfying and rewarding thing for people to be involved in. And one of the surprising things about it is that those dividends are returned in relatively short time. You talk to any of the volunteers, the landholder groups, the land care groups, who are engaged in this sort of work, and that's the driver for them, seeing results, seeing wildlife return, birdlife returning, just feeling that these landscapes are re-birthing, they're coming alive again.[62]

Restored land.

Simon first came to Australia from New Zealand in 1996, before moving permanently to take up ecological work in the Gondwana Link program. His initial impression of the landscape came from the air.

> I remember taking a fixed-wing flight over the landscape and looking down and realising what a fragile landscape it is and what a precarious existence it would be trying to wrest a living from pastoral enterprise from a land subject to frequent droughts and infertile soils. The native flora is so well adapted to these conditions but trying to grow wheat and keep sheep is a huge challenge.[63]

Coming from New Zealand's fertile, green, well-watered landscape to south-western WA was, for Simon, 'a huge learning curve. The transitions are very subtle. Everything here relates to the extraordinary mosaic of soils and the gradations between them'.[64]

In this region soil mosaics (patterns of varying soils) govern the task of land restoration and demand painstaking preparation, involving detailed analysis of soil on a particular site and of:

> ...*reference sites for those same soil types in existing vegetation within the same locality. From that we can build a picture of what a normal vegetation community would look like across that mosaic of soil types and then design a seed mixture appropriate to each soil type.*[65]

Replacing natural vegetation in previously cleared land presents a considerable challenge, partly because the local flora here are, as Simon Smale sees them, 'dispersal limited'. They may grow in only one locality.

Another major challenge in restoring and managing country is that it's not just about plants, soil and animals.

> *My job is looking after properties that we own and manage directly. We're operating in a mosaic landscape dotted with fragments of protected landscape and small farm communities and with remnants of Aboriginal communities. We've got lots of boundaries with neighbours: waterways that flow out of upper catchments and through neighbours' farms. I thought we might encounter opposition because we are putting hard-won tracts of farmed country back into bush. But there's a silent acknowledgment that the land has been pushed too far.*[66]

Interestingly, restoration work often has to run on a scale comparable to traditional farming.

> *We're using similar machinery and we're also cropping. It's just that we're cropping complex natural vegetation rather than a single species as farmers do. So there's a bit of mutual respect and understanding. We all have to understand the landscape we're operating in.*[67]

For Keith Bradby, through his growing friendship with Nyungar elders, and for Simon Smale, from a long association with Maori people through his Landcare work in New Zealand, there was a determination to involve the original locals in land repair, right from the start.

It's hard work in this landscape because of the fragmentation of Nyungar culture. Fragmentation of the landscape also fractures culture as people are dispersed and lose contact with traditional country. The land and culture go hand in hand and you can't disconnect them.[68]

Nyungar leader Eugene Eades comes from the Albany region and now heads up a bush centre, The Nyungar Meeting Place, at Nowanup, a name that also means 'place where the mallee hen (Gnow) nests' and which was an early property secured for the Gondwana Link program.

Eugene runs a self-supporting 'reconnection' centre at Nowanup. Much of his work involves cultural mapping: re-connecting with pre-European life in the bush.

We're going back in time to when our old people had trails throughout the Stirling Ranges and throughout the Porongorups and right through this whole country. They were the Dreaming trails where there were different locations set aside to teach our young men and our young women about how to care for country, about the way to best respect the land and all that lives on the land. These trails are cultural corridors. The cultural corridors concept is one of the ways we take our young men and young women back to teach them about the cultural values of this country.[69]

Stirling Range looking south

For Eugene himself, many of those trails needed retracing because of twentieth century European agriculture – an ecological invasion that caught up his own people.

I can remember growing up on the native reserve and seeing many of the Nyungar families, the menfolk in particular, being picked up by the farmers and they'd take them out each day to do sucker-bashing, cutting down all the young suckers and clearing the way for the chain to be grubbed through by two big bulldozers or tractors at the time, and after that they'd come down and plough up all the mallee stumps. Then they'd employ the Nyungar people to go out and pick the mallee stumps, heave them up and then burn them.

It could have been an honest mistake. Maybe the early settlers who gathered up Aboriginal people to take part in work clearing land, may not have recognised that the clearing was going on over sites of

Nowanup 2007 men's gathering.

significance to the Nyungar people, over ceremony grounds, over birthing places, places which were used as bush universities to teach the young people about cultural values in the past. And amongst all that there was this destruction taking place, destroying the Nyungar food, fruit and medicinal plants.[70]

Aboriginal people had been employed as rural labourers well before the Great Depression of the 1930s, and even twenty years later, in the 'million acres a year' land clearing, not much had changed for local Nyungars. There was still the problem that much of their farm work went against long-held cultural beliefs about country.

They were very difficult times. I mean if you didn't go out to work all you could do was to go to the local Native Welfare office and apply for a ration. And that ration would be no more than something like $30 to get you through the next week or so. And that was basically the only backup you had if you refused to go to work because of your connection to country and your respect for the land.[71]

'Healing Land, Healing People' is one of Eugene's current projects. This involves taking men and women, and frequently younger people, back onto land where they or their predecessors once lived.

For older people taking people back to land evokes memory, while for teenagers – youths at risk, sometimes in trouble in nearby towns – a week-long camp at Nowanup can impart bush skills, music and knowledge of culture through nature. Part of that knowledge lies in an understanding of distinctive seasons conferring the certainty of a nourishment calendar, beginning at the season Wadjellas (whitefellers) call summer.

The first one was Birak, it would come about in December to February, and in that season there was goanna and the goanna eggs. There was also fruit which is called chuk, a fruit high in vitamin C; pane, another one high in vitamin C and there were tubers as well, potatoes, and the mungart, the jam tree, had seeds that would be collected and ground to make the flour for damper. The wattles were also there as well, with seeds that would be ground for flour. That was one of the seasons that the old people shared in as they journeyed through the landscape.[72]

These stories and similar bush knowledge were not easily recovered. As Nyungar people lost the ability to live on traditional land, generational knowledge was also lost. But for Simon Smale, as an observer,

The power of restoration projects on country is an analogy for 'Healing People' and is really very powerful. When you start to focus on something, people then come out of the woodwork, perhaps remembering something that their grandmother said or seeing where she once lived. It's the power of oral history, reviving memories buried in the landscape. Land becomes the narrative.

At Monjebup, one of the properties acquired by Bush Heritage within this biodiversity hotpot, you can drive round the property all day and not see a living soul but if, as we did, you do an archaeological survey, you find stone fragments, evidence of tools strewn across the landscape and you know that there have been people here for tens of thousands of years everywhere in the country.[73]

For Keith Bradby the Indigenous input from the Nowanup Meeting Place has enriched his own view of healing landscape.

I also increasingly understand how fundamentally different is the Aboriginal way of looking at country and life and community and family. Fundamentally different and at the same time fundamentally the same. We are all members of a human society.[74]

So how do some of those individuals who have taken on the task of caring for country see the future of this unique region of south-western Australia? Eugene Eades, optimistically, believes that we've turned the corner.

I believe that the way forward for all of us is to make sure that we get things right both for the past and the future. There has been a change in commitment and a working together to learn and share about both ways

forward. It's about learning how to go forward into the future; it's about many cultures, sharing different ideas on the one land.[75]

Simon Smale also considers that his only option is to be optimistic.

I think we often leave things too late, like climate change, with which this is connected. The cost will be more than it should have been if we'd acted earlier but at some point we'll wake up. And I think ecological restoration is at a turning point. We're going to have to restore land if we're to have a future.[76]

Professor Stephen Hopper sees climate change as an additional pressure and not just on this particular patch of country.

The way global warming is going, if you're talking about the next three to four decades, water is going to be the scarce resource if it isn't already. Therefore there's a need to develop both new cropping systems and [to achieve] a better balance in looking at the landscape and asking 'Which bits really are well-suited for agricultural production; which bits are better restored and repaired to perennial cover, to control salinity and restore biodiversity?' Without that sort of intelligent use of the land, the alternative is that more and more people will walk off the land.[77]

Dr David Pannell suggests that we can only hope that, in this story of unforeseen land abuse, hindsight can tell us something.

If decision makers had known then what we know now (and had been willing to apply current values to the outcomes), they would have retained more large blocks of land in a natural vegetated state for biodiversity conservation purposes. I don't believe they would have chosen to go to 'no clearing', but might have taken a more balanced approach.[78]

Keith Bradby returns to his original feeling for a part of Australia that has adopted him and which still sustains him.

You get out here into the bush and you look at the huge horizons, the big sky, the millions of years of continuous biological forces that have been in play around you. And you see immense detail in the little shrubs and herbs. And just watching a little trigger plant bursting into flower in a way that matches a little native bee that's going to come and pollinate it, makes you realise that there is something quite magnificent playing around us. It's not just a matter of being a bit more humble about who we are, in not seeking dominion over the earth, but also in realising that there is a great mystery in how all this works together, and we're not going to fully understand that mystery, nor should we.[79]

Wildflowers, Monjebup.

Chapter 4

Salinity – it's always been there

This chapter title comes from a comment by Carl Beck, Chief Executive Officer of South Coast Natural Resource Management (NRM), Albany and previous Acting CEO with the Shire of Katanning.[1]

In the adjacent shire of Kojonup there are also long memories of salt in the soil and water of this region. In her history of the shire, *First the Spring*, written in 1971, Merle Bignell cites an Aboriginal legend told by Dinah, a local woman, to a Mr. Lilford.

> *The country was gripped by drought and the only known water was salty. The health of the parched Aborigines, birds and animals deteriorated. An eagle-hawk, soaring about the sky and swooping to earth, observed that a fat and shiny crow had a wet beak, wet with fresh water. The eagle-hawk, seething with unparalleled fury, attacked the cunning crow. In so doing his claws split the rocks and the blood of the attacked crow spattered over the surrounding rocks and earth. So a freshwater soak is to be found in the Wakhinup area, hidden among rocks and surrounded by rich, red loam.[2]*

Katanning and Wagin are just two of several shires in the Great Southern that have had to cope with the effects of salinity. In the Shire of Katanning the effects have been felt most acutely in the farming country. In Wagin the problem has also shown up; manifested, along with flooding, inside the townsite itself.

This chapter explores both rural and urban salinity in these two communities.

As Carl Beck suggests, salt was present in the landscape long before pioneer farmers turned the soil with ploughs.

> It has built up in the landscape over hundreds of thousands of years with salt coming in from the ocean with rainfall. Obviously while the landscape was largely covered in native vegetation, this kept the water table down. That meant that the salt was also lower down in the soil profile.[3]

Dr Richard George is Principal Research Scientist, Land and Water Development, with the Department of Agriculture and Food, WA (DAFWA). He has worked on the salinity issue for more than thirty years right across the Western Australian wheatbelt.

> There is a pre-history of salinity in WA which goes back thousands and millions of years. The way we approached agriculture here, removing native vegetation to make space for agriculture, meant that the water table below the ground rose and brought up the salt. Generally to initiate salinity you need only ten or twenty millimetres of the annual rainfall to get beyond the root zone and to build up the groundwater systems.
>
> The wheatbelt is a pretty arid place. There was water around big rock outcrops and salt lakes but, in between, and until we cleared, the country was generally dry down to a depth of forty to fifty metres.[4]

Clearing of the native bush in what is now the Shire of Katanning occurred from 1860 onwards. Lynne Coleman, with her husband, Bill, lives and farms on one of the earliest cleared farms in the district. Her maternal great grandfather, William Grover, took up land on the Carrolup River in 1865.

It took them a long time to clear the land. They ringbarked the trees. You can still see huge old trees that have been ringbarked. They didn't realise that what they were doing would, in time, cause problems.

And they used to cart big trailer loads of sandalwood down to Albany. The only way they had of getting money to clear more land was by harvesting sandalwood. This whole property was covered in sandalwood like most other properties. Now there is not a single sandalwood left on the place.[5]

From the 1840s onwards, what became the Katanning townsite was used as a sheep camp and as a temporary base for a few nomadic workers involved mainly in sandalwood cutting. There was no significant land clearing until Elijah Quartermaine settled with his family at Yowanup in 1960 and formed the nucleus of a small group of pioneer farmers.[6]

Katanning was given official recognition when the first policeman was appointed to the district in 1861 and became a recognisable township with the arrival of the Great Southern Railway in 1889. The train tracks, which were to play a significant role in the salinity story, now connected two ports, Fremantle and Albany, via the inland town of Beverley. Designed to reach Albany, the new line had its origins in 1873 when entrepreneur Anthony Hordern approached the Colonial Office in London with a scheme to put ten thousand migrant settlers into the Great Southern region of Western Australia.

With the growing potential of rail transport in mind, Hordern suggested the notion of a land-grant railway to the Western Australian Legislative Council. He later formed a syndicate in England to finance the scheme to encourage immigrants, thus creating an incentive for farming east and west of the new line.

By 1901 land adjoining the new rail line was opened up for conditional purchase. Hordern himself did not live to see the fruits of his venture, dying at sea in 1886. He was buried at Albany, where a monument commemorates his contribution to the Great Southern.[7] At the unveiling of the monument to him on 3 July 1890, it was noted that 'by the work he achieved for the colony and especially for Albany, he [Hordern] proved himself a man among ten thousand'.[8]

By the turn of the century farmers enticed by Hordern's scheme to the Great Southern had begun to clear and cultivate the country through which the railway ran, initially selecting the lower and flatter areas which had proved easy for line laying. This terrain also gave some new farmers level ground which was relatively easy to clear and gave good access to the railway sidings when they needed to send away wheat and wool to market.

As Richard George notes, there was early evidence of salinity rising to the surface.

> *When early settlers cleared land they saw wet patches developing low on the landscape and twenty years later they saw salt start to develop. But the railway engineers were probably the first to notice it. Railwaymen relied on dams along the Great Southern Railway and cleared many of those small catchments to generate sufficient run off for their locomotive boilers. But by the 1910s and 1920s many of those dams were beginning to grow salty from clearing of the upper slopes.*
>
> *While other railwaymen had noticed the phenomenon, it was an engineer, Walter Ennis Wood, who wrote the first description of the link between clearing the land, water infiltrating to a certain depth, raising the groundwater levels, moving down slopes and eventually appearing as scalds and saline seeps in dams.*[9]

Present-day farmer Adrian Richardson, who farms both hilly and low-level country north of Katanning, is now dealing with those consequences, notably where the higher ground has lost its tree cover.

> *In a nutshell, the land out here has been dramatically over cleared. So that when rain falls it runs. It hits a desert and runs off. It runs down the slopes and then sits in the valleys and the low-lying country. So the low-lying country is getting two or three times the amount of water it used to get and the high country is a bit starved because the water has all run away.*[10]

The problem is not unique to Katanning, the Great Southern region as a whole, or the entire wheatbelt of Western Australia. In these areas continued clearing of native vegetation during the last hundred and twenty years, and the increasing use of water for irrigated agriculture and domestic use, has caused the groundwater table to rise and the salt stored beneath the ground to surface in many districts.[11] Richard George has studied that long view.

> *You will find stories on salt in the agriculture journals right back to the turn of the twentieth century. Salt problems started in the eastern and central wheatbelt where there were large areas of red clay type soils. These were inherently saline, and depending what tillage you used, you could leach those soils. So a lot of agriculture then was about managing those inherently salty soils.*

The first association between salinity and land clearing appeared in print as a response in the Journal of Agriculture under the heading, 'Does clearing increase salt in the ground?'. The reply indicated that a farmer's query had been referred to the Government Analyst for attention and the answer stated that it had been 'pretty conclusively proved' that the removal of trees affected water supplies because rainfall passing through the soil took salts with it. It was considered that to prevent salting it would be necessary to replant a very high proportion of the trees that had been removed.[12]

According to Dr David Pannell, a small group of people already understood the nature of the salinity problem:

> *And even that it would 'salinise' creeks. I doubt that they appreciated that salinity would spread widely. But I guess the countervailing feeling was a national and state enthusiasm for development and a great need to do something for returning soldiers from World War I, to seemingly reward them for their war service, but also get them off the community's hands. And there was a pretty heroic view of development of the land, of taming and overcoming the country; a view that didn't brook any negative*

sentiment about salinity. So it just got buried within the enthusiasm of post-war land development.[13]

As land clearing in the south-west of the state continued and increased in the 1920s, more information about salinity and its causes accumulated. In 1929, Laurence Teakle, who had been appointed research officer and advisor in plant nutrition at the WA Department of Agriculture the previous year, reviewed overseas and local work on soil salinity and published the first technical article of any consequence on the topic.[14]

As a result of Teakle's work (he continued to undertake research on soil salinity issues for many more years[15]), it can be said that by the early 1930s, much was known about salt problems in WA soils and, in particular, that removal of vegetation was the basic cause of salt encroachment. He had also suggested that possible treatment measures included:

...drainage, surface mulches, the use of salt-tolerant plants, and soil management to maintain a surface cover of growing plants. It had also been observed that one approach to preventing salt encroachment was to replant the hills with trees.[16]

However, as Professor Geoffrey Bolton has pointed out, agricultural scientists tended to be damned when they brought bad news and praised only when they brought good tidings such as, for example, the information leading to the 'cure' of 'Denmark wasting disease' (cobalt deficiency). Thus 'experts' were derided in 1929 when their use of scientific soil analysis showed that poor crop results in some marginal wheatbelt districts were due to excess salinity.[17]

This early research by the Department of Agriculture had also found that salt problems were more prevalent in areas with low rainfall, and that occurrence was also influenced by topography and soil type.[18] This is especially true of the Katanning area where, as Richard George points out, the salt problem is exacerbated by physical factors in the landscape.

Katanning does not have any large prior drainage systems below the surface. These exist north of Katanning, as part of the Beaufort/Arthur system. But Katanning itself sits on twenty to thirty metres of very slowly permeable weathered granite.

The district is 'riverless' and the landscape that the water moves through is composed of granite rocks that have rotted over tens of millions of years. So its soils are not the product of river channels or erosion. They are the product of the bedrock dissolving and the hard rock has become deeper and deeper, leaving behind a skeleton of whatever the parent rock's fabric once was.[19]

The problems within the Shire of Katanning don't stop with salinity. It also experiences flooding, increased by the clearing of vegetation and unhelpful topography and drainage that, as we will soon hear, is an even greater problem for Wagin.

A settler who spoke with Peggy Webse in 1958 evokes early-twentieth-century images of the landscape at Ewlyamartup, a settlement east of the town of Katanning:

In the year 1906, Ewlyamartup was so heavily timbered that it was difficult to see far in any direction. The lake itself was timbered on all sides and was drying up rapidly from the summer heat, leaving a surface of salt and gypsum on the dried ground. Settlers had blazed a track from the Badgebup Road to their holding by knicking bark off the trunks of trees and gradually wearing a hardened surface with the tracks of their wagons and horses.[20]

Peggy Webse quotes this extract from a private letter written by Mrs M. Foulds.

I remember our own shack on the night of our arrival…The sun was setting about the time we arrived and we were rather dejected by the gaunt ring-barked gum trees that were soon to be burnt down to clear a patch for cropping.[21]

Over time, the landscape continued to change. Katanning resident Martin Kowald, born in 1908, lived on the Carrolup

River as a boy. He gives us a glimpse of a landscape changed for cropping.

> *After my school days I helped in clearing the land. It was hard work, felling the trees with axe and cross-cut saw and then the burning up. We used horses to drag the large logs into heaps (no tractors or chainsaws then) and we gradually got rid of the stumps left in the ground.*[22]

Once the land was cleared, environmental changes soon followed.

> *Dad bought another farm on the Carlecatup Road around 1930 in the Cherry Tree Pool area…When we first had this farm the river had lots of marron and perch and the wild ducks were plentiful. The wildflowers were a delight to see in the springtime with a profusion of kangaroo and cat paws, orchids, everlastings, smoke-bush and bottlebrush. We gave this farm the name of 'Birdwood' because of all the native birds and habitat. The river was fresh in those days but now has turned salt and all the beauty has gone. Much of the water is too salty for the stock.*[23]

As Carl Beck sees it, government conditions of land purchase in the mid-twentieth century also contributed to the initial over-clearing and the result: salty water.

> *A lot of the farmers who took up parcels of land were required to clear a certain amount of that land each year. It was called Conditional Purchase. And they tended to clear areas that were low in the landscape. These were the easiest sections to clear. The low-lying areas were also where the water collected, so the farmers thought that was the best place for sheep and crops.*
>
> *Some of the settlers might have been quite experienced farmers, but not in this kind of landscape. They had been thrown into a different country with a totally different list of problems. They had probably never experienced a drought. They were very isolated and had to be very self-sufficient. So they were doing the best they could, based on the information and experience they had.*
>
> *Obviously it's always easy to say, with hindsight, 'We shouldn't have cleared so much land', or 'We should have cleared in different spots',*

or 'We should have planted different crops once we had cleared'. It's easy to say that now.[24]

Originally from England, hydrographer Joe Burdass first worked for the then WA Department of Agriculture in the Great Southern region in 1966.

You didn't have to go very far before you encountered the salt lake systems around Katanning. Most of the creeks by that time were saline…We did advise leaving bush in the creeks but the salinity often moved up the creek and frequently the vegetation there was not very salt-tolerant. The die-off also created erosion. So some farmers were losing productive land. And as the lower land went out of production they lost some of the natural water supplies that had been fresh.[25]

However, at that time, salinity was not yet seen as a major problem.

At that stage a few individual farmers were being adversely affected but most of them not greatly. The problem manifested itself further east on the broad acres. Large chunks of farms came under threat.[26]

Mike Quartermaine is a fifth-generation farmer in the Katanning area. As a small child, he became aware of the growing problem.

As a kid I first noticed a bit of scald, degraded land, on the farm, but then we'd go for drives with Dad and go to Lake Towerinning at Moodiarrup, north-west of Katanning, and we'd pass through some land that, as a three- or four-year-old you'd think, 'Why isn't that looking like the rest of the land?' It was visually different and that was probably the first time I thought about it. 'There's something sick, the land looks sick.'[27]

But by the late 1970s salinity was highly visible. Steve Blyth now runs Blyth Tree Farm on the outskirts of Katanning, a wholesale plant nursery he took over from his father.

My folks started this nursery in 1978. Dad was a fencing contractor and a super-phosphate spreader, so he was contracting out to all the farms around here. Over the years he began to realise that there were some paddocks that he had previously been able to drive into but couldn't anymore. He'd just get bogged all the time.[28]

The Blyths starting thinking about a different kind of business and in 1978 they grew their first lot of trees.

I think it was 5,000. People came out and bought the first lot of trees. That's how it started. So my childhood was planting trees in little pots and then going out, when I got a bit older, helping Dad plant them out all over the place.[29]

Childhood over, Steve took off to see the world. Some ten years later in the late 1990s, he came home to Katanning to:

Devastation. The country was looking worse than when I left. The creeks were all filthy and dead. The pools were still there but they were very brackish and horrible. It was the same with Norring Lake where we used to sail. Now it's just too salty.[30]

Steve remembered his childhood playground as it was, over thirty years ago. He returned to a changed landscape.

As a kid you'd get a bamboo pole, get a bit of line on it and you could go and fish, especially at Cherry Tree Pool. I remember that vividly as a kid, and now there's no way you could do that. So I suppose travelling overseas, seeing some beautiful places and then coming back here and thinking 'This is not good' made me want to do something.[31]

Steve's parents were still running their tree nursery, so enlarging the scope of that operation was an obvious move.

I came back here and I noticed that there was a lot of planting being done. But a lot of the seedlings being planted were coming in from out of the district. So I saw that there was a lot of scope for this business to grow.

Mum and Dad were only producing about 300,000 seedlings, a year in those days. So I thought, 'Right, we've got to work out how we can get into that as well'. From 2000 through to 2007 I worked with all the

112

*farmers and all the nurseries in this area and we planted fifty to sixty
million seedlings in those seven years.*[32]

It was the right time to be able to 'do something'. A lot had
been learnt about salinity and its effects since the 1970s when, as
Richard George found, farmers began to be really concerned and,
increasingly, to ask departmental advisors:

*'Why is my best country going salty and what can I do about it?' Initially
advice from the Department of Agriculture was to manage the surface
water by planting salt-tolerant species.*

*Up until the mid-1970s there were many debates about why salinity
occurred, where it came from and about the principal causes. When I started
work in the eastern wheatbelt in the early 1980s I would get questions on
field days about water being generated from the Eucla or the Pilbara or even
the Kimberley, when it rained up there. I have even had field days where
I was told it came from Asia, with a subterranean flow to the wheatbelt.*[33]

Salinity had spread fast across the wheatbelt during the wet
years of the 1960s.

*The growth in demand for knowledge came from the period following
the 1960s which were wet years, and it was then that the Department of
Agriculture, the CSIRO and the state's Public Works Department had
to lift the level of research into salinity. Some work was done in the 1960s
but it really kicked off in the '70s and '80s. By the early 1980s we had
resolved the technical details on salinity in the Darling Ranges but we
probably didn't have strong evidence about the cause of the problem until
the middle of that decade.*[34]

Hydrologist Ruhi Ferdowsian, originally from Iran and now
retired in Albany, began work for the Department of Agriculture
(now the Department of Agriculture and Food or DAFWA) in
the Katanning district in 1987.

*When I started working in this area some farmers were resisting change
but it is good to use gentle persuasion. Some of them were struggling
financially...*

A farmer often thinks in terms of one season, growing a crop, financing that crop and getting the crop to the bin. In a lot of cases I found the women were thinking further ahead than one season because they were concerned about succession. They did not want to leave things in ruins for their children. But I think a combination of men and women thinking together made things work much better.[35]

Steve Bligh also found that the women were in the forefront of addressing the growing concern.

You know the blokes are out there too busy trying to get the dollars in. It's the ladies who really started this conversation around the kitchen table, saying, 'You know we've got an issue here. We've got a dam that's gone all salty', or, 'In that paddock, we can see that where we used to crop twenty years ago, we can't do it anymore. The salt is rising'. So there was a lot of that talk going around all over the district.[36]

Lynne Coleman was one of those farming wives. Lynne and husband, Bill, like many of their neighbours in the Katanning Shire, could see the situation getting worse. The first challenge they faced, when they took over the property from an uncle, was to repair the banks of the Carrolup River, which runs through their property. This waterway had been subjected to misguided weed-control measures.

There was Cape Tulip, a declared weed, right through the river. And my old uncle, Ernie Grover, was very vigilant in getting rid of it. Later the Agriculture Protection Board came out and sprayed it. But before that, Ernie would burn the river, burn all the reeds and rushes. Every year he would chuck a match in and away it would go. So the river actually became quite bare. The old paperbarks that were there and beautiful old banksias mostly went. He did that in good faith, thinking he was doing the right thing.[37]

Each year, the river was spreading out further and further because there were no stable trees on its banks. If there was a wet winter it spread out even further.

Carrolup River on Bill and Lynne Coleman's property, spring 2014.

When we took over the farm, Bill said, 'That's it. We are not burning this river any more'. But then I found that the Carlecatup people had got funding to fence the Carlecatup River. So I thought, if they can do that, so can we. Initially we fenced off twelve kilometres and then extended it to twenty. And just by fencing off the river we now have beautiful riparian re-growth. We no longer have flooding. Now the river is defined.[38]

Lynne Coleman was also one of the instigators of what became the Katanning Land Conservation District Committee or LCDC.

In the mid-1980s a lot of farmers were getting quite concerned about salinity problems, waterlogging and wind erosion. So we got together and approached the shire and decided to form a land conservation district; this became the LCDC in November 1989. Most of the time we 'white-boarded' for the first year to set up ideas as to what we wanted, as a conservation district. We identified the catchments in the Katanning Shire and for each catchment, we had a voluntary coordinator. No-one got paid.[39]

Jenny Gardner began remediation work as a part-time Katanning Creek Landcare co-ordinator in 1991.

> *There were a few that just couldn't be involved at that stage and I found that over the seven years, most of those people were coming on board and by the time I left and one way or another, eventually, they could see it working on other people's properties.*[40]

Adrian and Jill Richardson, farming north of Katanning, saw the beginning of local partnerships.

> *I think everyone had different problems with salinity, depending on the type of country you farmed but everyone had a feeling of needing to do something. You can tackle it on your own but it works better if you tackle it as a group. Obviously, adjoining neighbours in a catchment have to work together, because if they don't, one neighbour can create problems for the other.*[41]

The Richardsons had purchased their farm in the early 1980s.

> *We're both from the country: I am from Boyup Brook and Jill is originally from Brookton, and we'd had three children fairly quickly and I didn't want to bring them up in the city. Giving them the opportunities I had I suppose, and the freedom to be outside and work and play on a farm.*[42]

But their new purchase came with a lot of problems.

> *It was a desert. I could stand on the bank of the dam, on the top one hundred acres, look west, unblocked by trees, and see for four-and-a-half kilometres. And you could check every mob of sheep that we had because you could see right across the whole farm. A high percentage of our land was salt-affected or waterlogged. Initially we did what most people do and attack the problem where it is, rather than look to where it is coming from.*[43]

Lack of tree cover, lost through over-clearing, was soon recognised as a large source of the salinity problem. But as Carl Beck noticed, many farmers tended to plant their trees in the wrong place.

Early days – the Richardson family on the farm.

A lot of people could see water coming up to the surface so they said, 'We need to lower the water table. Let's get a few trees back into the landscape. Let's plant the trees close to where the water lies'. It took time to find out that the trees would work better if they were planted higher up in the landscape, and also to determine the types of trees that would work best.[44]

Given the considerable variation in the local landscape, from extensive hill slopes to flat valleys between ranges of hills, this was a useful step.

You have to address where the water is coming from. So, if you can plant the trees higher up in the landscape, they will often use up the water before it flows down to the valleys. Whereas if you try planting trees right next to where the salt is already showing on the lower ground, there's a fair chance that the soil has already become saline, even if you can't see it, and the trees won't grow so well.[45]

Jenny Gardner sees salinity as a long-term problem with equally long-term solutions.

Salinity in the south-west of Western Australia was first recognised as a problem soon after clearing. It runs in cycles from clearing trees off the land to showing up as salt-laden land thirty years later. So you can't expect to take two or three years to deal with the problem when it's a thirty-year cycle.[46]

On Adrian and Jill Richardson's farm, the first steps to repair country took several years. Their land varied in topography: a mixture of higher hilly country and flat lowlands in a long valley. They worked out what they had to do for each land level.

You just look around to see what naturally grew here, and on the good country you can go back to exactly what was here originally because the conditions are still the same. On the low country you have to plant differently...because we've brought up the salt water from underneath the ground, you've got to have more salt-tolerant species on this sort of country, otherwise they won't survive, grow and thrive.[47]

Adrian recalls encouraging signs of early recovery.

Improvement, surprisingly, was almost immediate. In 1989 we started planting trees high up in the landscape and we were putting in two to three kilometres of drains each year. That involved surveying the slopes, digging the drains. Not deep drains like the ones you'd use to drain low-lying land. These drains were designed to guide water down the slopes, into dams and then into safe outlets. It took us ten years to put our whole landscape plan into effect on this property.

We would do two to three kilometres of drains a year. It involved surveying it, digging it, fencing it and treeing it, because there are four lines of trees behind every drain on the high ground. That had an immediate effect.[48]

In her other role as Katanning Landcare District Manager, Jill Richardson had already found that aerial photos helped pinpoint some of the problems farmers were facing.

Aerial pictures give them much more perspective on how their property looks when you're looking down at it rather than driving around looking across your paddocks. But they also show the connectivity between how a landscape feature on someone else's property, three farms away, is having

Channelling water – Adrian and Jill Richardson's property.

an effect on your property, on that of your neighbour or on other farms downstream of a salty area.[49]

Adrian also looked directly at the ground.

The paddocks tell you. You could pick up things from the photos and then if you went out to the paddock and had a look, you'd think. 'Ah! I didn't realise that was there'. We've got one paddock called the channel paddock and the very old black and white aerial photos show lines across it that look like sheep tracks, but in fact they're sand seams that carry water. The ground there was going bare, not from sheep walking on it, but from salt underneath in those sand seams. And, sure enough, when we put our water management system in, we found a sand seam that we had to cut out.[50]

Further south, Bill and Lynne Coleman were also re-routing the water on their farm. Contouring is about trying to capture the water before it runs into the valleys: to catch it and put it into dams.

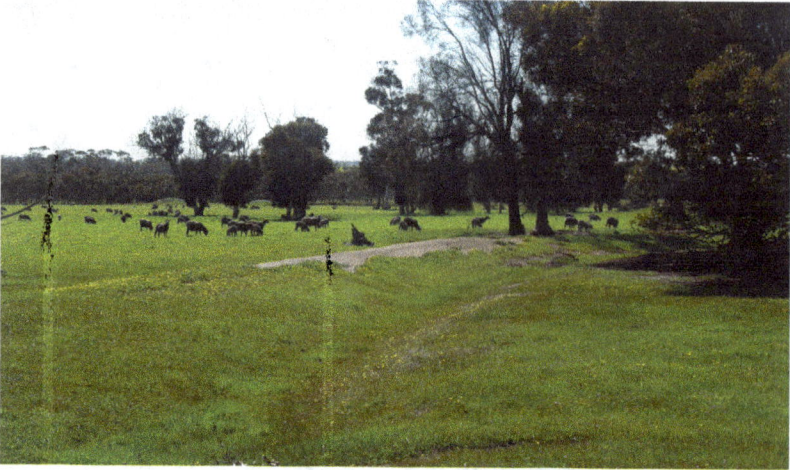

Ridged paddock on Bill and Lynne Coleman's property, spring 2014.

We put in contour banks. Our banks all feed into dams. So we're catching our water and using it so that now we haven't got the run-off problem we used to have. We also put down roaded catchments – ridges of earth with a channel to direct water into our dams. Some people said, 'You will regret that. They'll get washed out'. But the ones we put in have never washed out.[51]

Adrian Richardson stresses the value of not only fencing the drains they put in to keep out livestock, but, in addition, planting four lines of trees behind every drain on the higher ground. He saw an immediate effect.

I often say a tree does a thousand things that you and I don't know. When I look at our place the trees aren't there just for aesthetics, although that is one of the important benefits. They are there behind every drain to soak up anything the drain misses, so that the bit of land immediately adjacent to it, below it, starts with a clean sheet in that it only receives the rainfall that it would have received for the last, however long, thousand million years.

Trees also bring back the insects, ants, every sort of insect you can imagine, and so they bring back the birds and the insects. Both balance

120

Dam and tree lines, Adrian and Jill Richardson's property, spring 2014.

each other out and therefore you don't get huge populations of bad insects on your crops and pastures. And those are just the things going on above the ground. There is ten times more activity under the ground doing exactly the same thing with microbes and the soil itself.[52]

Adrian also saw the practical benefit of planting trees in reducing the damaging effects of winds.

Wind is one of the most damaging elements. It is a drying factor and an erosive factor. A tree can't stop the wind but it can lift it off the ground and slow it down. That has a dramatically positive effect on your production. Your growth rates of pastures and crops are far better.[53]

Planting trees to combat salinity is not always viable in areas with lower rainfall, as former DAFWA employee Ruhi Ferdowsian explains.

When we come to some of the areas with low rainfall — less than 600 millimetres — trees are not very viable. Or you have to plant them with a good distance between them. You can't have densely planted plantations in those situations. The trees will survive and produce quite good timber if they are not densely planted. They will struggle if you plant them too densely.[54]

As a Landcare Manager, Jill Richardson agrees that tree planting, while important, is not the only means of dealing with over-clearing and its end result, salinity.

> *Twenty-five years ago the big push then was all about planting trees. Planting trees or woody perennials is still an answer, but it's not the only approach. So our group doesn't have a culture of 'It's all about planting trees'. It is 'Look what you can do with trees as part of your landscape', and we have worked on that.*[55]

The Richardson's next big repair task was dealing with saline land at the lower end of their property.

> *We re-vegetated the paddocks in-between the tree lines with perennial pastures on salty land that we were losing. And now they're becoming our best paddocks in the summer because they carry green feed. It's not all green grass, there's more saltbush but they can still provide us with a week or a month of grazing. If you let sheep graze there for a short time and then take them out, the pasture recovers and you can do it again.*[56]

Nurseryman Steve Blyth, concerned with producing plants that combat salinity, has seen both the benefits and limitations of saltbush plantings.

Recovered pasture, Adrian and Jill Richardson's property, spring 2014.

Yes, there has been a lot of land out this way planted back with saltbush. And you think 'Yes, brilliant!' But now they're realising that while the sheep will go in there and eat it, if they just eat saltbush that's not quite enough nourishment for sheep, and maybe they've got to tweak it a bit more and maybe put some perennial grasses in between. And all these things help to drop that water table back down.[57]

Fortunately, more recently other plants have come to the rescue when dealing with salinity. Richard George sees lucerne as high-quality grazing forage, ideal for providing good stock feed in the Great Southern at times of year when there is little or no green pasture, such as in summer months, and on salt-affected land.

The principle of salt lake grazing is that you can set up a 'living haystack'. Lucerne has a significant attribute here. It is a perennial, deep-rooted plant that can successfully hold down water so that salt doesn't flush to the surface. It is also handy for long periods of rotation between, on average, four to six years, enabling farmers to feed cattle or sheep while waiting to re-crop again. Lucerne is also high in nitrogen and after it is harvested the soil will be more fertile and nitrogen can be extracted by plants that you grow after the lucerne and that reduces the fertiliser inputs.[58]

Ruhi Ferdowsian worked with farmers planting lucerne in the Great Southern.

I think we can show a hundred examples of farmers successfully reversing the salinity trend. Especially in the areas that have got very low rainfall, 300 to 450 millimetres per annum. In those areas the best treatment is growing lucerne in a kind of rotation. We found the best plan is to grow lucerne for four to five years and then you can go back to cropping for seven to ten years. This system is called phase farming.

This system will become sustainable, because during the period that lucerne is growing, groundwater levels will drop considerably: maybe around two to four metres in some places, depending on the landscape and the attributes of the aquifer. But then, when you remove the lucerne and put a crop in the groundwater will rise again for a short time...It is a kind of long-term rotation which has successfully reduced salinity in many parts of the western south coast.[59]

However, as Richard George points out, lucerne does have some limitations.

It is harder to manage than conventional pasture and costs more. Lucerne is suitable for some but not all farms in the Great Southern. It is not tolerant of high soil salinity, preferring sloping land where the water tables are deeper than two metres. Lucerne's main mode of action is preventing recharge of rainfall getting to the water table.[60]

Farmer Mike Quartermaine believes in improving his land by planting a variety of nitrogenous grasses.

I'm trying to get away from monoculture as well trying to grow an understorey and be a bit more diverse. But I grow hay silage, not necessarily just grain, for fodder. I try and go clover based – something nitrogenous – and feed the system. I plant Italian rye grass, an annual crop, along valley floors. Around here especially people are growing tall wheat grass, fescues that are doing quite well, as a perennial.[61]

The Katanning story suggests that a variety of solutions and much hard work can help, if not totally repair, salt-stricken land. But how should we assess the severity of the problem in the overall context of WA's enormous wheatbelt? Richard George offers an overall view.

Throughout most of the landscape farmers are getting good yields but problems remain on the valley floors, a perspective about salinity that is often under-estimated. Allowing for variations between shires, about five to ten percent of the Great Southern region is salt-affected.[62]

The largest percentage of land may not be saline, but as David Pannell explains, treatment depends on what you are trying to fix.

If you are dealing with cases where the soil is already saline, you look for salt-tolerant productive plants that can be grazed or plant salt-tolerant crops. In other cases you may be dealing with areas at risk of going salty. That involves planting perennial crops and trees that are economically beneficial and can generate an income. Sandalwood is an example. Oil mallee is another. There are quite a few quite oil mallee plantings spread through the wheatbelt. They haven't hit the home run yet as a well-established commercial industry. But those are two approaches to dealing with salinity.

Tree planting alone has helped to both repair and limit salinity, but important lessons have been learned along the way. For nurseryman Steve Blyth, there were plenty of trees to choose from. But which trees should he promote to farmers?

We didn't know where to start, what we should plant, and that's where a lot of experiments and different ideas emerged. There were about twenty to thirty different species of trees that people could use. Sometimes they based their decision on name alone. 'We've got a salt area, so we want the Salt River Gum'. But in the last five, six years there's been a lot more focus on variety. So now we grow over three hundred different species compared to the thirty that we were planting all those years ago. That has meant more biodiversity, trying to ensure that you get different types of flowering trees.

If you've got a shelter belt of only one species that flowers for perhaps only two to three months of the year, then you need other flowering trees for the rest of the year. That way you'll get little pygmy possums who feed on one tree in September and another tree in November.[63]

Carl Beck agrees with Steve's views on the importance of trees and of diverse plantings.

Trees bring in more rainfall, insects and bees, all of which help to pollinate your farmer's crops. All our crops rely on pollination. If you haven't got any native vegetation you haven't got anywhere for bees and birds to live. You get much less pollination and your harvest rates go down. It is pretty clear that having good quality native vegetation or biodiverse vegetation as part of your landscape has to be beneficial to your crops.[64]

Tree Regrowth on the Carrolup River, 25 years on

But as David Pannell has pointed out, tree planting ventures have had mixed success.

> *In the southern parts of the state there has obviously been a fair bit of enthusiasm for things like blue gums. Those strategies haven't worked for everyone. Some who have advocated those approaches have had success whereas other farmers have not, for understandable reasons. They have had different soil types or different rainfall zones or those systems just haven't worked for their particular farm.*[65]

Farmers are now recognising that restoring native vegetation is an important weapon in tackling salinity. Adrian Richardson recalls that, back in the 1980s when the Katanning Landcare District Committee began remedial work in the area, this was not the case.

We had less than 4 per cent of original vegetation left in the area. In effect the country was almost ninety six per cent denuded through clearing. So let's assume our farm was the same; probably also 96 per cent cleared. We've taken it back to probably 15 per cent of restored native vegetation because we plant native species behind our drains. And there is a figure, probably between 12 and 20 per cent, where you can keep on adding vegetation and increase your productivity dramatically as a result.[66]

Jill Richardson adds that when Landcare promoted tree planting, it was often assumed that this was solely for aesthetic reasons.

I know there are still people who totally dismiss the word or the concept 'Landcare' because they think it's only about planting trees to make the landscape look nice. Yes, they do, but look what else they do. We have worked hard on that perspective and I believe our farmer constituents are now very happy with that wider view.[67]

Mike Quartermaine was one farmer who initially planted trees largely to make the landscape 'look nice'. But he has been influenced by the work of the Katanning Land Conservation District Committee.

I planted trees on a very over-cleared farm in the 1980s but that was for shelter and aesthetics as much as anything to do with salinity. Once the Katanning LCDC started, I got involved in the early 1990s.[68]

Looking at the big picture, Richard George estimates that

We have about 5 to 10 per cent of the wheatbelt, depending what shire you are talking about, that is salt-affected. This means conversely that 90–95 per cent of the area is fine. Even at the worst of the forecasts we would probably still say that 80 per cent of the wheatbelt is non-saline.[69]

So what can further tree planning achieve?

We run about twenty or so tree-planting experiments across the wheatbelt with various farms, groups and individuals and us as experimenters, and we plant trees at varying scales on the whole landscape, on patches, around contours, in belts and in alleys.

Twelve decades of monitoring that work suggests that to change the overall extent of salinity you would have to re-plant over 50 per cent of the landscape with trees. To return it to non-saline conditions you would probably have to re-plant more than 80 per cent of the land with trees. So you would have to re-plant five to ten times the area of land that is salt-affected with non-commercial species in order to save the 5 per cent of land which is salt-affected. This is something which, clearly, farmers could never afford to do.[70]

As Jill Richardson has found from her work with Landcare, it is not easy for all farmers to even think about the bigger picture and the benefits of tackling salinity.

That's a challenge for farmers who are struggling with going to the bank with cap in hand for half a million dollars to put this year's crop in. It's not easy for every farmer to think in that bigger picture way and the banks don't seem to want to think in that way either, especially when things are very tight.[71]

Jenny Gardner also understands that it is sometimes not possible to make the investment needed.

There will always be some farmers who are at that stage in life where they've got four children away at school or have other commitments, and there's no way that they can afford to make changes to their property while their children are young.[72]

At the same time, Jenny has seen many farmers achieve great improvements. 'Great changes were made on some properties where there were two sons at home and they had their workforce ready to roll out'.[73]

Most families are happy to achieve limited repair and prevent further saline spread. Mike Quartermaine believes that farmers are already:

…doing a lot of good work to reduce the effects of salinity without even realising it or thinking about it. Just minimum till for one. Over time, root systems can get down deeper with minimum till. So you can get

an increase of organic matter further down in the system. Previously, ploughing allowed water to run off under the ground and end up on the lower valley floor.[74]

Tree nursery specialist Steve Blyth knows there is no silver bullet:

I have seen some great successes but it is very site-specific. I know of lots of farmers who have changed things around. They have done a lot with banks, and they've drought-proofed their farms, harvested their water, and in an area that once was completely saline and devoid of any vegetation so that it couldn't be used, they can now harvest clover. Now that's just huge. That's using all the tools they've been exposed to through the Landcare network.

But I have seen other areas where they've spent thousands, hundreds of thousands of dollars, and that hasn't worked. They've achieved nothing, because there is no silver bullet.[75]

However overall Steve believes that:

We are winning. We are getting there but they say it's going to take many years to see results. It used to be called the 'vegemite approach'; spread a bit there, do a little bit here, do a little bit there. People were quite critical of that at the start. 'It's not going to work', they'd say! But it will. We have still got several years of hammering away at it. We'll never get the land back to how it was originally but what we will get back is something significantly better than what it was when we started.[76]

The historic town of Wagin lies 50 kilometres north-west of Katanning on the Great Southern Highway. As in the Katanning shire, farms within the shire of Wagin are also prone to salinity and so is the town. But the townsite is especially vulnerable lying on the edge of the Coblinine River, a series of a long, flat wetlands and salt lake chains. It has a long history of urban flooding — inundation in the lower part of the town. This threatens homes as well as the historic buildings which form an important part of Wagin's cultural heritage.

It was that rich heritage which struck Mark Pridham, Senior Development Officer with DAFWA, on his first visit to the town in the late 1990s.

The first thing that caught my eye was the heritage, the buildings. I would say that Wagin had one of the most attractive façade streetscapes of any of the wheatbelt towns. From a heritage architectural perspective, it was one of the best-looking towns. And that was due to the preservation of those buildings from the 1920s. A lot of reclamation work had been done since then: the Palace hotel, Moran's hotel, the town hall and the courthouse. There are a lot of heritage buildings that have been preserved and they are an important feature of Wagin.[77]

Current Shire President Phillip Blight recalls a baptismal experience in one of those buildings.

As a young fellow I remember going into Moran's hotel for a darts evening in 1978. I went down to the cellar to get the dartboard. The cunning old sods behind the bar, they got me well and truly. They said something like 'Look out for the water when you walk down the ladder'. The water

Part of Wagin's heritage

was crystal clear with no ripples and quite invisible. So I went down the ladder, leapt off the end and I was immediately two feet deep in water.[78]

Like Katanning, the town of Wagin came into being close to the turn of the twentieth century with the advent of the Great Southern. Parts of the Wagin townsite have experienced occasional flooding over a long period. As Mark Pridham reiterates, there's a good reason why Wagin gets wet.

The townsite is on the edge of the main drainage line of the Coblinine river and lake system, which is the catchment area that feeds the Blackwood River. It's the overflow from Lake Dumbleyung. A lot of it is naturally saline. The salt was always there. It just wasn't always being mobilised. But the water table started to rise again once the land had been cleared.[79]

The district soon attracted settler farmers and others who sought an income from the new town. The Spratt family had previously set up an inn at Arthur River on the Albany Highway west of Wagin. When the railway arrived in the town, they were tempted by the prospect of passengers looking for a meal and a bed. This seemed to suggest a better guarantee of business rather than awaiting the occasional horse-drawn coach on the rough and ready Albany Highway. So they moved east and established the first hotel in Wagin Hotel, now known as Moran's Wagin Hotel.

Charles Moran (1868–1936) was a Queenslander who as a young man qualified as a pupil teacher before deciding to emigrate to WA in 1890. Here he found employment with Andrea Stambuco, a Florentine by origin, who had been a prominent Brisbane architect but who came to WA at the same time as Moran looking for better opportunities. In Perth, Moran supervised the construction of some of Stambuco's buildings and then went into politics. After he lost his seat at the 1905 election, Moran became uncomfortable with the polarisation of political parties and moved to Wagin where he became a prominent publican and farmer and, for a time, a trustee of the Agricultural Bank. His experience in working with Stambuco may have stood him in good stead when he was planning what became Moran's Wagin Hotel and other local constructions.[80] Moran's is now one of Wagin's most historic buildings, and the cellar, like that of other hotels, has seen its fair share of flooding over the years.[81]

In 1998 Mark Pridham was asked to help to find solutions to flooding problems in wheatbelt towns, including Wagin. A visit to the pub became an almost obligatory method of water divining.

> The old 'go to the pub' trick was one of the first things I cottoned on to when I started on the 'Rural Towns' program. The pub was usually one of the oldest buildings. It would be near the railway line and low in the valley because that's where the town centres usually were. And because all pubs had a two-and-a-half-metre-deep cellar, that was where the salt and water table were going to appear, if they were going to appear.
>
> So yes, go to the pub, talk to the publicans, ask them about the history and condition of the building and my opening question was often, 'How's your cellar?' And I usually got one of three answers:
> 'It's OK now because we pump it out',
> or, 'No, it's got half a metre of water in it – we don't use it anymore',
> or, 'We had to fill it in because we couldn't control the flooding'.
> That third answer became a yardstick as to whether a town really had a problem. And we're are talking about a water level at the cellar floor, a good two to three metres below ground level and in an area of town which is pretty close to the valley floor anyway. So before you needed to drill a groundwater monitoring bore, the pub often gave you an indication as to the depth of the underlying water table.[82]

Mark sees urban salinity as different from rural salinity partly because the effect of salt on townsites is often masked.

> In a townsite there are complicating factors. There is irrigation which doesn't normally occur in the wheatbelt landscape. Townsite infrastructure creates many hard surfaces producing new and unusual drainage patterns which interrupt and divert runoff and often create flooding elsewhere.[83]

Flooding was quite often disguised as something else.

You would see cracking roads and people would look at that and say, 'That's probably due to heavy traffic'. In any main street in these old towns like Wagin you might look at the road surface and assume that some of the damage is due to heavy traffic breaking up road surfaces. But it is compounded by something else: flooding or shallow water tables. These disguises have helped hide the problem for decades.[84]

Shire President Phil Blight agrees.

Urban salinity probably wasn't recognised anywhere very early because in rural areas the impact is more visible and in some instances rural salinity has been here since the dawn of time I suspect. Some of the lakes in this area have always been saline. But I think that townsite salinity is more about flooding and high water tables than salinity.[85]

Like Katanning, Wagin formed a Landcare Conservation District Committee (LCDC), and in 1999 the Wagin Woodanilling Landcare Zone was established. Phil Blight became the secretary of the Wagin LCDC.

I happened to see a funding source that mentioned groundwater investigations and, together with Ned Crossley, DAFWA Project officer for our Landcare committee, we looked at doing a sub-surface investigation and then we obtained funding for a Wagin Townsite Salinity Management Study.

That involved groundwater drilling, investigating groundwater. We found enough money to put down some bores, just to see what was going on around the town, and then we ran out of money. But Mark Pridham, from DAFWA, came along at just the right time and with the resources to expand the project.[86]

The DAFWA Rural Towns Program, established in the late 1990s, was an initiative of the State Salinity Strategy. It aimed to arm communities with the right tools to fight townsite salinity.[87]

When Wagin Shire put its hand up to be part of that program, Mark Pridham and his DAFWA team assisted.

We suggested drainage combined with pumping to control groundwater. But it's not very often that you can apply all the available techniques because groundwater control isn't always feasible. You just can't get water out quickly enough or across a big enough area to make a difference.

Or you may install a bore and get water out but will it draw down the groundwater? Will it actually stop water table rise? Quite often the answer is 'no'. But in Wagin it was possible. So we identified that quite early on as an option.[88]

What helped in the Wagin situation was what Mark Pridham describes as the groundwater 'zone of influence' and, more specifically, its shape, as an inverted cone (an upside-down funnel).

If you've got a cone that looks broad and deep then you can do a lot of good with one or two production bores. But if you've got a cone that is steep-sided and narrow you will need to put in dozens and dozens of bores. Usually this would not be feasible.

De-watering spears might be an option but you wouldn't use spears in Wagin. Spears wouldn't work as large-diameter bores in that town because under Wagin there are a lot of unconsolidated coarse sediments from an old riverbed that flows from the north-west corner of the town. We have tapped into that layer with three of what we call 'production bores'.

You don't always find those conditions and get that lucky. You can find situations where there is a badly salt-affected valley floor and you can't get the water out as easily as we managed to extract it in Wagin.[89]

Engineer and Manager of Works with the Shire of Wagin, Allen Hicks, worked closely with Mark's DAFWA team.

We helped them do test holes and we assisted them in putting in pipes to drain the water away. We put in major bores throughout the town. These are still pumping today.

Bores can reach down to about twenty metres or a bit lower and they do keep the water level down. But as soon as they shut off, or we have to shut them off, within two weeks the water level can rise about six metres. So it doesn't take long for the water level to come back.[90]

However salinity still presented problems. 'All the galvanised pipes that we first put in became corroded. They don't last long with the high salt content. So we had to put in new stainless steel pumps. Now all our pipes are PVC.'[91]

The bores themselves were described as production bores, but, as Mark Pridham pointed out, that is a bit of a misnomer.

If they were installed simply as a water production bore you would be aiming to produce water for a particular use. But we are producing water to get rid of quite salty water to keep water levels down to a safe level. A water table greater than two metres below ground level is considered safe and we are trying to achieve that. We know from our testing that by lowering the water table, getting rid of water from those sites, we will be reducing water levels generally across the town.[92]

However, some water carried away from the town can be put to further use, because:

Much of it is surface water from storms and winter rain and runs off the streets; from the hard stand areas, the roads and roofs. It runs into the

A townsite bore – part of the answer.

135

main town drain as storm water. This water would become saline as it moved down through the catchment and pick up contaminants, but before it can do that the drain runs into a weir near the shire depot and is captured.[93]

Mark Pridham points out that because these towns have rain in winter and a drought in summer, there is potential for them to use this non-potable but high-quality water that is captured for irrigating public facilities.

You could be fully self-reliant on locally harvested water for all your townsite watering needs. Your townsite irrigation requirements are approximately 70 per cent of your town's water consumption and it is going to be consumed in parks, public gardens, golf courses, bowling greens and the footy oval.[94]

And in Wagin's case that's exactly what happened, as Allen Hicks and Phil Blight recall with pride.

New irrigation sources.

We built a weir down behind the shire depot and that holds two million litres of water. We were catching 100,000 litres of water from 1 millimetre of rain. That was just from one quarter of the total town catchment, not the whole lot. Because we were catching so much water, Council built another dam. We extended our weir and today we can hold four million litres of water, just from that little section of town, and we've got two Grundfos pumps now pumping it up there.

Rainfall decline has not affected the situation because we catch every little bit of water that hits the bitumen road and goes in those drains. We've had years here where, if we had not had this set-up, our ovals and gardens would have died. The water we have pumped and caught each year has been a saviour.[95]

Shire of Wagin's Chief Executive Officer, Peter Webster, is convinced that the recapture of storm water has also helped lift community spirit.

I was in Kondinin in 2010 when we had a very dry winter. We ran out of water by December. We made the decision to reduce watering the oval to just once a week for about twenty minutes and community morale just went down.

Wagin Weir.

People in a rural area need to see something green or something positive. We've been talking today about drier winters. If communities want to have green towns, as they used to, they have got to develop ways of catching water, as Allen Hicks has done with the weir here in Wagin.

If we can get some of this fresh water back to use that around the town instead of buying it in, that's all part of making the environment and the town look good into the future.[96]

For Mark Pridham the Wagin project has emphasised the value of thorough investigation of the importance of getting the science right.

A million dollars has been spent on Wagin in the last fifteen years. If we got that wrong we'd have wasted a lot of money. You can analyse how much has been saved in terms of what the damage and long-term costs would have been if untreated. But you also have to get your hydrogeological investigations right.

You've got to know that those groundwater de-watering bores are going to work before you invest a lot of infrastructure in the project. You work out where to place bores, how many, the spacing needed, and then how to draw on them. The aim is not to empty the aquifer but to reduce water levels and maintain them at a safe level so they are not at or near the surface.[97]

Shire engineer Allen Hicks has noticed the reduction in salt water damage to the bitumen on the town's roads. 'Since the pumps have been going we have had fewer problems with the roads. There are a few bad ones around, but not as many as there were'.[98]

And for Allen the Wagin townsite salinity project has been a valuable learning experience.

I have also learned a lot about salinity and salt water; how it works and how to keep it out of the town, together with the water catchment that we built. It has been good for the town.[99]

Importantly too, as Shire President, Phil Blight says the project has helped to protect the town's historic legacy.

> *We don't know how rapidly that heritage might have declined if we hadn't done it. What would Wagin look like without this or that building? And it would be disastrous to have lost any of those heritage buildings. So that alone says that the work we've done has been worthwhile.*[100]

Roadside drain, Wagin.

Chapter 5

What are forests for?

You get in the middle, deep in the forest and you look around you and you just can't imagine how the rest of the world can behave as it does.

Ron Meldrum,
a south-west tree-faller and later long-time forest officer.[1]

In previous chapters we've looked at site-specific case studies of environmental issues: salinity, land repair and water quality. Forests, however, present a wider challenge. The south-west region of Western Australia, despite extensive clearing, is still home to large and often divergent forest species, including major tree types which vary widely in their characteristics, growth patterns and geographical distribution: tuart, wandoo, marri, karri and jarrah, to name but a few. Forest history in Western Australia has been contentious and contested, and forest issues today are still the subject of widely differing opinions.

We might first ask what constitutes a forest? Is it any wooded area, and what values does it hold? The Macquarie Dictionary defines a forest simply as: 'a large tract of land covered with trees'.[2]

And certainly most of us will think immediately about trees. But there are a myriad of definitions, similar to the one below, most of which relate to the impact of forests on both the living and non-living things within our world.

> *Forests are areas of land dominated by tree cover that can reach at least two metres height at maturity, and include all other living and non-living things within, such as animals, plants, soil and water.*[3]

So a forest, by this definition, is a lot more than a collection of trees and, in addition,

> *Forests are ecosystems: a dynamic, constantly changing community of living things, interacting with non-living components. Forests are valued on social, environmental, cultural and economic factors, and are used, loved and appreciated by most people.*[4]

So in the same vein we might now also ask: 'Who are forests for?'

Our discussion in previous chapters has often come back to conversations about trees and the ways human beings have treated

South-west forest.

them. In that sense the forest is the key to the entire south-west environment. In itself a forest is an oxygen factory, offsetting carbon dioxide discharge into the atmosphere, but it can also be evaluated in terms of water, rainfall and land use, including competition between forests and the increasing demands of agriculture for cleared land. Then deputy conservator of Forests WA, W. R. Wallace, in a 1965 presentation, commented that:

> One of the main reasons for the colonisation of Western Australia was the vast expanse of its forests and the great demand for suitable timber for shipbuilding by the Royal Navy, following the decimation of its oak forests over previous centuries. Utilisation of this forest wealth commenced immediately after the arrival of the first settlers and one of the first export records (1836) of the new colony includes 10,000 cubic feet of Western Australian mahogany, as it was then called, for the naval dockyards in England. For the following ninety years exploitation of the jarrah forest continued unabated and uncontrolled.[5]

And, as historian Geoffrey Bolton has commented: 'Of all the human activities which might have been thought to affect the climate of nineteenth-century Australia, few were carried out more zealously than the cutting down of trees'.[6] Expanding on this theme, Bolton points out that:

> In Western Australia alone from the 1850s, only about 20–30 years after white arrival, timber was seen to be as a resource to be cut down and exported. Thus generations of Western Australian school children were brought up in the belief that it was our hardwoods that were paving the streets of London and providing piles for Indian jetties that were conveniently resistant to the ravages of the teredo worm. Timber was largely seen as a non-renewable asset but one which we, in Western Australia, with limited resources, had to make the most of while it lasted.[7]

And perhaps hopefully, at least in the mind of the Premier of the time, those resources would not last long. 'It was said of James Mitchell that he thought an acre of turnips was a finer sight than an acre of jarrah or karri'.[8]

Mitchell and others before him had their way. There were soon far fewer forested acres, as Wallace noted in his 1965 presentation: 'The jarrah forest...originally covered an area of some 13 million acres, of which more than half has been alienated for other purposes – mainly agricultural'.[9]

So at a time when we still have the odd 'hectare or two of jarrah and karri', it seems useful to pose questions about the problems facing today's forests and to look at potential solutions for maintaining the health of the varied woodlands which are a vital part of our natural heritage.

Ron Meldrum's comment, which heads this chapter, might now resonate with an expression coined almost a century ago by one of Western Australia's most far-sighted and conscientious foresters, Conservator Of Forests Charles Lane Poole. He used the word 'conscienceness' to describe how the Western Australian community could, and in his view, should, treat the forests bequeathed to them by nature and time.

Associate Professor Michael Calver, at WA's Murdoch University, has made a study of the history of forestry in WA. He sees 'conscienceness' as a very helpful term today, when we look at the current state of the forests of south-western Australia, even if Lane Poole's choice of expression may have been unintentional.

Whether it was an accidental misspelling or a deliberate coinage, I guess we will never know. But I am rather tempted to believe that he was feeling for a word that combined both the idea of awareness, being conscious, and also having a conscience about the natural environment. In other words, through awareness you can develop a moral position. You are conscious of your conscience.[10]

When Charles Lane Poole used that term, Michael Calver suggests, it was very appropriate for his own time.

As WA Conservator of Forests in the early twentieth century, Lane Poole had to deal with a situation of frontier mentality. There had been attempts before to regulate the forest industry in WA and they had fallen down very badly. As an exceptionally well-trained forester, with experience in other parts of the world, he was very keen to establish a sustainable forest industry in WA. And he believed that the community needed to understand and appreciate the value of forests; the source of richness that came from a sustainable long-term forest industry.

Lane Poole felt that when people had actually reached what he called 'forest conscienceness', then they would also arrive at a position where they believed that forests need to be used responsibility and sustainably. And he thought that this would put an end to the exploitation of the state's forest, which he was very, very upset about.[11]

What Lane Poole strove for was not what today some might call an 'extreme green' perspective, but one that valued a timber industry based on sustainable values.

As a wildlife biologist, Michael Calver sees this policy as economically influenced, but also as an approach which embraced broader values including the importance of native animals.

It is clear from Lane Poole's training manuals that he held a utilitarian view of forest. He saw it as an indefinite source of timber, if it was well managed. He also had a sense of conservation and preservation. In some of his publications he refers to 'the maintaining of groves of older trees' as a reminder of what forests were like before they were modified by timber production. Lane Poole was also very aware of forest fauna, and again his instruction manuals include references to the kinds of animals that would be found in a forest, which ones were possible pests, which ones he considered helpful to the forest industry.

So, on the one hand, his was very much a utilitarian perspective, and, on the other, he had a sensitivity to the aesthetics of forests and to the wildlife the forests sustained.[12]

However, in the early twentieth century, the south–west forests were already under threat from a rival 'utilitarian' perspective.

There were those who believed that timber should be removed from forested country and that the land would be better used for pastoralism or crops. Today what remains throughout the south-west is effectively a compromise between that view and the belief that the best use of the land was long-term timber production. The finest agricultural land lay along water courses which held the most productive soils. Inevitably forested areas, with poorer soils, were fragmented by agricultural clearing. Any area found unsuitable for intensive agriculture ultimately wound up in timber reserves.[13]

There were contemporary concerns about the sustainability of forests as they faced agricultural expansion. Former WA Premier Hal Colebatch was commissioned by the then state Premier Philip Collier to produce *A Story of a Hundred Years: Western Australia 1829–1929*, a book commemorating the state's centenary. In a chapter entitled *Giants of the Forest*, Colebatch wrote:

Shade for man and beast in summer and shelter from cold winds in winter are often lacking in our more progressive country districts, where the axe and fire stick have done their work too thoroughly. In a hundred years we have sacrificed forests which Nature has built up through the centuries, and one of the lessons waiting to be learned from older civilisations of Europe and Asia is the wisdom of planting crops of trees side by side with fields of wheat.[14]

Colebatch, in this 'official history', also expressed concern for the future of the state's forests.

Big advances have been made since the passing of the Forests Act 1918 but forestry cannot be regarded as having been placed on a sound basis until the total volume of timber extracted each year no longer exceeds the estimated increment of the growing trees.[15]

Neil Burrows, Senior Principal Research Scientist at the WA Department of Parks and Wildlife, has written and spoken extensively about the science of forest management, and also about this aspect of its early history.

A consequence of the competition between forest and the demands of agriculture in the early days resulted in a lot of land being permanently cleared. In the jarrah forest the situation is not good. A much higher proportion of jarrah has been cleared for farmland. And the wandoo woodlands in the eastern part of the forest have fared even worse. Most of the wheatbelt was once woodland and is now about 90 to 95 per cent cleared. So there has been a horrific loss of forest and woodlands as a result of agriculture.[16]

Perhaps paradoxically, despite subsequent over-cutting, we still have forests in the south-west, if only because their distinctive trees were valued as commercial assets. While forests clearly have other values, these were seldom considered in the nineteenth and early twentieth centuries.

The current highly cleared state of the WA wheatbelt gives some idea of how our southern landscape would look now if forest had given way entirely to field. Fortunately, for reasons that Neil Burrows explains, other factors intervened.

A lot of the remaining forest lies on rocky lateritic soil, and farmers didn't want it. Another perhaps less important factor was the occurrence of poison bush throughout the forest. It wasn't very palatable to stock and even dangerous to let them graze it.[17]

The provisions of the *Forests Act 1918* went a long way to prevent further loss of woodland. The Parliamentary Bill was largely drafted by Charles Lane Poole himself and reflected his views on how the forest should be managed. It was to be an act for the better management and protection of forests.[18]

Section 19 of the Act gives some idea of its scope.

19. (1.) The Conservator shall, with the approval of the Minister, cause a classification of the forest lands of the State to be made for the purpose of determining which of the lands are suitable to be:

(a) Permanently dedicated as State forests; or

(b) reserved from sale as timber reserves.

19. (2.) The Conservator shall cause plans to be prepared of the lands so classified showing the quantity of timber growing thereon, and indicating those portions which, in his opinion, do not carry or are not likely to produce marketable timber.[19]

According to the Forests Act the scope of what the forest could offer was very comprehensive. It covered potential commodities right down to the forest floor.

Trees, timber, firewood, piles, pole wood, wattles, branch wood, slabs, chips, sawdust, plants, grass, reeds, rushes, bedding, creepers, fibres, leaves, moss, flowers, ferns, blackboys, grass trees, roots, bulbs, galls, bark, gum, kino, resin, sap and charcoal; and in any State forest or timber reserve also includes stones and earth (except gold and other minerals, alluvial, and coal, as defined by the Mining Act, 1904), shells, indigenous animals and birds (not being game within the meaning of the Game Act, 1912–13), honey and bees-wax.[20]

Section 11 covered situations, including misbehaviour and competence and *incapacity to perform his duties*, in which the Conservator of Forests could be suspended from office.

Sadly, the question of 'performing his duties' perhaps comes close to the problems faced by Charles Lane Poole, not from failure to carry them out conscientiously, but rather because, despite his concern for ensuring that the forests under his jurisdiction were sustainable, he felt increasingly undermined.

Matters came to a head when the state government, under Premier James Mitchell, extended concessions and leases to a timber company, Millars, whose harvesting practices showed, in Lane Poole's view, little evidence of 'conscienceness'. He had previously requested, to no avail, that Millars' permits to cut timber should be controlled by the Conservator of Forests, in the interests of maintaining a sustainable forest yield.[21]

Lane Poole resigned his post in 1922 and moved to Canberra. He then pursued a successful and lengthy career as Commonwealth Inspector General of Forests and acting principal of the Australian Forestry School, which he had helped to establish.[22]

Lane Poole's successor was Stephen (known as Kim) Kessell. The two conservators shared similar views about forest management. However, Kessell was less acerbic than his predecessor and managed the politicians and the timber industry more astutely. But he too lamented that:

> The *Anglo-Saxon settlers who populated Australia brought with them no traditions of forestry as a rural industry, and for 100 years or more the forests were looked upon as an enemy to be slaughtered.*[23]

Silviculturist Jack Bradshaw values the legacy that both Lane Poole and Kessell left to their successors.

> When Lane Poole resigned and Kessell took over as conservator, they wrote letters to each other in which they discussed, and agonised over, a number of issues including how much timber should be cut and the silviculture of jarrah in particular. They knew nothing about the way jarrah regenerated but they were trying to work that out. That knowledge is continually being refined, but they worked out a lot of the answers very early on from clear observation.[24]

Jack Bradshaw believes that foresters of his generation benefited considerably from their pioneering efforts.

> What always amazes me is some of the early work that was done by the Forests Department in the 1920s. At that time they had no research background, were mostly European-trained and had next to no resources. They devised systems on the basis of very, very educated observations, to the extent that the silviculture practices that we use today (and which I had a part in reinstituting in the mid-1980s) are virtually a copy of what they started in the 1920s, because those systems worked best.[25]

Roger Underwood, former General Manager of CALM, which became the Department of Conservation and Management, also built on the knowledge of south-west forests that Lane Poole and Kessell had begun to acquire. As he describes it:

> The forestry profession in this state gradually came to understand WA forests through processes of research, trial and error, and experience and observation over decades (a process known these days as 'adaptive management'). Remember, they started knowing nothing, and from this

they developed an entire system of forest conservation and management. This required the build-up of an encyclopaedic body of knowledge from forest botany and soils, to silviculture, forest inventory, forest growth patterns, fire control, ecology, catchment protection...and even more mundane matters such as surveys and maps, and telephone and radio communications.[26]

Roger believes that 'if you don't get your bushfire management right, no other forest management objective is achievable'.[27]

Joanna Young, a botanist who has worked on forest pathology in both the United States and south-west WA, believes it essential to manage forests ecologically.

A lot of work has been done worldwide on how to manage native forests. There is a whole world literature on the principals of ecologically sustainable forest management and the values that you manage for. The current forest management plan does try to address a wide range of values including water, soil, biodiversity and forest products. I have concerns that, at the landscape scale, many values are still being degraded. For example, just because we have a certain percentage of forest in reserves, there might not be enough mature forest retained within some forest types to ensure that the local tree-dwelling fauna survives.[28]

So, in the twenty-first century, how should our forests be managed? In addressing this question it might be worth considering the nature of the south-west landscape prior to European settlement and what our forests looked like prior to 1829. A better understanding of this scene might help us in working out how to care for our forests into the future.

It is likely, as historian Geoffrey Bolton suggests, that long-term Aboriginal occupation and hunting practices involving fire inevitably changed the Australian eco-system well before Europeans arrived to survey and modify their surroundings.[29] Nobody is certain as to how long ago this process began, but historian Bill Gammage has thoroughly surveyed a significant feature of Indigenous activity: fire regimes. In his recent publication, *The Biggest Estate on Earth: How Aborigines Made Australia*, Gammage depicts a very different landscape to the one that we see today.

> *An important clue, but one which was long misinterpreted, can be found in the manner in which early European settlers depicted the country in paintings and sketches. For a long time, well into the twentieth century, it was assumed that the park-like appearance of much of the landscape reflected a wish by the artist to project 'romanticised landscapes, invented landscapes, to depict a romantic view of Australia'.[30]*

But many of these early depictions of country show no evidence of romanticism.

> *They were painted by artists or surveyors or landholders. These pictures tell us a great deal, because most artists were unconscious of the implications of what they saw: park-like landscapes which usually included associations of dissimilar plant communities like grass and forest or grass, forest and water together. These painters were not, as people have often assumed, depicting something that wasn't there.[31]*

What early sketches and paintings perhaps unconsciously reveal is a landscape carefully managed to ensure the continuing existence of both humans and animals; a strategy that called for the preservation of diversity.

> *There has to be a habitat for every creature in the landscape. That concept was enforced through totems that connected people to creatures in the natural environment. An emu totem, for example, meant that you would be responsible not only for emus but also their habitat. In other words, the law is ecologically based and recognises the interconnectedness of life. It says that you must create these habitats and, if you don't, your own soul is at risk because you are linked by your soul to your totem.[32]*

Fire was a key management tool used to implement the law. In traditional life in Australia, the old saying 'fight fire with fire' could perhaps be better expressed as 'prevent fire with fire'. In conversation in January 2015, Bill Gammage reminded me that he was:

> ...struck by one of the fire controllers in the recent bush fire in Adelaide saying, 'No Fire Service on earth could have put out this fire'. And I remember a Fire Controller saying the same thing in South Australia in 1983, Ash Wednesday, thirty years ago. So twice in thirty years you had a huge fire which our modern services couldn't put out.
>
> Now how could Aborigines have dealt with fire before Europeans came? They didn't have the means to flee or fight fire. So their remedy was to prevent it and their chief means of prevention was to reduce forest fuel. Hence European accounts of Europeans being able to step over fires. They were so low to the ground.[33]

Another strategy, in effect, isolated separate potentially flammable areas such as scrub.

> You must have scrub because it is habitat and also contains totem animals and plants. They broke up those areas with open grassy areas and that alternated fire control zones with fire-prone zones so that you always had safe areas.[34]

In south-western Australia there was a burning calendar. Indigenous historian and Edith Cowan University lecturer Noel Nannup describes the process.

> It was to burn in unison with nature. When Aboriginal people burnt, they burnt during the right times of the year, when there was a fuel load to burn. So, for the Aboriginal people, through their total connection to everything and immersion in the land they lived in, they knew which area would burn and carry a fire and which area wouldn't. They knew the weather conditions which would make fire possible. They also kept the forest open in some places and that is where the animals would feed for the next two to perhaps three years and where the grass was the sweetest.[35]

Surprisingly perhaps for twenty-first century dwellers facing hotter, drier summers, burning could be and was carried out in our warmest season, summer. Cattleman Lew Scott recalled for forester David Ward, a memory of south-west farmers burning the coastal land around the lower Donnelly and Warren rivers in the 1920s.

> The real oldies followed the burning patterns of the natives in keeping the place green...learned to burn little patches that they wanted for their existence, same as the black fellow. Of course not winter and not spring, because you kill all the little birds and animals – and so summer burning.[36]

In this southern damp and watery landscape, winter burning was not feasible anyway.

Terry Cornwall (known as Koodah, meaning 'mate' or 'friend'), was born in Wagin and is a Nyungar man from the Wiliman Clan. He also describes traditional practice in the south-west.

> They wouldn't burn one big patch. They would burn in a mosaic pattern; it was for their own safety. If they fired the land up and it got too hot they could lose all the animals and plant life and their medicine trees. So they knew when to burn with the weather and the seasons.[37]

And, as Bill Gammage emphasises, the First Australians lit cool fires.

> If you got a dry day with no wind in summer, then you could burn more safely. But you might also burn in winter, late in the afternoon because you knew that the dew would put the fire out and dampen the fuel. There would be fires pretty well the whole year round. The fire would only burn a few metres but that was their purpose, and enough of those small fires become mini fire-breaks when the country dries out later on.[38]

The role of fire in Aboriginal culture also varied.

> It depended on what you wanted to do, what you needed in a particular area. Do you want this just as a fuel control area or do you want grass to grow long because you want to harvest the grass seed or protect lizards or grass wrens or provide seed for birds?[39]

Mike Quartermaine's great-great-grandfather, Elijah Quarter-maine, was the first European to establish a farm in the Katanning district. Mike has some understanding of Aboriginal land management practice, partly from a family account of how this local landscape once looked.

There have been farms here since 1855, and my grandfather said that his father told him that his father told him, in turn, that there were mainly big trees with not much undergrowth, and so they just ring-barked them to stop taking the nutrients and water from the pasture.

It didn't dawn on me for a long time what that meant until I started to grow better crops and then I noticed these wild oats and native grasses coming up in the crops all the time.

Then it dawned on me why there was no undergrowth, because the Aborigines had been burning for thousands and thousands of years and had just left these big trees, because they wanted to promote the grasses that have evolved over thousands of years to keep the 'roos' and other animals close to their water sources. Parkland clearing is what they used to call it when they cleared land like that, but it happened with human (Aboriginal) intervention.[40]

As Bill Gammage emphasises, this fire strategy increased the variety of habitats.

It created grass where there might once have been dense forest and it also created edges. Edges are very important. A great many species hover on edges between grass and trees, grass and water, which offer food and shelter. Burning increases the number of edges and of course animals can wander in and out of them. And that strategy creates more and more habitats. And keeping country open makes it easier both to hunt and travel.[41]

Michael Calver suggests that, when European travellers or would-be settlers journeyed in the south-west of WA, they benefited from this long-established practice.

If you look at many of the early photographs of either karri or jarrah forest, horses or mounted riders are very often included in the photographs.

And I suspect that whoever posed for the picture was thinking; 'I need an indication of scale; hence the horses. This inclusion will reveal big trees and indicate the nature of the under-storey'. Putting a horse into the picture must suggest that the understorey is open. And the fact that horses are there in those photographs is strongly suggestive of the open state of the forest.[42]

Open or otherwise, how might that country have looked to an early-nineteenth-century Western Australian settler like John Garrett Bussell, when he looked down on the well-watered Busselton coastal plain in 1831? For Bill Gammage there are complexities in resolving this kind of conjecture.

If somebody talks about an open forest or an open plain we can't be absolutely sure that an 'open plain' means no trees or few trees. But there is no question that when somebody says there is an open plain they

Open jarrah forest.

*mean it is much more open that would be natural. I would say that the
Busselton coastal plain was open in general, probably mainly grassland,
perhaps with some open woodland; stretches of trees or bush.*[43]

The Busselton area was also well-treed, as described by Shann.

*The country here was so clear that a farmer could hardly grudge the fine
spreading trees of red and white gum and peppermint the small portions
of ground that they occupied only to ornament.*[44]

However Neil Burrows notes that the early European settlers
generally misunderstood the Indigenous use of fire.

*They attributed the really low soil fertility of our Western Australian
native forests to frequent burning by Aboriginal people.*

*These apparently infertile soils, worn down, heavily oxidised and
eroded, have, nonetheless, nurtured and sustained the south-west forests.
The amazing thing is that our forest trees, including jarrah, marri,
karri, blackbutt, wandoo: all those wonderful species that we have, the
remarkable thing about them is that they do so well on such poor soils.*

*Quite some time ago, a colleague – a forester and a soil scientist –
from Switzerland came to visit and I showed him the statistical profile
of our forests, which demonstrated how poor they were in nutrients.
When he actually saw the forest, the huge karri trees, he was blown
away. He could not believe that such poor soils could support such tall
forests. In that respect the south-west is quite unique. There is nowhere
else in the world which has a Mediterranean climate and poor soil that
supports forests.*[45]

This country also appears to be unique in that fire, the
management tool of the First Australians, plays a vital role in
forest health and nourishment.

*Fire is a very important part of that process. It helps the breakdown of
eucalypt leaves and twigs that fall from the trees. In our dry climate,
without fire, these would take forever to break down, unlike in a tropical
rainforest where in humid, moist conditions, breakdown of plant matter
is very rapid.*[46]

Acknowledgment by Europeans that fire can play a valuable role in forest management has been relatively recent. As Neil Burrows notes, their nineteenth-century experience of fire 'was with very savage bush fires' and they were concerned about the damage fire did to the timber quality of the forest, to the re-growth of young trees.[47]

As Roger Underwood also notes, although Charles Lane Poole was revered as a conservator of forests and understood the need to nurture and protect the forest, he regarded fire as the enemy.

> *Lane Poole thought that all fire was a bad thing. He was imbued with the European concept that was also adopted later in India in the nineteenth century, that fire was something that must be expunged from the forest altogether. He thought fire would destroy the humus layer on the forest floor, as it did in European hardwood forests. He did not understand that Australian forests had evolved in an environment in which fire was a frequent visitor, either lit by lightning or deliberately lit by Aborigines.*[48]

As Neil Burrow reminds us:

> *Fire also releases minerals and triggers the germination of legumes, the acacias, the wattles which, once they grow, capture nitrogen from the air, store it in their root system as nutrients and, when they die, the nitrogen becomes available to the forest trees.*[49]

While Aboriginal people had effectively made use of fire, it took many decades for Europeans to understand its role in the forest and ways of managing it.

> *They had an attitude that fire was nothing but bad. So they had a policy of fire suppression and fire exclusion. That lasted right up to the 1950s and 1960s. The famous Dwellingup fire event was a turning point. Although the policy had changed before that, nothing had changed much on the ground.*[50]

Roger Underwood was a Field Forestry Officer at Dwellingup in the summer of 1958–9 and almost daily saw the danger of fire.

In the entire summer our main job was fire-fighting. Fires were starting all the time everywhere, one of the sources being steam locomotives. I described them as the perfect mobile incendiary machine. They chuffed through the forests spitting out sparks. Fortunately most of the areas along the railway lines were ignited by the locomotives so regularly that it was quite easy to handle the fires in those areas.[51]

So by the long, hot summer of 1961 there was a lot more forest fuel to burn and the potential for fires to do a lot more damage, partly, as Neil Burrows explains, because the region was changing and growing.

There had been bush fires before that. The south-west was sparsely populated so nobody cared; but by the 1960s we had some sizeable towns there with industry, mills and farms. So you had this combination of many more people, much more industry and heavy fuel loads built up all the way from north of Perth through to Albany. A string of dry thunderstorms from the north-west set light to the bush at very, very high intensity. It destroyed a number of settlements and farms but, remarkably, no-one was killed.[52]

A Royal Commission was held after the fires and a new approach to fire management, based on 'prescription' or controlled burning, resulted from the Dwellingup fire and other major fires of 1961.[53]

In the twenty-first century, we are now more aware of the role of fire in our native forests, as well as the dangers that uncontrolled fire can bring, especially in more populated areas. 'Sea-change' towns, settlements on the south and west coast and on the fringes of the outer Perth metropolitan area are now seen to be particularly at risk.

However, conservationists became increasingly worried about the controlled burning policies then advocated and practised by the WA Forests Department and its successors. Bolton suggests that first impressions of burnt forest were powerful factors here.

I guess for anyone who comes for the first time to an area that has been burnt through, even with controlled burning, it does look a pretty sorry spectacle and it is easy to underestimate the capacity of Australian bush to renew itself if it is given a chance.[54]

However, fire is not the only danger that our forests face. We are also increasingly aware of changes to our woodlands brought about by two centuries of human intervention. From early settlement onwards, axe and saw took out many of the big trees. The forest canopy shrank and the forest floor became more open to the sky. Michael Calver describes the effect.

The first European uses of the forests of the south-west were, of course, clearing for agriculture and felling for timber. And back in the 1960s, Roy Wallace, who was Deputy Conservator of Forests at the time (later Conservator), wrote a paper on fire in the jarrah forest environment in which he presented some fairly blunt statistics. In particular he refers to the area of the jarrah forest that had been cut over by the early twentieth century. So we had a situation where both removal of timber and clearing for agriculture resulted in a reduction of 50 per cent in the forest canopy over the area Wallace described. That has to mean increased understorey. Increased understorey means an increase in small shrubby plants that are ideal fire food.[55]

Old growth forests have been protected from logging in more recent times but the overall health of our south–west forests is of increasing concern.

Changes in the pattern of forestry management have played a role here. Until the 1970s, as Geoffrey Bolton comments, all Western Australia's woodlands were in the hands of the WA Forests Department, an establishment that had existed since Lane Poole's time in the early 1920s.

Even in the early 1980s you had a cadre of professional foresters who all had a similar training and background. And they were an independent department. But in the 1980s the Labor Government under Brian Burke thought it was wise to throw forestry in with the wildlife people from Fisheries and the rangers previously employed by the National Parks Authority. So they set up Conservation and Land Management

(CALM) as a government department with environmental themes and a conservation focus. They tried to amalgamate at least three different administrative cultures but they weren't always a very good fit.

Today there is no longer a Forests Department. The 1918 Act was repealed by the *Conservation and Land Management (CALM) Act of 1984*; an act which made no specific mention of forests but which was intended to:

> *...make better provision for the use, protection and management of certain public lands and waters and the flora and fauna thereof, to establish authorities to be responsible therefore, and for incidental or connected purposes.*[56]

So for the last thirty years the woodlands of south-western Australia have been managed by government agencies: departments with other responsibilities and interests besides forestry. On top of that, Geoffrey Bolton points to:

> *...from the 1970s, the growth of a keenly critical environmental movement, comprising people who, rightly or wrongly, were critical of some of the practices employed by the foresters. And that is still a subject of contention. The result is that the foresters are not able to stand as a united professional stand-alone group defending their practices. They now have to negotiate through the whole of the CALM (now the Department of Parks and Wildlife) system.*[57]

Looking back at these changes, one could ask whether they were ecologically or administratively motivated.

> *I think it was partly a desire for rationalisation. The Burke government attitude was that there were a lot of areas like the Office of the Surveyor General, for instance, that had been around forever but it was necessary to move with the times. So there was an element of business theory involved.*
>
> *What triggered it was the decision in the 1970s, which was taken before Brian Burke's government, to develop a woodchip industry. The timber industry and the foresters both saw that woodchips would mainly*

be taken from marri waste and that it would be small branches that had
been cut but were of no use for anything else. However the critics argued
that chips didn't stop there; that high-grade old-growth forests, karri,
jarrah, tuart were being cut down for no benefit other than chipping. And
claims and counterclaims were made by both sides.[58]

As professional foresters working in the south-west, Jack
Bradshaw and his staff were in favour of woodchipping as a means
of using the otherwise unwanted marri trees. 'We were highly
supportive of woodchipping as a means of using the marri to
enhance regeneration and of preventing a karri/marri forest from
turning into a purely marri forest'.[59] However, as Jack admits,
even within his own department, the advent of woodchipping
was not heralded with universal enthusiasm. 'Some foresters in
the department were not initially supportive of woodchipping.
Like the general community, they saw this practice as clear-felling,
motivated by wood chipping for profit'.[60]

For Michael Calver, woodchipping represents a dilution of
the potential value of the forest.

At one time, there was a feeling that the forest was inexhaustible. So
people used timber for all sorts of things: paving, railway sleepers etc.
But, if you then find that the forest is not inexhaustible, you get into
low residue use; trying to wring the last drop of value out of it. So wood-
chipping and the downgrading of the quality standards for prime logs are
an indication of the diminishment of the resource and a direct consequence
of over-harvesting.[61]

The fact that woodchipping suggests, for many people, a
reduction in timber resources has influenced the community
response to forests and foresters. Independent forest dieback
consultant Joanna Young has seen significant changes in public
attitudes to forestry in the last quarter of the twentieth century.
In the old days it was possible to selectively log the jarrah forest:

But once you have made, say, two or three selections during the long
history of cutting, there are fewer good trees left. So the foresters said,

'This isn't working, we had better start allowing bigger gaps in the forest to allow the lignotuberous stock to re-grow and regenerate as jarrah forest'. But where the loggers were cutting intensively and extensively, it looked like clear-felling. The gaps in the forest were often many hectares apart.[62]

Joanna sees this practice as influencing public demand for the establishment of tracts of forest to be legally protected from logging.

So I think there was pressure that, if an area was made into a reserve, people didn't want that forest touched. People did not accept the level of disturbance. They did not like wood chipping and clear-felling, whether karri or jarrah. Trust was lost and hence many conservationists developed the view that the forests should be left alone. 'Leave them, don't touch them, don't disturb them, don't burn them: their values are being degraded.'

Boranup forest, 2014.

I believe that if the timber volumes extracted had been smaller, sooner and if the logging had looked less destructive and less wasteful, we might well not have needed the Gallop Government policy of no more old-growth logging.[63]

Argument between foresters, the timber industry and the critics of both parties remains a constant factor in more-recent forest deliberations. Foresters have been criticised for being too close to the timber industry, for an over-enthusiastic attitude to fire management and for clinging too long to their own culture. But given their long tenure as keepers of the forests, Geoffrey Bolton sees merit in still hearing their voice.

By training and temperament there is a lot to be said for bodies where there is a strong professional identity and a growth of accumulated knowledge and wisdom. Now sometimes that can ossify into conservatism, but the foresters were never of a mind to cut everything out. There was a sense of the forest being a harvest; something that you reaped when the time was right, but you were going to replace it. And I think that good forestry recognised that.[64]

Roger Underwood was General Manager of CALM and previously a regional and district manager with the Forests Department. He and his colleagues saw themselves as people with broad interests and a deep regard for all the values that the forest represents.

Foresters would spend all week working in the forest and then go out in the forest again at weekends just for the love of it. I did that all the time when I lived at Pemberton and Manjimup, and later I took my family with me. I am pleased that this grounding gave my children a love of the bush as well, and I am proud to see that this is rubbing off onto the third generation.[65]

Professional work and out-of-hours relaxation went hand in hand and often led to new interests and areas of expertise.

A great many of my forester friends had forest-related hobbies: bird watching, botany, photography, painting, history, Aboriginal culture, fishing etc. One of my friends, Dick Perry, was so fascinated by termites that he eventually became a world expert on them. Another became an authority on Boronia.

My primary interest was forest history and I would spend hours exploring old settlements or abandoned bush homesteads, walking the former railway formations, measuring bridges, climbing and documenting lookout towers and so on. Jack Bradshaw and I actually restored an old lookout tree in the Dryandra Forest.[66]

The picture that Roger paints of the relationship between foresters and the forest that they managed is one that David Worth recognises. His work has explored the conflict over the logging of native forests in the south-west of Western Australia from a sociological perspective.[67]

You have loggers who just love living there and I talked to them in their homes, amidst the forest, in a superb environment. But they would go out the next day to cut down some old growth trees. I suppose they were of the view that you could do it sustainably but, on the other side, you had quite well-known scientists who did not hold that view.

Roger Underwood, however, is quick to point out that foresters are not loggers.

Forestry is a profession, a calling, like engineer, historian or architect. It is not an industry. The role of foresters, practising forestry, is to manage forests and thus management need not have anything to do with cutting timber.[68]

At the same time relations between foresters and the timber industry inevitably raise questions of conflicts of interest. Until the year 2000, when the Forest Products Commission was established, budgets in the Forests Department, and later CALM, had been closely tied to timber production. Foresters managed forests. Timber companies cut into them. Jack Bradshaw, formerly a manager with CALM'S Forest Management Branch, recalls their association.

It was a bit mixed. In this relationship I always felt there was a great degree of honesty. Industry had their job to do. We knew what that was and it was the same with us. We had a job to do and they understood and respected that. So we had lots and lots of bun-fights but I think there was respect on both sides.

In the long run we were both trying to achieve much the same thing, but with different ways of going about it. They wanted the best timber to sell. So they were continually trying to 'up the grade' and we were trying to push it down. If an area was being cut, we didn't want them just to pick the eyes out of it. If you cut a tree down, you used as much as you could from it. Every tree was marked for removal (or later marked for retention) by the department's tree-markers. So there was a very close relationship between the tree marker and the people in the bush. There was daily contact.[69]

But less contact, it is evident, between foresters and their environmental critics. It might appear pointless to revisit this situation, years on from the division that grew between them in the 1970s and '80s. But it may be worth looking at what gave rise to their differences, if only to ask what each group might have learnt from sharing thoughts and experience, a dialogue that could still help us in caring for our unique south-west forests.

Changing technology was perhaps an irritant here. By the late twentieth century, heroic images of tree fellers as strong-armed men taking out majestic karris with cross-cut saws were very much part of the past. Now chain saws swiftly despatched trees and as they did, silenced bird song in the forest. Joanna Young sees increasing mechanism as a factor in the growth of public concern.

People also saw the forest industry as dominated by more and more machinery. Bigger trucks, mechanised felling machines. And the native forest, particularly the karri, started to look a bit more like a plantation, and I think the public started saying, 'We don't like our production forests looking like this. Large clear-felled areas looked terrible after they had been logged and burned and nothing seemed to have been left'.

This practice would result in maximum log production in relatively short rotations but diversity would be lost at different scales. I don't think the public were prepared to accept it. Values other than wood production had to be given greater consideration.[70]

Geoffrey Bolton was initially hopeful of an agreed approach to forest management that could, in turn, benefit the forest itself.

In 1997 I was one of a group that tried to get conservationists and forestry people to sit around the same table and see if we could work on some measure of agreement. The first meeting was fairly good tempered and there seemed some hope that they might be able to agree on a few points in common. But unfortunately that didn't follow through and in the end people went back to entrenched attitudes.[71]

David Worth has studied the relationships between the varying parties in the last quarter of the twentieth century.

Most groups had a clearly painted picture of their opposition which didn't allow for a lot of movement into the middle to establish common ground. We did have the regional forest agreement in the south-west. This was an agreement about putting certain limits on logging of old-growth forests. But both sides never really agreed with that. They wanted their position to prevail and that is what the anti-logging groups achieved with Geoff Gallop.[72]

Geoffrey Bolton sees the Gallop Old Growth Forest Agreement (2001) as a reasonably successful attempt to bring some sort of order and rationality to the debate.

It wasn't seen by either side as perfect but at least it was something they could live with and it provided much stronger legislative protections for a good deal of the remaining old growth forest. It meant that timber harvesting, including woodchipping, could go on, but it was much more strictly regulated.[73]

Now, well into the twenty-first century, we are looking at a forest facing dangers that include not only the potential for excessive logging, but also the physical health of the forest itself, a concern that has been around for some time and is certainly not diminishing.

Giles Hardy is Associate Professor at Murdoch University's Centre for Excellence on Climate Change and Woodland and Forest Health. He specialises in forest pathology and related issues.

> *There were reports of canker in marri and red flowering gum going back to the 1930s and 1940s, when they planted King's Park with red flowering gums, and all the trees there died from this canker pathogen,* Quambalaria coyrecup. *It has been observed, but at very low levels, and it is only in the last ten to fifteen years that we have recognised that this problem is something quite significant. This pathogen appears to be at its worst in areas of human disturbance, along roads, on farmland, remnant bush, semi-urban and urban landscapes. These trees will die and result in big changes to the landscape.*[74]

Other harmful pathogens, including *Phytophthora cinnamomi*, are, Giles Hardy suggests, also taking a toll on other plant species, using them as hosts. There are over 116 species of Phytophthora (pronounced Fy-tof-thora, and meaning 'plant destroyer' in Greek), but it is *Phyophthora cinnamomi* that causes the most severe and widespread damage to native plants in Western Australia. This introduced plant disease was sometimes known as jarrah dieback, but, since it attacks a large number of native and introduced species, it is now referred to as Phytophthora Dieback.[75]

> *Wherever the plants are, Phytophthora Dieback will kill them all. In areas where there are banksia woodlands, we find no individual plants left, once it has moved through the landscape. Marri is also just one of many hosts and, under disturbed conditions it appears to be, quite susceptible to Phytophthora.*[76]

Tuarts, trees unique to the south-west coastal areas, have also been affected by another harmful pathogen, *Phytophthora multivora*. But there is some good news. 'We can return a really sick tree to one that is magnificent by boosting its immune system with nutrients, and with phosphite, a fungicide chemical we use to control phytophthora'.[77]

Drought and frost, both possible indicators of increasing climate change, have also begun to take their toll, particularly to jarrah and marri trees.

> *We are seeing a lot of frost damage on marri and jarrah now affecting some very big trees. We have seen frosts in 2006, 2010 and 2013 and they are reducing the tree height and also the flowering patterns. Marri, for example, takes two years to produce seed.*[78]

Marri is one of the giant trees of the south-west. For Cielito Marbus, a researcher with Murdoch's School of Veterinary and Life Sciences, this tree:

> *…is a keystone species. In a lot of areas where jarrah has been largely cut out, it is the dominant over-storey species. The marri tree is much appreciated by apiarists because it flowers profusely and is a rich source of pollen and nectar for bees.*[79]

Her current work is a study of the effect of yet another pathogen now affecting marri. She showed me affected trees near Margaret River.

Marri blossom, autumn 2015.

I am looking at the impact of a fungal disease Quambalaria pitereka, *an introduced pathogen that infects the leaves, flowers and flower buds of the marri tree. The question I have to answer is, how much of an impact will this have on the availability of nectar and pollen for bees, and on fruit and seeds for our native birds such as the black cockatoos?*[80]

Cielito is also examining the effects of *Qualambria coyrecup*, which, as Giles Hardy has noted, affects many, if not most, marri trees in the south-west.

It causes the limb to swell and crack. Sometimes the canker bleeds as well and it is easy to spot the blackened areas, even from a distance. This particular pathogen can kill a marri tree but it takes up to ten years to die, so people don't always notice it. They get so accustomed to seeing the tree looking scraggly and bleeding that they don't notice that it is dying.

We are concerned about the impact that these two pathogens together will have on the marri forests and the ecosystem services they provide. And, if you skip a marri season, for example, it can impact negatively on the bees' health. They are not as productive or as big and the young they produce are smaller.[81]

Dying marri, Caves Road.

Bee health is critical here.

Not just because bees rely on the marri for a lot of honey and need the marri to flower prolifically. But it is really important in the cycle of moving beehives from one stock of trees to another. Bee-keepers follow the flowering cycles of a number of Western Australian eucalypt species and marri pollen provides essential fatty acids that are really important for the health of the beehive. It has been called 'WA's best pollen'.[82]

And not just beehive health. The health of the marri itself is also vital to the survival of some of the local native birds.

This floral pathogen is also going to reduce the ability of the marri to contribute to the ecosystem. If, for example, the flowers are dying, there are no fruit or seeds for already endangered birds, the native cockatoos, to eat.[83]

And Cielito adds that 'if the WA honey industry is to be developed to its full potential, it is marri pollen and honey that offer the most promise in that direction'.[84]

Other factors affecting marri survival may well include changing weather patterns in the south-west of WA.

Temperature and rainfall are the main factors affecting when the marri first flowers and how much it flowers. So, if the climate is changing gradually over time, by just a degree or two, that will greatly affect the timing of flowering. We don't know whether we are going to see a longer or a shorter flowering season. Are we going to have fewer resources available to the bees and the birds? And how will this impact on the resources available to birds, bees and us?[85]

The impact of climate change raises more questions than it than answers, and they apply to the entire forest system. Two forestry scientists from Murdoch University, restoration ecologist Katinka Ruthrof and Joe Fontaine, who describes himself as a 'disturbance ecologist', are currently studying sites in the Darling Range once densely forested with tall jarrah and now changed or disturbed by drought or fire. Drought sites, already highly visible from aerial photographs, are due, Katinka Ruthrof suspects, to

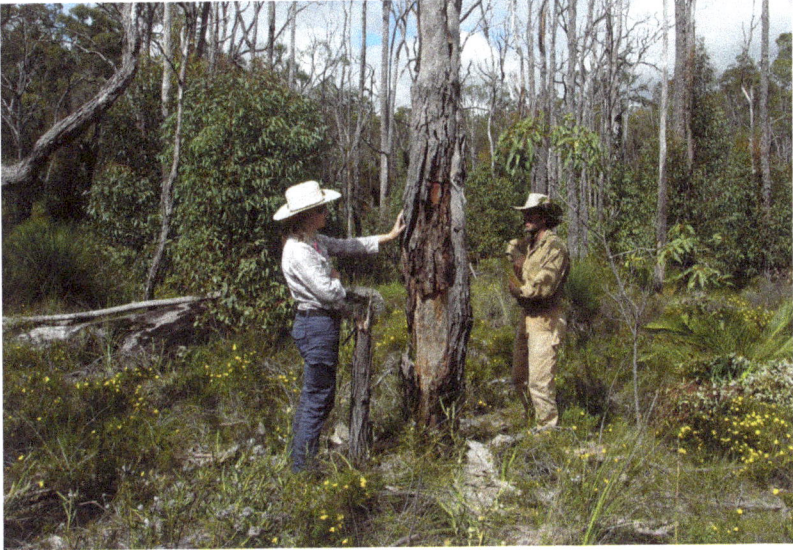

Joe Fontaine and Katinka Ruthrof checking a drought site of jarrah forest.

shallowing soils, possibly due to decreased forest cover. But these sites now face another predicament.

> *These sites can show us what could happen in the future if the climate continues to dry and we keep getting hotter and hotter days in summer. These trees will die back and re-sprout and these drought areas could get larger and larger.*[86]

I caught up with both researchers on one of their regular inspections of a site in the northern jarrah forest. Joe Fontaine described the situation they were monitoring.

> *Drought alone suppresses what might have been flourishing re-growth in previously logged areas; especially where the forest canopy has now gone or has been opened up.*

Katinka Ruthrof sees the resulting drier conditions as increasing the likelihood that these drought sites may worsen because 're-sprouts' from dead trunks use more water in a drying climate. 'A lot of these harvested areas would be more vulnerable to drought'.[87]

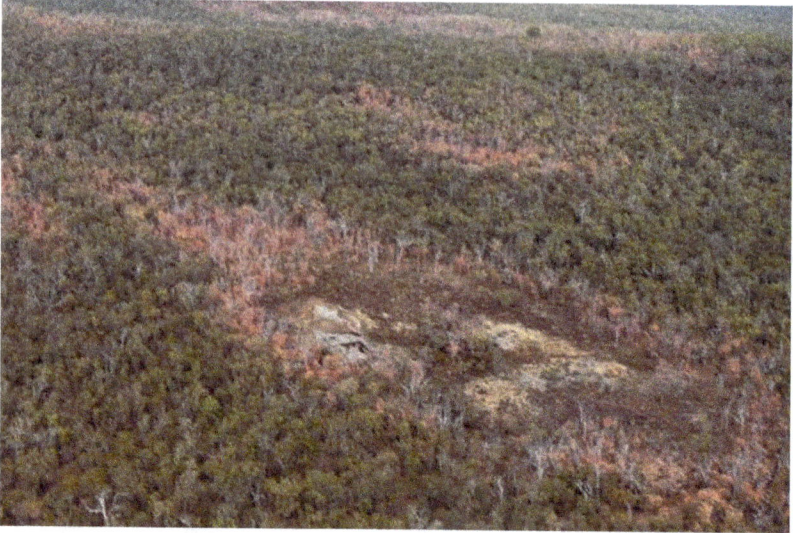

Aerial view, drought site.

A suggested solution in sites like this with too many small trees is to 'thin' the forest. Drastic though this practice might appear, Neil Burrows thinks that it would benefit our brooks and streams because, with too many trees in a given area:

> ...the less water there is for the catchment. The higher the area of the tree stems or the leaf area of tree canopies, the more water they use. So there is less water available for creeks, streams and catchments.
>
> Currently creeks in the jarrah forest that once ran for most of the year are now becoming ephemeral. They are just little pools, and many of the creeks just don't flow anymore. Until the 1970s, when we used to have good reliable rainfall, these creeks ran every winter. So if we want the creeks to run and we want the catchments to recharge with water and to recharge the ground water, we are going to have to thin the forest.[88]

Roger Underwood considers that 'thinning' in the northern jarrah forest catchment areas in the Darling Ranges should be a priority because, in his view, reducing tree numbers would improve water supply.

Thinning would not only enhance the growth of the trees and the health of the forest but it would also maintain the hydrological system so that water could flow into the streams and dams. Because that thinning has not been done, we now have forests that are choked with trees, and Perth's reservoirs, Mundaring Weir and Canning Dam, Serpentine, Wungong and so on, are not receiving sufficient runoff and are drying up. These are areas that were cut over for timber a long time ago. They were then regenerated and have become dense stands of regrowth forest. But it was always the intention that these re-grown forests would be thinned.[89]

Roger believes we would soon see results.

Once an area has been thinned, the whole hydrological system picks up immediately. So, within a year or two, you will start to see water flow into streams. The impact is almost immediate.[90]

However, thinning on a large scale, especially in jarrah, is not an easy option, as silviculturist Jack Bradshaw explains:

With karri you can do that pretty easily because karri is so vigorous that once you create a gap by thinning, karris fill that space very quickly by expanding their crowns and prevent more regeneration. You can thin karri and the effect of thinning will persist until the remaining trees again reach maximum density.

Jarrah, however, is more difficult, because it coppices strongly and also grows from lignotubers. It is also very tolerant of fire and moisture stress. So it is very hard to kill, and after reaching maximum density it persists (instead of dying) and slows down its growth rate. You can remove trees, but to prevent them coppicing and negating the thinning, you need to poison the stumps. The trouble with jarrah is keeping it low in density. If you thin and leave some trees behind, they will grow as single trees. But if you don't poison a stump it will quickly coppice and compete again. In a very vigorous area you can be back to where you were within ten years.[91]

While Neil Burrows favours thinning, he thinks it is a matter of balance.

It is a 'trade off'. We need to thin the forest sufficiently to give runoff, but not to thin so much that we destroy the integrity of the forest. I think if we were to thin the jarrah forest to about half the natural basal area of the forest, we would both protect the forest ecology and the integrity of its biodiversity as well as providing a level of runoff to streams, rivers and catchments.[92]

Des Donnelly, a forester with many years of experience of work in the south-west, holds firm views on the value of thinning.

Keeping the forest healthy is paramount. Jarrah has the ability to grow from lignotubers. Mild fire will go through, burn them, but they will re-grow and keep on doing that. We should be able to thin out at the various stages of that life cycle to allow fewer trees to reach maturity much sooner.[93]

This is a practice, Des believes, we should extend to our national parks and other forest reserves. But Jack Bradshaw asks:

Even if you do thin, the question is can you do enough to make any difference? The current rate of harvesting affects only about 0.25 per cent of the forest per year. And, for the life of me, I can't see anybody wanting to do it in national parks. If you don't thin, then you accept the fact that, if the climate changes, then there won't be sufficient water to maintain the same stand density as it does at present.[94]

Restoration ecologist, Katinka Ruthrof, thinks some more practical research is needed.

We need to establish some fairly large trials to determine whether some of these areas could be thinned in such a way that that they don't re-sprout with multiple stems. We want to allow that structure to come back to the way we have always seen the forest to be, rather than this re-sprouting jungle that we see now.[95]

As I suggested to Katinka, beyond any projected trials, it would surely be very hard to assign a completion date to thinning on a large scale. It would pose an immense challenge, requiring a large labour force, a lot of machinery and access to difficult areas. She agreed.

Obviously not all stands need that sort of intensive management and I know that often people don't want management intervention in the forest. But in certain areas of the forest, reducing re-sprouting and allowing individual stems to grow singly could be best for forest health.

However, I would be concerned if a particular thinning regime was applied across the entire forest, given how diverse and widespread the forest is. It is a big task, made more so because we don't have a market for the small stems of timber that we're taking out.[96]

This is a challenging trajectory, as her colleague, Joe Fontaine, sees it on-site.

We are looking at a big-stemmed stump with three large sprouts from its base. Could we cut these back to only one stem per tree? One of those could become dominant, grow larger and taller and then we begin to regain that forest structure instead of the bushy, shrubby appearance of this patch of ground.[97]

The big-stemmed stump.

175

Jack Bradshaw is also conscious of both the lack of a market for 'thinned' timber and the reluctance of many people in the community to support this treatment of trees.

> *In order for thinning to be an operational reality, you really want to be able to take out the poorer trees, and to do that you need a market for them. This is difficult to achieve and almost impossible from a social point of view. Poor quality jarrah would be ideal to sell for biomass. People are happy for you to cut saw logs but not the poorer and smaller trees and that is the opposite of what is needed for forest health. The greatest challenge for forest management is to find markets for low-quality material.*[98]

For botanist Joanna Young, loss of diversity and nourishment of forest health is a concern if thinning takes place. What else might get thinned? She cites the example of the shrubby *Banksia grandis*.

> *The foresters didn't want* Banksia grandis *in the production areas of the northern jarrah forest because it competed with the growth of regenerating jarrah. They wanted trees to grow with less competition from the understorey. So they cut out and poisoned* Banksia grandis *all over the place. But such flowering species are a very important food source for birds and other animals. It is not ecologically sustainable to keep removing species such as banksia, snotty gobbles and grass trees in the quest for wood production from our native forests. Many vertebrate species are dependent on them.*[99]

Like Jack Bradshaw, Joanna argues that thinning is not a one-step process.

> *If you thin the forest down to a low level, you have much loss of understorey and if a fire goes through, in my view, the remaining trees could be lost, with future regeneration less secure. For increased water runoff repeat thinnings would be required. The structure of the forest will permanently change. You have to keep doing it, effectively turning a forest into a parkland.*[100]

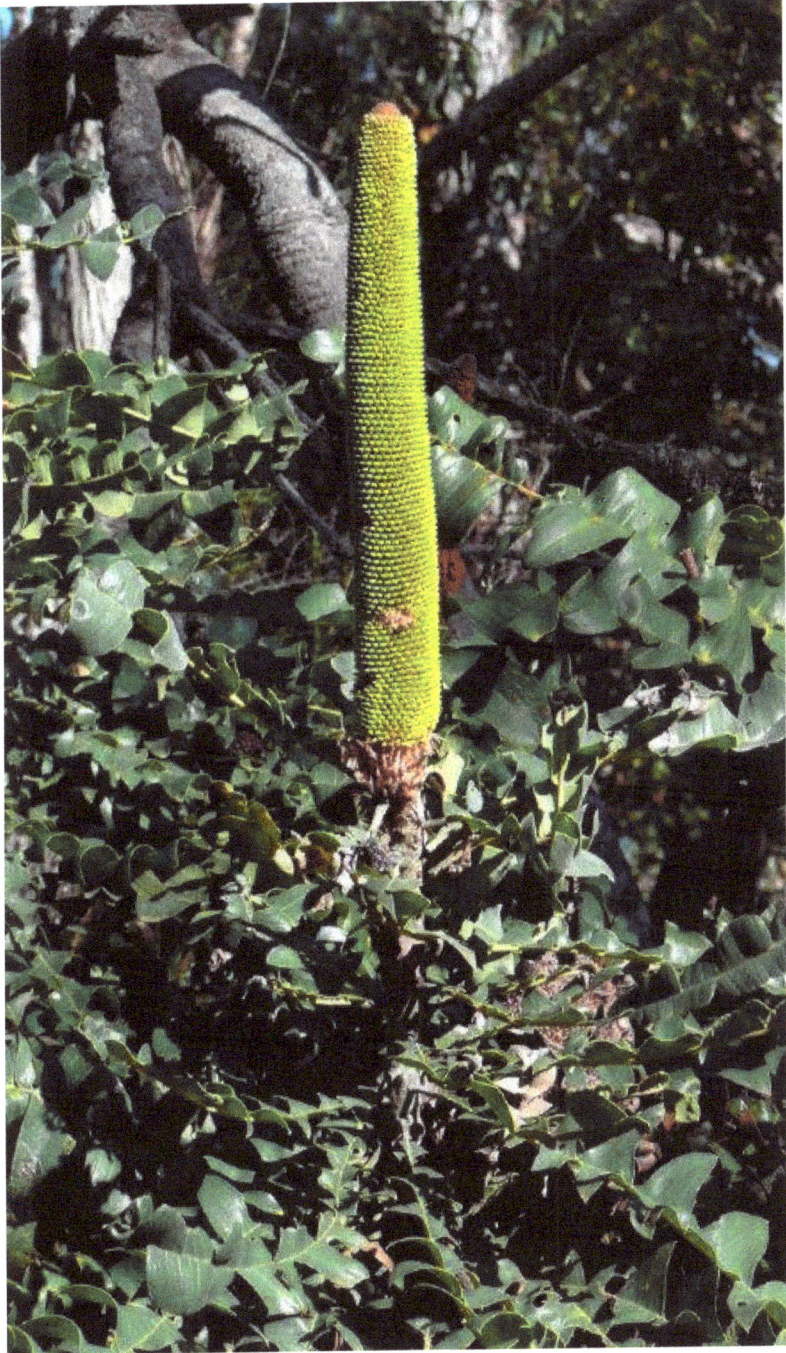

Banksia grandis.

A threat to the jarrah forest, in particular, in the last half of the twentieth century, has been the intrusion of bauxite mining. This has worrying implications for jarrah regrowth. As Roger Underwood points out, one of the weaknesses of the former *Forests Act of 1918* was that it was 'made subservient to the *Mines Act*'. In fact, Lane Poole, who drafted much of the bill for that act, was obliged to include that provision, because if he had not done so, the bill would not have been passed by Parliament. The effect of mining in the jarrah forest, as Roger Underwood sees it, is that much of the jarrah forest now looks more like a plantation.

> *The bauxite miners don't just only clear away the forest. They remove the forest soil completely to a depth of several metres and what is left is the sub-soil, the impermeable clay, over which they lay a little layer of topsoil. It is a total destruction of the native forest ecosystem. The areas are replanted afterwards but nobody knows what is going to happen to them. Early growth is as you would expect. They bung them in, give them lots of fertiliser and a fluffy cultivated site and early on they grow quite well. But it is not jarrah forest again. It is a plantation, in some cases and in the early days, made up of pine trees and eastern states eucalypts.*[101]

And, as botanist Neville Marchant suggests, re-growing a jarrah forest is not a simple process.

> *We all know now about eco-systems being so incredibly complex but we don't fully understand them. When they cleared the jarrah, they took the topsoil off and stockpiled it for a number of years before replanting. But they didn't understand the role of the small organisms in the soil, the micro-organisms, the fungi, for example. When you stock-pile soil you lose its structure. You lose that tiny litter layer on the surface and when you expose the soil by bulldozing it and stockpiling it, any fungi that were in that soil may well not survive. So if you're going to replant a jarrah seedling in an area where you have no idea what the soil structure is like underneath, although it's been deep-ripped, it is now in a very different situation and you may very well have failure over a wide area.*[102]

Ecologist Joe Fontaine believes that good research and good public dialogue are both important in discussing all current forest issues.

> *When we begin to talk about managing the south-west forests, it is absolutely vital to actively engage with the community, because at times initial management might look a bit ugly to some people and that can cause angst in the community.*[103]

So what kind of engagement is needed?

> *I think we need to do some sound science: some research to understand what the likely impacts are. We can learn from previous actions and where we might have made mistakes. But we also need to think about some practical management options, work with the community in certain areas, and do some demonstration projects to show these things can work.*[104]

Sitting on a fallen jarrah tree, Joe comes back to the need to manage fire carefully.

> *There is now quite an emphasis on burning the forest frequently and extensively. The stand where we are now is probably at a point where it is very susceptible to fire. If we burn it using prescription burning, it might cause more harm than good. So we need to re-think where to place burns on the landscape.*[105]

Joanna Young shares that concern.

> *Prescribed burning, not only of production forest areas but also of the conservation estate, was often portrayed as 'very mild fires trickling around in the understorey of the jarrah forest'. Foresters dominated fire policy development in CALM and started prescribed burning very widely, although the practice had been primarily developed in the jarrah forest.*
>
> *That was the image that was often portrayed about how prescribed burning works. But you can't apply that model universally. When you deal with higher rainfall areas, including swamps which accumulate aerated fuels, peaty communities, granite outcrops, tingle, karri, heaths and coastal woodlands, and start trying to burn them about every seven*

*years in the spring, you are going to change the species composition in
those communities. There are real risks to biodiversity when bureaucrats
prescribe blanket prescriptions and don't take on board local knowledge of
the values being managed.*[106]

Fellow botanist Neville Marchant also stresses the risk of
losing diversity through excessive and hot fire.

*We know a lot about forest ecology now but managing a forest to produce
timber is a very different issue from managing to ensure attractive wildflowers and diversity. And while a lot has been written in the past
suggesting that unburnt areas are poor in flora, that is not my experience.
There are different species. They may look overgrown and heavy with
litter but they present a different suite of species from a regularly burnt
area. And if there is too much burning in some ecosystems then you don't
get replenishment, you get a real change in ecosystems.*[107]

Neville believes that, where flora is concerned, too much
reliance is sometimes placed on the efficacy and necessity of burning.

*You can see examples in Melville in Perth or Applecross where a garden
has been established since the 1950s or 1960s. There are enormous grass
trees there which flower without fire. So it is not necessary to use fire to
induce lots of flowering. If you do induce flowering by lots of fire, by this
disturbance, you could actually cause a huge imbalance.*[108]

An imbalance not always immediately apparent.

*Over the years people have said you need a fire. Three or four years after
a fire it looks wonderful. All the flowers come up. It looks all fresh and in
a way it is rejuvenated. But I don't know whether it is necessarily a good
thing. It may well be that you quickly have a fantastic show of orchids.
But I believe that diversity is actually achieved by natural selection.*[109]

Professional forester Des Donnelly holds another view about
where the threat to diversity lies.

*Ultimately, if we don't put fire into our national parks and burn them
under cool conditions, they will burn under severe conditions and we will*

gradually lose the biodiversity that they hold. We have got to use it as a tool to manage our forests and our bushland areas for the good of the flora and fauna. History tells us that the land was burned on a regular basis and we have to work out how we can do that effectively.[110]

On the other hand, Neville Marchant believes that human intervention, whether European or Aboriginal, is only a part of that story and that our floral history is both very ancient and complex.

One thing we have to remember is that, if Aboriginal people have been here for 40, 50, or even 60–70,000 years, that is only a fraction of the time frame of the evolution of our south-west flora. Western Australia has been isolated from eastern Australia for 50 million years. That is a long isolation and we're looking at five, six or seven million years for the evolution of lots of our species. So our flora evolved well before Aboriginal controlled burning.[111]

However environmental historian Sylvia Hallam suggests that, despite that lengthy evolution, WA flora may well have been

Post-fire National Park, 2015.

modified by Aboriginal fire regimes. Given that they probably burned the country for 30,000 years, there have been:

> ...*long-established vegetation effects. Botanical work has long indicated that most of our 'virgin' bush is fire climax vegetation and that Aboriginal firing of the bush must have been an important factor in the establishment and maintenance of this vegetation pattern.*[112]

Dr David Ward, who has made a special study of the impact of fire on forest environments, believes that we could and should learn from Aboriginal fire management practices. 'It would be difficult here to reintroduce Nyungar fire but I think it could be done and I think eventually it must be done. It is the only way we can manage'.[113] He recalls an occasion on which he spoke to a group of Nyungars about fire management:

> *A lot of them kept quiet. One old lady listened patiently to me explaining, from the work I had done, that I believed that the jarrah should be burnt every three or four years. And she sat and listened patiently and at the end she said, 'Why are you telling us what we know already'. And there were smiles around the table.*[114]

But Joe Fontaine, looking at what is generally described as the northern jarrah forest, questions whether what might be good for jarrah might not always be appropriate for the overall forest context.

> *We are seeing here in the forest the three dominant tree species: jarrah, marri, and casuarina (sheoak). But in the jarrah forest there are something like 800 species of plants. The bio-diversity is in the understorey. We need to think very carefully about that and look at the sensitivity of some of these groups of plants; their ability to cope with fire, different frequencies of fire, susceptibility to drought and so on. The bush environment is more than just the trees.*

These diverse views on how we should manage the unique forests of south-western Australia suggest that none of us have yet fully understood the complexity of our distinctive ecosystem.

Our efforts to manage our forests are thus likely to be based on incomplete knowledge of exactly what we are dealing with. Moreover, as humans, we have only been here for a tiny fraction of the slow evolution of our ancient continent. As Katinka Ruthrof suggests, this is not an issue for scientists alone.

> *There is so much that we don't know about our ecosystems. There is so much that we can learn about ourselves, about our community, about our relationships through these forests and I think that is an opportunity that we shouldn't miss. Given the gap that seems to be ever increasing between humans and their environment, we all need to reach out to managers, to policy makers, the community and Indigenous communities. We need to share our knowledge.*[115]

The edge of the jarrah forest.

Chapter 6

When do we get it?

As human beings we have to remember and acknowledge that we are all here on a journey. We are passing through this land and our sole role is to look after it, preserve it and hand it back to a younger generation the way we found it.

Wadjellas (whitefellers) have also got to 'get it'. If they don't, all they will see is destruction through mining, trees being cut down and fires increasing. What is happening to our environment is because people are not getting it.[1]

Koodah Cornwall, otherwise known as Terry Cornwall ('people know me as 'Koodah', which means 'mate–friend') was born in Wagin, which got its name from the (Waitch) emu, and a little bird the (robin red breast) in the south-west of Western Australia. He now works and lives near Pinjarra at Fairbridge Village, a non-government centre that aims to create opportunities for young people to find meaning in life, appreciate their heritage and live harmoniously with the environment.[2]

I teach them about our ancient Aboriginal culture and help them understand the importance of the environment that we live in. Mother Earth doesn't see colour. She just needs to be respected and understood because she provides for all our needs. We humans all need to care for her for the future of the human race.[3]

In previous chapters we've looked at environmental issues of varying complexity that have faced nineteenth- and twentieth-century arrivals to our shores. Some are stories about partial repair and rehabilitation. These 'success stories' result from the commitment of individuals and communities affected by the economic impact and environmental degradation of problems such as salinity and water pollution. Other challenges, such as protecting our forests, appear more difficult to deal with, especially in the context, that most of us now accept, of a changing climate, a drier south-west WA and less predictable seasons. In these circumstances is it less likely that we can, in Koodah's words, 'hand the land back' in good condition?

We now need to examine more closely the changed circumstances in which we find ourselves and consider carefully how we might cope with them. The issues under review are not necessarily solely environmental but are also closely tied to social perspectives and changing ways of living. Nor are they confined to life and work in rural areas of south-west Australia.

One major shift in Western Australia in more recent times has been a marked change in the way city and country relate to each other, and that change affects the community's appreciation of environmental issues such as climate change.

This is a major concern for epidemiologist Dr Fiona Stanley, Professorial Fellow at the School of Paediatrics and Child Health at the University of Western Australia.

We are losing our relationship with country. As sophisticated citizens of an urban world, we don't think we need that connection. But urban values are not rural values. It is strange because in fact we are still hunter-gatherers in our genetic makeup. Our health and well-being over the next thousand years is going to be determined by a much more intimate earlier relationship with land.[4]

Does this suggest that we are now more likely to be hunter-gatherers at the smart coffee shop in the city or shelf-shopping the vast DIY centre in our nearest suburb? Are we becoming conditioned to ignore our natural environment by so much urban living, as this childhood reminiscence from ecologist Cielito Marbus perhaps suggests?

We lived in a street with about fifteen houses and by the time I grew up all the houses had manicured lawns, and edging around the flower-beds. But there was one couple in the street, two doctors, who had left the native bush as their front yard. Banksias and things like that. I remember as a kid thinking it was ugly, partly because of what all the adults around me said about it. They all complained about this one house. They said, 'This street would look so nice if it wasn't for the doctors' garden. Why don't they sort it out? They are so lazy'. Then someone else bought the house, cleared out all the banksias and planted palm trees. And everyone loved it. I look back now and I just think that is really tragic that this 'neatness' is our perception of what a garden should be.[5]

Cielito's story also suggests a not uncommon sense of alienation from the natural vegetation of the continent we proudly claim to be part of and proud of, even if many of us no longer live alongside native shrubs and trees in our ever-expanding cities. Former farmer Chris Evans reminds us that for Western Australians, this divorce from the country is a relatively recent occurrence.

My brother was at boarding school in the 1960s and we would drive down to watch him play football and, as we were driving up and down the Brookton Highway, you would see people parked on the side of the road, mushrooming, and I think there was a sense that the bush and farmed country were easier to access. The rural areas weren't far out of Perth. Wanneroo was all market gardens. Middle Swan was all market gardens, wine and orchards. So our rural areas were very close to the city.[6]

Damien Postma, CEO of the South West Catchments Council, also sees that city/country 'disconnect' as coming at a cost.

One consequence of intense urbanisation is a 'disconnect' from the environment and a lessening of its importance in the minds of many. People in places like Perth can now spend months on end without ever getting out of their local suburb and their local environment. Thus their appreciation of the value of natural areas reduces, and that is then reflected in politicians' views and priorities.[7]

Urban Planner Peter Ciemitis is conscious of the need for governments to pay more attention to the provision of trees and green spaces and help our urban areas relate more closely to nature.

The increased urbanisation and suburbanisation of our cities brings with it a continuing loss of tree cover. And we are not just talking about removal of natural tree cover. People are often unwilling to replace tree cover, whether in streets or parks or on their residential properties. It seems to be something that is happening in parallel with urbanisation, this particular feature of 'arborphobia'.[8]

Denmark River estuary.

Arborphobia, in effect, means not just a fear of, but also a dislike of, big trees. Peter Ciemitis believes that this particular 'phobia' is often rationalised as a justification for removing a tree because it is seen as a safety risk, with a chance of someone, or something, being hit by a falling limb. Sometimes a tree is also seen as a 'litter bug', dropping twigs and leaves.

> But it seems that there is a somewhat deeper feeling that trees no longer have relevance in people's day-to-day lives and that they see trees, not as an attractive contribution to their surroundings, but almost something that transgresses against the sense of their own space or street. 'Wouldn't it be much cleaner if streets all had nice straight lines and no trees to mess them up?'[9]

But how might the presence of trees compensate for their homicidal tendency to drop limbs onto the heads of passing residents or making a mess of suburban streets? Peter sees vegetation as potentially playing an increasingly important role in a concrete- and bitumen-dominated environment. 'The urban "heat island" effect is one of the biggest impacts we are going to see in the evolution of our cities, particularly associated with climate change'.[10] Wealth and health may well go together here.

> It is universal code that a 'leafy suburb' means a wealthy suburb. But it is also a healthy, wealthy suburb and carries other infrastructure and economic compensations. The presence of canopy cover and thus abundant shade over streets significantly reduces the rate of degradation of bitumen road surfaces. Bitumen is a material that degrades very quickly in a heat wave and if you can reduce heat on a road surface, then evaporation and degradation significantly decline.[11]

And while science tells us that road heat might decline under tree cover, contentment with an arboreal sunshade might well increase personal well-being. Peter Ciemitis invokes a 'happiness factor' here.

I know, myself, from walking in parts of Perth's central area, that there are sections of walkable links that, despite great aesthetic design qualities, don't have the same quality of life if they lack the shady presence of trees. When you move from one of those spaces to an area with trees and grass, you immediately feel intrinsically happier walking through these spaces. Anecdotally we see a greater conviviality within those spaces. You can see it for yourself when you move around in them. You see more smiles on people's faces. Areas of 'green' possess a quality that is important to our happiness and our spiritual response to city life.[12]

Peter also identifies trees with improving the starker surroundings of urban life.

In a tree-canopied urban street one immediately experiences two things. Firstly the presence of the trees diminishes the sense of the scale of the buildings. It doesn't matter whether they are three or thirty storeys. Space starts to become defined by the presence of trees. Secondly, they add another sound element to the streetscape. The sound of leaves in a light breeze creates a masking background that diminishes your awareness of traffic.[13]

Royal Street, East Perth.

The recent spread of housing estates in Perth, and even in major south-west country towns, has not always been accompanied by the spread of or retention of trees. Peter Ciemitis suggests that we have a long way to go.

> But that is not to say that authorities do not recognise the benefits trees confer. The problem often lies in the impact of many well-meaning policies, standards, practices that necessitate either the removal of trees or the decision not to include trees in particular spaces. These may be things like simply the need to keep a safe distance from a kerb line because a high proportion of accidents happen where trees are close to kerbs.
>
> That rule usually applies to roads, not so much to streets, but often we take those rules from highway design and apply them to local streets. And so, even in local streets, trees are not planted because the only available space is very close to the kerb.
>
> However there is a lot of evidence to suggest that if you plant trees along a street you diminish accident rates by introducing what is known as 'friction': a sense of risk, a sense of enclosure which makes motorists slow down, take more account of their immediate environment and moderate their behaviour in tree-lined streets.[14]

Woodvale subdivision 1988 – trees retained.

When new suburbs are planned, he believes, developers are increasingly sympathetic to the inclusion of trees and tree cover. 'They certainly try to retain trees wherever they can'. However Peter singles out building contractors for criticism here.

> *The practice we see today of almost total clearing of land for housing estates isn't now driven by developers. They tried to retain tree cover on the blocks they sold. That made sense. It is also much cheaper to retain trees where they grow on natural slopes than spend several months pushing mountains of soil around, and building retaining walls etc.*
>
> *However, the home-building industry has adopted a total clearing practice because it delivers flat sites for the construction of cheaper homes. And of course the community has called for cheaper homes because they can get more space and more product for their money.*[15]

Damien Postma believes, however, that authorities do now look beyond social interaction requirements when they are laying out a new suburb.

> *Historically urban planning was considered to be a social science because it was about social geography: how to lay out a suburb well for good social interaction. But now it is recognised that interaction with the environment,*

Contemporary land development practice.

including water flows and increased proximity to native vegetation, to habitat for wildlife, is equally important.[16]

Living and working in Bunbury, Damien Postma also notes that Perth people, while they love to visit the south-west, sometimes fail to understand the special challenges of rural life and the nature of this more natural environment; a failure with importance consequences, because:

It is in the cities that a lot of big decisions are made about how our state runs. That then leads to increased urbanisation and a 'disconnect' from the environment and its importance in people's lives.[17]

Any 'disconnect' between city and country also hinders people from understanding the special challenges that face farmers, foresters, water managers and others who earn their livelihood in rural areas. Because most of us live in larger communities we are not always aware of the predicaments smaller places, country towns or settlements within the landscape of south-west WA, often face. Sometimes on our travels we might pass a lonely 'village hall' almost surrounded by bush, an abandoned homestead or a disused tennis court, indicators of a once-thriving farming community.

Abandoned farmhouse.

While the south-west of the state has become popular for city dwellers wanting a few hectares as a weekend hideaway or hobby farm, the number of long-established farmers on the land has been declining for some time. As Dr David Pannell reminds us:

> *I think we are observing a continual trend. The wheatbelt in particular is becoming a less populated environment. That means that a farmer now has fewer neighbours and those neighbours can live some distance away.*[18]

Variations in international demand, fluctuating prices, a less predictable climate, increased fuel, machinery and fertiliser prices and land degradation, not to mention the provision of good education for their children, all drive an imperative 'to get big or get out' as Dr Henry Schapper, agricultural economist at the University of Western Australia, famously told farmers back in 1970.

Vic Rodwell, a dairy farmer on the coastal plain near Bunbury, is one primary producer driven by economics to get bigger.

> *Farming has greatly changed. When my father farmed here, when I first came home, we were milking forty cows on the home farm. That was before we bought the neighbours' place and leased the land across the road. We got up to three hundred on the same dirt.*[19]

Many other farmers have 'got out', but getting out can be accompanied by very difficult emotional responses and stark challenges. Mike Quartermaine, a fifth-generation Katanning farmer, who is still adopting new methods of land care, is now involved in assisting other farmers, not necessarily in the traditional role of helping a sick neighbour, for example by getting his harvest in for him, but rather dealing with issues beyond the paddock, and not just physical problems. The most stressful issue may well be leaving land that has been in the family for generations.

> *The biggest mental health issue for farmers is that they feel they become nothing without the farm. And that's why some farmers leave it too long before they get out of farming. It's the biggest psychological hurdle they*

have to overcome. They always hope that next year will be better. The warning bells are ringing but they don't want to listen because they think, 'Who am I if I'm not a farmer?' Those who have made a good transition from farming are the ones who have been open to the notion of 'That's the end of one life. This is a new life. The old life has gone'.

But some ask, 'How can I get a bit of my old life along with the new life, like keeping the home block or the farm house?' Well, the answer is none, or very little. You need a special ability to stand back, not reflect on the old, and embrace the new.[20]

Sometimes, thinking that they have to make a clean break:

...farmers feel that they have to cut themselves off from the old life and surroundings completely and move to the coast, when really if they stayed in their community, they could pick up more work than they believe is possible. They've been told that they're not qualified for anything other than farming but they're qualified for lots of things. It's important for them to know that there are other lives, other ways of making a living.[21]

Environmental Sociologist Angela Wardell-Johnson, from the School of Social Sciences at the University of the Sunshine Coast, has spent time with economists and farmers looking at the profitability of farming.

Farmers have an attachment to landscape and to place, as well as to the communities they belong to. That attachment transcends economic viability. In fact, if you look at the economics of any farming enterprise, viability is not what drives whether or not farmers stay on farms. They stay there because they have a very strong attachment to place.

They also have a strong attachment to their community because a sense of place is driven by social relationships as well as landscape. Their sense of belonging and connectedness to that place absolutely transcends the economics of farming. So people don't lose farms, they give them up only if they have to, and economics don't drive that decision.[22]

Former farmer Chris Evans now works for *Beyond Farming*, an organisation set up to help farmers who need to, or want to, leave the land. He has found that tradition is also a strong influence in decision making.

There is a strong psychological connection to the land you have farmed. And it draws not just from your association with the land and its environment but also the family history. Many farming families have this sixty-, seventy-, eighty-year tradition of farming. So you draw a lot of beliefs and values from that history. 'Grandad always said that paddock was good for wheat but not for barley'. That intrinsic knowledge of the land, of the capacity of each paddock. 'Don't put sheep in that paddock in case the wind swings around when they have been shorn and there's a cold snap. Grandad lost a hundred sheep in there one day'.[23]

When farmers either leave or lose farms, the community loses too. Chris Evans sees this as a loss of social capital, and it doesn't affect farmers alone.

A lot of people who leave farming, but don't intend to retire, stay in rural or regional areas. But you can't rely on agriculture or farming to employ these people. You have to have allied industries and non-farm businesses in those centres to develop an economic strength that works hand-in-hand with social development. The biggest thing that our small farming communities are up against is the depletion of social capital.[24]

Social capital is depleted when the population of rural areas declines. There are fewer people in the landscape, fewer people to provide local services and fewer people to make up sporting teams and organise events like the annual agricultural show.

Social capital is directly linked to economic viability, and that is the biggest problem in rural areas. Banks have pulled out of small towns. So you lose a bank manager, and probably an accountant. When families with children leave school numbers drop. So you lose school teachers. You also lose diversity of ideas and thinking. A bank manager would come into a town and develop his network, become treasurer of the bowling club etc. We had a bank manager who stayed for years in Brookton. He became friends with his clients. So when they came in for a loan, he'd say, 'As a bank manager I would say "yes"; as a friend I would say "no, don't do it"'. And that was important because he stopped people from over-committing themselves. And many rural towns have lost their locally based priests. When farmers or their wives or the family were having emotional or psychological issues, the local priests were often the first stop. They could talk to them confidentially. That's gone in many places.[25]

When Chris Evans himself left farming he pursued a university degree and now helps former farmers faced with leaving the land. In his own case he reflects that he could have had another career much earlier in life but felt tied to the farm by tradition and filial obligation.

I went straight back on the farm from school and it was something that really bit into me. I met contemporaries who had spent five or six years away from the farm, guys I went to school with in Brookton, and they were having really interesting lives. And I thought 'I am stuck on the farm'. It wasn't my first choice. The army was my first choice but Dad intimated that he was expecting me to come back because he didn't have many years left on the farm and my brother needed a hand. I see that situation now with a lot of farmers in their forties and fifties. I ask them, 'Was it your first choice?' And a lot of them say, 'No, it was just expected of me'.[26]

An expectation Chris now turns on its head in his work for *Beyond Farming*. In his case he left agriculture for a variety of reasons: financial pressures, farm viability, the concept of 'get big or get out', and the educational needs of his children; all factors that also face the people he now works with. But Chris suggests that, while resilience in the face of adversity is usually seen as a virtue, it can sometimes be a hindrance to making the right decision.

He argues that while people living in the city might admire the way cockies battle on in adverse conditions, the qualities of self-reliance and stoicism that farmers have acquired through tradition, while admirable, can also be their Achilles heel.[27]

Knowing when to leave, and whether you are doing the right thing by selling or giving up the farm to relatives, is also sometimes accompanied by a sense of guilt. Talking to other farmers I have noticed there is that sense of 'Have I left this to a good steward?'[28]

David Pannell has observed that farmers who stay on the land often experience an isolated lifestyle.

A growing number of farming families are choosing not to live in the farming landscape, but in regional centres or even in Perth. They divide their time between commuting to the farm and living with their families in town and can live quite lonely existences on their own in agricultural areas. Another factor is that labour has largely been replaced by machinery for cropping and ever larger and more efficient machinery, requiring even less labour.

In Australia in 2011, there were 19,700 fewer farmers than there had been in 2006, a fall of 11 per cent in five years. Nationally in the thirty years from 1981 to 2011, the number of farmers declined by 40 per cent.[29] Western Australia is no exception to this trend and there are now fewer people to take care of the land.

Empty landscape.

Simon Smale, who works with Bush Heritage Australia in the Great Southern, argues that that depopulation of rural landscapes probably works against efforts to protect the environment:

Because we can't leave nature to fend for itself anymore. Nature, everywhere around the globe, has to be actively managed if we are going to sustain its values, including biodiversity and the intrinsic values of our environment for our successors. So we need to have people actively working in the landscape, actively managing to sustain those values. Where small farms have been merged into large holdings, there are farmers who manage to work in ways closely allied with sustaining ecological values.

On the other hand, small farmers, whom we might think would be closely connected with their landscapes and doing the right thing, don't always find themselves in a position to do so. Farmers in difficult circumstances find it hard to fence off streams and explore alternative options for land management that might be a bit gentler on the country.[30]

David Pannell agrees, but adds that, 'Without a strong financial driver, there will never be sufficient motivation to do more in the way of land repair'. But he suggests that, wherever economically possible, farmers should aim to derive ecological benefit, if not cash, from improving their patch of country.

Obviously water table management helps. And there is potential for some financial gain from planting and harvesting woody perennials. For livestock farmers, trees offer benefit in terms of shelter from wind. Crops probably suffer more from competition with trees because trees use a lot of water and that is why they are there. But the presence of trees also means that crops growing close to the trees have lower yields.

There are also benefits from reducing wind erosion by planting trees and shelter belts and rewards in terms of biodiversity; encouraging habitats for local wildlife. These are benefits that some farmers value very highly.[31]

Katanning Land Care Centre Manager, Jill Richardson, values land restoration in a human health context.

It's widely acknowledged that there are a lot of mental health issues everywhere, but particularly with farming. It can be a pretty soul-destroying business, as well as a hugely rewarding business. Wherever possible we try to get funding for people to do things on their land. And it's my view that if we can subsidise people who normally couldn't afford to do this work, that will improve their feeling of well-being, because when you get into a difficult state financially you're probably thinking 'well I'd like to improve this bit of my land but I can't afford to'.[32]

Carl Beck, CEO of Natural Resource Management in Albany, suggests that in this context nature and economy can sometimes work together.

It is always hard to figure out the dollar value of land improvement; being able to justify the return on the dollars spent. Take, for example, the money you spend to help fence off a bit of woodland with a Carnaby's Cockatoo flock living in the trees. That might then bring people down to look at that site and spend some money in the local café. It is hard to measure. Without agriculture we won't have anything to eat. But without a good natural environment we won't have a thriving economy either.[33]

Agriculture claimed much of the original forest in the nineteenth and twentieth centuries. However, as Gondwana Link's Keith Bradby notes, 'agriculture and forestry are different cultures and they don't seem to meet that well'.[34] Field and forest, much in contention over two centuries from the beginning of European occupation of Australia, are still literally competing for space. Keith sees the economic drive to 'what passes for efficiency' as a particular threat to the environment.

The current definition of efficiency is to get in quickly, get the crop in and get out again and not worry about the nuances of the landscape. This seems to me to be the opposite of where we want agriculture to go.

The whole country has convinced itself that we are going to become food resource millionaires from feeding the Chinese. However it is a pretty competitive food production world and the inputs in WA are extremely high and extremely expensive. And I think the ever-relentless and remorseless squeeze is forcing our farmers down the line of what is called efficiency.

A particular example was given to me yesterday. There is one property north-east of Albany where the farmer can run a tractor in a straight line, putting in a crop for three kilometres before they have to turn around. They have taken out all the contour banks, all the paddock trees, all the fences.[35]

So is there much effort today to shift the balance between cleared and wooded land? When Keith Bradby looks at the current landscape, his answer is equivocal.

Agriculturally, we still have a moderately viable agricultural system. There are farmers out there who have integrated forestry alleys into their farming system immensely successfully, but the take up by their neighbours is close to zero. However farming is becoming very unviable in large sections of the wheatbelt, because rainfall is decreasing and continuing to decrease. Possibly it has become more viable in the wetter areas because they have become drier and made cropping more viable.[36]

This decrease in rainfall can be attributed partly to climate change but also to the clearing of land for agriculture. There is now clear evidence that declining rainfall is associated with climate change. Carbon storage declined when trees fell to the axe or bulldozer.

Dr Mark Andrich is a research consultant in sustainability (energy, climate and water). He recently conducted experiments which show that rainfall, and thus sustainability, is significantly affected by the clearing of native vegetation.

If you went from 60 per cent native vegetation to 30 per cent native vegetation, you reduced the rainfall noticeably. But if you reversed that from 30 per cent back to 60 per cent of forest cover that might be enough to reverse rainfall decline. But a lot more research is needed to be certain of that effect, and the increase in CO_2 in the atmosphere may change this significantly.[37]

Mark Andrich describes an interesting relationship between trees and rainfall. He suggests that this subject is likely to become increasingly important because south-west WA now receives, on average, less annual precipitation.

Clouds, as they move across a land surface, release rain where there is elevation, provided by hills, and especially mountains. It's called the orographic effect. The land also provides friction. Forested land attracts rain and reduces the horizontal wind speed as cold fronts move across with rain-bearing clouds.

Other factors in attracting rain include the ability of trees to send additional moisture into the air, as well as releasing volatile organic chemicals upwards, a process parallel to cloud-seeding carried out by aircraft. Rainfall data can vary widely from locality to locality but there is strong evidence that woodland areas do acquire more rain than levelled and cleared areas.[38]

Mark adds that it has been shown that uncleared land east of WA's rabbit-proof fence attracts more rain than land to the west under plough or pasture. So more woodland might give us more rain.

If one farmed carefully, and there are farmers who do, you would whack your GPS on the header, work out which soil types you'd make good money from and which ones you wouldn't. And given your soil mosaic, you could probably put about 30 per cent of the farm back to bush and still be better off, especially if you focus your efforts and input costs on the better soil. And there are good people in the wheatbelt who have done exactly that.[39]

Landscapes, whether farmed or forested, are inextricably connected. Water, soil mosaics, topography and 'disturbance events' like fire are all factors in the total environment of the south-west of WA. Changes in the landscape can result from natural events such as climate or geological change. They are not necessarily due to human activity. But people have influenced our landscape, not just since the first permanent settlement of

Europeans in Western Australia in 1826 or 1829, but from the time when the first Aboriginal groups arrived on this continent.

A case in point is what we today call national parks. As forester Jack Bradshaw reminds us, these now exist in a very different context.

Often the declared objective of a national park is 'to manage it as it would have been naturally'. But we are no longer in a natural environment. A national park is now a relatively small area surrounded by towns and farms. Allowing a fire to run, for example, might be seen as natural for the original forest but it is not tenable now partly because of the impact on other areas.

So when you talk about 'developing it naturally', do you mean pre-European? Do you mean pre-Aboriginal? Do you mean the 1920s? Do you mean the year 2000? You really have to say, 'Forget about "managing naturally"'. I think the question is: 'What do we want national park management to achieve in the twenty-first century?'

Porongorups National Park and surrounding farmland.

If you can decide what you want from a national park you can develop a management scheme to create it. People are very happy to write a prescription to say, 'Do this, do that'. But it is much harder to get people to divorce themselves from a particular line of thinking and say, 'This is what we want to achieve. This is our long-term goal'. I believe it is the role of government to decide what it wants from a forest and the role of foresters to develop the means of achieving it.[40]

And perhaps it is the role of people in the community to tell governments what they think that goal should be. However it is worth keeping in mind that, as Jack says, national parks are not a 'natural environment'. They are, however, a resource that the public values and, in Jack's view, 'the trees do not have to be harvested for the forest to survive in a drying climate. The forest will survive but changes have to be accepted'.[41] Furthermore, in his view, some intervention is needed to limit the risk of catastrophic fire.

To decide to leave fire to chance is in itself a 'decision'. You need to decide on a specific regime and to recognise that 'no decision' is a decision. For example, if you decide not to burn an area, you are really saying, 'I prefer to burn hot and uncontrolled' than 'cool and controlled', because 'not to burn' is unrealistic. We used to say that our aim was fire protection. The emphasis of fire management is now to maintain biodiversity. That is a relatively new concept, but it is now an accepted fire regime, an ideal to aim for that can be adjusted with experience over time.[42]

Botanist Neville Marchant agrees that we can't 'throw away the key' to national parks.

We now have too many people living too close to these dangerous areas with lots of undergrowth. We are forced into controlled burning and I accept that. It would have been nice to have fenced off some national parks and thrown away the key for a while. But you just can't do it. Roadways alone through these areas bring the incursion of weeds and dieback disease.[43]

Fellow botanist Joanna Young sees time as an important element in developing any forest plan for the future. She asks whether we still have time, when planning, to adapt to changing circumstances, such as a drier climate and other factors.

> You definitely have to have time and you have to be really careful how you view the cumulative effects of repeated and different types of disturbance, whether it be fire, logging or storms. I don't think we often give some of the systems time to regenerate and I think we have to be very careful.[44]

Noel Nannup adds that, where the environment is concerned, we need to be prepared to adapt and to change our thinking quickly.

> We all exhibit the qualities of a listener but do we really listen? Adaptation is a word but do we really hear it? Aboriginal people adapted when the tall ships came and adapted quickly as a matter of survival.
>
> We are all now confronted with a desperate situation on a global scale. So we have to adapt and adapt quickly if we are going to cope with it. And when we are driven by a need for material things we lapse into a false sense of security, hoping that we will be able to invent something that will make everything OK. I can't see that happening soon.[45]

For Fiona Stanley, adaptation is something that more-recent Australians haven't yet adopted in their relationship with their land.

> I think there is a big difference between the long Aboriginal spiritual connection to country and the European perception of land. Even urban-based Aboriginal people are still connected with land in a way that Europeans are not, and never will be. We Europeans are much more likely to damage or exploit land and not feel the same anguish that Aboriginal people feel. And, if we had more spiritual connection to land, I think we would value our adopted home more highly and be less likely to abuse it.[46]

David Worth feels that he detected some movement in this direction when researching his 2004 thesis 'Reconciliation in the Forest?' He noticed:

> *A rise in people saying they didn't have a religious affiliation at the census. One thing that surprised me was that in a 2001 census, people in Augusta, Margaret River and Denmark came out with the highest level in Australia with no religious affiliation. But my sense is that, while in the census they stated no religious affiliation, they are deriving spiritual benefit from being in these environments. I don't think these people are atheists with no spiritual beliefs. They are people who get great value from living in that natural environment.*[47]

The spiritual aspect aside, Neil Burrows argues that, in the forest context, we need a much more informed debate involving a range of values.

> *What we need to do as a community is to articulate or define what we want these forests to do for us. Because ultimately, if the community does not value the forests, we will lose them one way or another, either by benign neglect, or if climate change bites, and parts of the wheatbelt become desert, there will be pressure to clear the forest to grow food elsewhere.*
>
> *So, the community needs to have an ongoing debate about what we want these forests to do for us. And rather than a debate driven solely by ideology or emotion and passion, it should be underpinned by knowledge.*[48]

Knowledge itself raises another issue. While knowledge is an obvious asset it can be 'lost in translation', or perhaps 'non-translation', as Neil himself comments.

> *For example, as an ecologist or as a forester, we have a particular language as all disciplines and professions do. We slip into jargon, accepting that everyone understands what we are talking about. And we think that everybody is equally interested in the forest and as passionate and knowledgeable about the forest as we are.*[49]

Michael Calver relates an interesting anecdote here. It concerns the scientist and film-maker Randy Olson, who wrote a book called *Don't Be Such A Scientist*[50] and later made the film *A Flock of Dodos*[51] capturing a debate between creationists and scientists. He then assessed the impressions of students who had watched the documentary.

> *What surprised him was what the students took away, as the primary message from that film, was the arrogance of the scientists, how dismissive they were of other people, of alternative views and how cocksure they were. The scientists came across very badly. So this, rather than the dishonesty of some of the creationist advocates, was the primary message. And the film had made it clear how dishonest some of the creationists had been in pursuit of their aims.*
>
> *I think there is a very, very strong message there for good communication and a need for genuine humility. There is a need to listen to the other side. It doesn't mean you have to compromise your position or to disagree but the arrogant 'I am right, you are wrong – shut up and listen' does not get anyone anywhere.*[52]

Keith Bradby is not surprised by that student reaction. He is well aware that scientists can use terms that fail to reach people they are hoping to inform.

> *A word like 'biodiversity' still remains a strange term for the mythical 'person in the street' thirty or forty years since it was first coined.*
>
> *You will get much more resonance if you use a word like 'nature' or 'wildlife'. In Victoria recently colleagues were having conversations with the then Minister for the Environment about cattle grazing in the high country. They had been arguing from a biodiversity angle, but when they explained that a big issue in the USA is 'fresh water', a term that everyone understood, they started to get a hearing and a positive result.*[53]

Keith's message is that scientists promoting 'biodiversity' should beware of being entrenched in their own discipline, and the jargon of their profession. They need to use terms that people understand and avoid incomprehensible acronyms.[54]

Murdoch University student Sam Walsham, who is currently pursuing a double major degree in sustainability and communication, would probably agree with Keith. 'I have always been interested in the point where science meets society. Communication between the two is not always the best'.[55]

Studying two separate disciplines, Sam has found that the students in his sustainability classes seem to have little in common with those studying communication and media.

> There is a massive divide between the two groups. In sustainable development the vast majority of students there seem to have a good understanding about global issues and what we can do about them and they understand a lot of the science.
>
> But the moment I switch back into my communications and media group there seems to be an underlying attitude that, whatever the problem is, they can't do anything about it. This is certainly not the case for everyone, but this slightly less optimistic attitude is definitely more evident among the media students. I think if people don't believe that they can make a difference there really isn't any motivation for them to learn about environmental issues. I think if we can address that feeling among people we can encourage a lot more inclusive action.[56]

Sam has taken a practical approach to inclusive action. He has founded an organisation called Sustainability Link[57], which aims to tackle global sustainability issues positively, creatively and inclusively. In addition to an online presence, Sustainability Link offers talks on climate change and sustainability to schools, workplaces and universities. In Sam's words:

> Sustainability Link recognises the unlimited potential for innovation for people of all ages and from all walks of life. The talks and blog aim to inspire ordinary people to investigate how their talents can contribute to effective action, while the presentations can create an initial commitment and provide audiences with effective tools with which to work. Sustainability Link is very much designed to be an introduction to the concept of sustainability and allows people to feel comfortable, but also excited and interested, in exploring the concept.[58]

Sam Walsham, founder of Sustainability Link, talks on climate change.

Forest ecologists from Murdoch University, Joe Fontaine and Katinka Ruthrof, are also talking about 'inclusive action'. They spend a lot of time in fieldwork or, more accurately, forest-work. Joe Fontaine feels that, in order to engage the community in these important conversations on the future of our environment, universities need to spend more time communicating and holding conversations with the public, a view endorsed by Katinka Ruthrof.

Because people are losing connection with the land very rapidly. We have to work very hard to develop those communication skills. It takes a lot of our time because, while there is a wide diversity of people who care for the land, learning their language takes the scientist a lot of time. It is also a two-way street. We learn from working with the community. They invest so much time and energy as well as helping us appreciate what they find important. That is incredibly rewarding.[59]

Joe Fontaine values the experience of discussing key issues with other professionals and on location with forest and land managers.

> You go out together. You come to a place like this. You sit around. You look at it together and you talk about it. It takes time and a lot of energy. But it pays and the dividends go on forever. It takes some instigation and a little bit of luck and the right person to be at the right time and in the right place. But I have seen massive success with this, with people who organise field trips for managers, communities and scientists. A lot of good comes out of that.[60]

Kath Lynch, District Manager with the Department of Water in Busselton, is working to reduce nutrient flow from farms and gardens into the Vasse-Wonnerup estuary. She also believes that a more participative approach is required to achieve change.

> I think it is behavioural science. We are trying to get people to change their behaviour in a logical scientific way. But I don't think we are sending the right messages. We are not giving the right cues. We should be going back to the farmers and asking them what they need and how we can work out the problems together.[61]

From his work as a restoration ecologist, Simon Smale knows that you have to take people with you.

> One of the great challenges for me, and what I love about my job, is that it's managing human relationships as much as land management. Just as you have to get it right in understanding the physical landscape, you have also got to get it right in terms of understanding the social landscape in which you work. If you are off-side with neighbours, if you're not carrying people with you, you won't achieve an environmentally friendly management system. So it is very much a whole of landscape and people approach.[62]

Not just in the paddock. Sharing constructive discussion is important for the whole community. Sam Walsham, whose studies bridge science and the humanities, is critical of the current role that the media plays in scientific debates over issues such as climate change.

If you look at the TV on a morning show like Sunrise, *you often watch a debate where a person who denies climate change is up against a scientist. At the same time scientific evidence has actually moved on from any debate as to whether climate change is real or not. So this debate is meaningless. But nothing makes for better TV than a heated debate. It is good business for a TV station, even though it is an out of date discussion. So I think, to a certain extent, the media encourages that kind of division.*[63]

However, Sam believes that the media, using approaches learnt from the humanities, can help scientists communicate important messages.

Especially when you consider humanities often deal with the consequences of such issues. So perhaps people who work in the humanities field might be able to bring a more human element to the science. If you bring a few more humanity students into the picture, the community could have a much more open and informed discussion about climate change.[64]

For Sam, improving the quality of the climate change discussion is a challenge, but one well worth embracing.

I don't fight for lost causes. I think the people who understand the science, the vast majority of people, approximately 89 per cent of Australians, support a renewable energy target and that is what we need to focus on now. Current technology can also help us solve some of our problems.

I have no doubt that we can avoid disastrous climate change. If I didn't think it was possible or worth the commitment, I wouldn't have spent so much time thinking about it.

I think it is easy to work out the scientific predictions and conclude that action is possible within a reasonable time scale. The moment we change our mindset about climate change and decide we can overcome the challenges, the required actions will follow naturally.

Keith Bradby agrees that the science on climate change is clear but senses that there is little evidence of effective remedial action.

Go down to the jetty and talk to anyone who catches fish about what is happening to ocean temperatures and the fish in our waters. I have been in the Wimmera in Victoria, the Sunshine Coast of Queensland and in Sydney in the last month and everyone is saying, 'Yeah, it is bit weird. It has been consistently dry for the last decade'. I think there is an increasing and widespread understanding that things are changing. Give it another few years and it will hit people with a 'whack'.[65]

While Keith concedes that human beings are resourceful it might take:

The ecological richness of the world 20 million years to recover from what is happening right now. But it will. Whether humans survive is another matter. But I think there is a very strong chance that people will realise the dangers of climate change and take the action necessary to reduce carbon outputs. We are very clever people and there is some stunning technology.[66]

However, Keith is less sure that we have acted in time to avoid the worst.

But will we do it too late? I suspect the horse has bolted. In this century, a two to four degree increase in temperatures is a 'dead cert' and a half to 1.5 metre sea level rise is a 'dead cert'. So whether we are smart enough to hold it at that level is open to debate. And the intriguing question is, will we all say, 'Oh dear, we have been silly. Let's put the smart people who knew this was coming in charge and let them help us mitigate the impacts'. Or will we adopt the classic cycle of getting more and more desperate and doing more and more silly things. That is also a great human tendency. And I fear that one.[67]

One can only hope that Sam Walsham's optimism wins. It could depend on whether people believe individual actions can make a difference.

When you ask me if I am optimistic, one thought comes to mind. The world we have today is really something worth fighting for but the world that we could have, if we were to move towards sustainability, is just simply too prosperous, exciting and rewarding not to fight for. I really believe that. We are going to take the challenges of today, discover the answers and, in the near future, look back and call these solutions our greatest accomplishments.

I think the world that we could have, rather than the world we are trying to avoid, is a concept that really excites me, and that is why I am in this business.[68]

Joe Fontaine, also an optimist, especially about the future of our diverse south-west landscape, places great faith in the benefits that science can bring.

I am also incredibly optimistic. If we can ask some good relevant questions and do some good science, we can get some reasonable traction on providing managers, policy makers and the community of the south-west with actions we can take. These could ensure that these crown jewels of biodiversity continue to be jewels in the future.[69]

Neville Marchant reminds us of that amazing diversity in our south-west ecosystems but questions whether we know how to manage them.

We have got these enormous national parks but we don't know how to manage them because they are so diverse. The Fitzgerald River National Park is just one park but with many different habitats and ecosystems. And you can't just draw a line around some of them. There is a continuum, a change from ecosystem to another.

I took some visitors, heads of Herbaria, down to the Fitzgerald River National Park. We reached the edge of the park, stopped and looked at what was there. We went another kilometre down the road, stopped and looked again because it was so different. If you just drive along it all looks much the same. But if you stop every few kilometres, the suite of flora is unbelievably different. The eco-system is incredibly diverse and the soil is much more complex than we think. We assume it is all sand or gravel. But it is not like that at all. It is a great mosaic of different soils and therein lies the secret of how our flora has evolved.[70]

But has our thinking about the environment of our adopted country also evolved? Koodah Cornwall has challenged non-Aboriginal Australians to 'get it'.

Wadjellas want a place to live. Aboriginal people have been living here for a long, long time. People who have come from other countries want to call this place home. But they don't always accept what the Aboriginal people say and respect their knowledge and what this place means to them.

Aboriginal people have never been anywhere else. They never went to another man's country. This was their country. This was their spiritual connection. They don't argue and fight over other people's country because they have no spiritual connection to another man's country.

Wadjellas have come here to build a place that they can call home. But they want to own something to which they are not spiritually connected. Once they sit down and accept the wrong that has been done to this country, then they will be able to reconcile within themselves and reconcile with the land.

When that happens we can all work together and find our role in mother earth. It is not about blaming people. It is about people taking responsibility for what they need to know and understand so that they can also become carers of the land.[71]

So do we, as Koodah Cornwall has urged us to, 'get it'?

Sam Walsham recalls 'getting it' while still at school and a long way from south-western Australia.

I was in year 11 and we had the opportunity to visit China. We visited quite a few places but one event stands out. We were in Beijing, walking into the Forbidden City and going across Tiananmen Square. We'd got about half way across the square when one of my teachers nudged his colleague. He seemed quite shocked and he told him to look at something, I followed the direction of his finger, expecting to see an interesting building or a famous person. But he was pointing at the sky and the sun.

This was a rare sight, because from the moment we landed in Beijing, the smog was so thick we hadn't seen the sun once. It was almost as if the sun was forgotten in this city until that moment. I just remember standing there and I thought, sunlight travels millions of miles and can incinerate anything that gets close to it. But somehow on our tiny planet, we have the ability to shut it out completely. I wasn't really sure whether I was excited or terrified about that power. But in that moment I realised that we had a choice.

We can use our capabilities and our intellect to build a harmful and aggressive environment or we can build a world that supports our economy and society. I believe we can make the environment an asset rather than a liability. It was once and I think it can be again.[72]

Pemberton in spring.

NOTES

Notes to Chapter 1: More than a single walk

1   C. Darwin, *Journal of the Beagle,* in *The Works of Charles Darwin,* P. H. Barnett and R. B. Freeman (eds), *Journal of Researches into the Countries Visited during the Voyage,* part two, vol. 3, Pickering & Chatto, London, 1986, pp. 535–6.

2   S. Hopper in interview with the author, 19 October 2012.

3   S. Hopper, *Origin of WA Landscapes,* lecture given at the Tattersall and Wilmore Theatre, University of Western Australia, 17 December 2012.

4   *Ibid.*

5   S. Hopper, interview, October 2012.

6   *Ibid.*

7   E. McDonald, B. Coldrick and L. Villiers, *Study of Groundwater-Related Aboriginal Cultural Values on the Gnangara Mound, Western Australia,* Department of Environment, Perth, WA, October 2005, p. 1, http://www.water.wa.gov.au/PublicationStore/first/82492.pdf.

8   *Australia's 15 National Diversity Hotspots,* Department of the Environment, viewed 10 August 2014. http://www.environment.gov.au/topics/biodiversity/biodiversity-conservation/biodiversity-hotspots/national-biodiversity-hotspots#hotspot8.

9   W. E. H. Stanner, *After the Dreaming, Lecture 4 Confrontation,* The Boyer Lectures, 1968. Typescript provided by Australian Broadcasting Corporation Archives.

10   S. Jackson, *Aboriginal Cultural Values and Water Resources Management: A Case Study from the Northern Territory,* 2004. Quoted in *South West Regional Water Plan: Workshops held with the Nyungar Community,* Brad Goode and Associates, report prepared for the Department of Water, Government of Western Australia, Perth, WA, 2008, p. 11, viewed 15 January 2015. http://www.water.wa.gov.au/PublicationStore/first/78932.pdf.

11   *Aboriginal Education, Noongar Towns and their Meaning,* Department of Education, WA, viewed 14 July 2014. http://www.det.wa.edu.au/

aboriginaleducation/apac/detcms/aboriginaleducation/apac/regions/albany/
aboriginal-place-names.en?cat-id=9192388.

12 Craig McVee in *Kojonup, Place of Healing: Encounter*. ABC Radio National,
    Perth, 14 September 2003.

13 Kado Muir in *A Turning Land: Hindsight,* ABC Radio National, Perth, 1997.

14 B. Bunbury, *Unfinished Business: Reconciliation, the Republic and the
    Constitution,* ABC Books, Sydney, NSW, 2001, p. 9.

15 *The Holy Bible,* authorised version, Isaiah 40: 4.

16 C. Von Hugel, *New Holland Journal 1833–1834, 7th December 1833,*
    ed. D. Clark, Miegunyah Press, Melbourne, in association with the State
    Library of NSW, 1994, p. 53.

17 *Ibid.*

18 M. Flinders (ed. T. Flannery) *Terra Australis: Adventures in the Circum-
    navigation of Australia,* Text Publishing, Melbourne, Australia, 2000, pp. 54
    & 56.

19 P. & I. Crawford, *Contested Country: A History of the Northcliffe Area,*
    University of Western Australia Press, Nedlands, WA, 2003, p. 4.

20 J. Mulvaney & N. Green, *Commandant of Solitude, the Journals of Captain
    Collet Barker 1828–1831,* Miegunyah Press, Melbourne, 1992, p. 407.

21 R. Glover, *Plantagenet Rich and Beautiful: A History of The Shire.* University
    of Western Australia Press, Nedlands, WA, 1979, pp. 6–7.

22 J. Bird, *West of the Arthur,* West Arthur Shire Council, Darkan, WA, 1990,
    pp. 13–14.

23 *Ibid,* p. 15.

24 *Ibid,* p. 177.

25 Crawford, *Contested Country,* p. 67.

26 F. Von Mueller, *Report on Forest Resources of Western Australia,* Reeve,
    London, 1879, p. B-(1).

27 Glover, *Plantagenet Rich and Beautiful,* p. 265.

28 L. & G. Fernie, *In Praise of a National Park: The Origins and History of the
    Walpole-Nornalup National Park,* Walpole, WA, c. 1989, p. 14.

29 Gary Muir in interview with the author, 27 January 2014.

30 *Report on the Forests of Western Australia: their Description, Utilisation and
    Future Management,* Western Australia Woods and Forests Department, R.
    Pether Government Printer, Perth, 1896, p. 47.

31 Fernie, *In Praise of a National Park,* p. 36.

32 C. Lane Poole, *Statement Prepared for the 1920 British Empire Forestry Confer-
    ence, London,* Forests Department, Government Printer, Perth, WA, 1920,
    p. 34.

33 O. Robinson in 'Something Unique, Something Majestic: The Karri and
    Jarrah Forests of SW WA', *Talking History,* ABC Radio National, 1983.

34 'Something Unique, Something Majestic: The Karri and Jarrah Forests of
    SW WA', *Talking History,* ABC Radio National, 1983.

35 K. Foulkes, *ibid.*
36 Crawford, *Contested Country*, p. 92.
37 *Ibid.*
38 L. Mumford in 'They Said You'd Own Your Own Farm: Group Settlement in WA in the 1920s', *Talking History*, ABC Radio National, 1983.
39 P. Cross, *ibid.*
40 G. C. Bolton, *ibid.*
41 J. Ricketts, *ibid.*
42 W. N. Clarke, quoted in Fernie, p. 8.
43 E. H. Wilson, quoted in Fernie, p. 47.
44 Gary Muir in interview with the author, January 2015.
45 Edward (Ted) Pickersgill, personal communication to the author, 1993.
46 Glover, *Plantagenet Rich and Beautiful*, p. 274.
47 Keith Barrett in interview with the author, 15 August 2009.
48 Bird, *West of the Arthur*, pp. 409–10.
49 B. Bunbury, *Till The Stream Runs Dry: A History of Hydrography in Western Australia*, Department of Water, Government of Western Australia, Perth, WA, 2010, p. 71.
50 W. J. Lines, *False Economy*, Fremantle Arts Centre Press, South Fremantle, WA, 1998, p. 262.
51 *Ibid*, p. 250–1.
52 John Thompson in *Something Unique, Something Majestic*, ABC Radio National, 1983.

Notes to Chapter 2: 'Two rivers, two plains'
1 A. Hasluck, *Portrait with Background*, Oxford University Press, London, 1955, p. 205.
2 J. R. Wollaston, *The Wollaston Journals Vol. 1 1840–1842*, G. C. Bolton and H. Vose with G. Jones (eds), University of Western Australia Press, Nedlands, WA, 1991, p. 128.
3 *Ibid*, p. 153.
4 Personal communication to the author from Emeritus Professor Geoffrey Bolton, AO, July 2014.
5 N. Ogle, *The Colony of Western Australia 1839: A Manual for Emigrants to that Settlement*, John Ferguson, in association with the Royal Historical Society, Sydney, 1977, pp. 240–1.
6 Wollaston, *The Wollaston Journals Vol. 1*, p. 128.
7 J. R. Robertson, 'Yelverton, Henry (1821–1880)', *Australian Dictionary of Biography*, National Centre of Biography, Australian National University, 1976, viewed 2 January 2015, http://adb.anu.edu.au/biography/yelverton-henry-4898.
8 Wollaston, *The Wollaston Journals Vol. 1*, pp. 122–3.

9   E. O. G. Shann, *Cattle Chosen: the Story of the First Group Settlement in Western Australia, 1829 to 1841*, University of Western Australia Press, Nedlands, 1926 (facsimile edition 1978), pp. 51–3.

10   J. R. Wollaston, *The Wollaston Journals Vol. 2, 1842–1844*, G. C. Bolton and H. Vose with G. Jones (eds), University of Western Australia Press, Nedlands, WA, 1992, p. 165.

11   Shann, *Cattle Chosen*, pp. 10–11.

12   J. R. Wollaston, *The Wollaston Journals Vol. 2*, p. 181.

13   Wollaston. *The Wollaston Journals Vol. 1*, p. 249.

14   R. Jennings, *Busselton: A Place to Remember 1850–1914*, Shire of Busselton, Busselton, WA, 1999, p. 87.

15   Jennings, *A Place to Remember*, p. 273.

16   *South-Western News*, 2 December 1910, cited in Jennings, *A Place to Remember*, pp. 274–5.

17   Shann, 1978, p. 13.

18   *South-Western News*, 7 June 1907, cited in Jennings, *A Place to Remember*, p. 274.

19   S. Slee in interview with the author, 2 December 2014.

20   *Ibid.*

21   T. A. D. Phelan, *A Survey of the Busselton District Drainage Scheme and its future*, 1968, viewed in the State Library of WA: Q627.54 PHE, p. 10.

22   *Ibid*, p. 14.

23   *Ibid*, p. 15.

24   *Ibid*, p. 18.

25   *Ibid* p. 21.

26   *Ibid*, p. 29.

27   C. Tarbotton in interview with the author, 7 November 2014.

28   *Ibid.*

29   K. Lynch in interview with the author, 13 May 2014.

30   *Ibid.*

31   Department of Water, *Vasse Wonnerup Wetlands and Geographe Bay Water Quality Improvement Plan*, Government of Western Australia, Perth WA, March 2010, p. 1.

32   D. Postma in interview with the author 7 March 2014.

33   V. Rodwell in interview with the author, 25 July 2014.

34   *Ibid.*

35   *Ibid.*

36   *Ibid.*

37   Lynch, interview, May 2014.

38   A. Pastega in interview with the author, 14 April 2014.

39   *Ibid.*

40   Lynch, interview, May 2014.

41   *Ibid.*

42 Tarbotton, interview, November 2014.

43 *Ibid.*

44 Lynch, interview, May 2014.

45 *Ibid.*

46 *Ibid.*

47 *Ibid.*

48 Tarbotton, interview, November 2014.

49 *Ibid.*

50 *Ibid.*

51 Lynch, interview, May 2014.

52 *Ibid.*

53 V. Rodwell, interview, July 2014

54 P. Casonato in interview with the author, 28 October 2014.

55 R. Underwood in interview with the author, Perth, 28 January 2015.

56 *Ibid.*

57 B. Ipsen in interview with the author, Augusta, WA, 30 January 2015.

58 *Ibid.*

59 Underwood, interview, January 2015.

60 Ipsen, interview, January 2015.

61 *Ibid.*

62 *Ibid.*

63 Underwood, interview, January 2015.

64 Ipsen, interview, January 2015.

65 Marchant in interview with the author, Perth, 4 February 2015.

66 Casonato, interview, October 2015.

67 P. Lane in interview with the author, 5 January 2015.

68 *Ibid.*

69 *Ibid.*

70 *Ibid.*

71 Casonato, interview, October 2014.

72 *Ibid.*

73 *Information for National Water Week, 2014*, Water Corporation, Perth, viewed 2 January 2015, http://www.watercorporation.com.au/about-us/in-the-community/events-and-activities/national-water-week-2014.

74 *Planning for the Future, Our Ten-Year Plan for Perth*, Water Corporation, Perth, viewed 2 January 2015, http://www.watercorporation.com.au/about-us/planning-for-the-future.

75 *Planning for the Future, Our Ten-Tear Plan for Western Australia*, Water Corporation, Perth, viewed 2 January 2015, http://www.watercorporation.com.au/about-us/planning-for-the-future.

76 Casonato, interview, October 2014.

77 S. Whittaker in interview with the author, 28 October 2014.

78 *Ibid.*

79   Lane, interview, January 2015.
80   Whittaker, interview, October 2014.
81   Tarbotton, interview, November 2014.

Notes to Chapter 3: 'We've cleared the paddock'
1   K. Bradby in interview with the author, August 2009.
2   Landgate (WA) History of Country Town Names, viewed 26 November 2014, http://www.landgate.wa.gov.au/corporate.nsf/web/History+of+country+town+names.
3   K. Bradby in interview with the author, 14 January 2012.
4   *Ibid.*
5   *Ibid.*
6   A. Chapman in interview with the author, 18 December 2012.
7   *Ibid.*
8   *Ibid.*
9   *Ibid.*
10   *Ibid.*
11   *Ibid.*
12   *Ibid.*
13   *Ibid.*
14   P. Luscombe interviewed by the author, 'Taking Down the Fences', *Encounter*, ABC Radio National, broadcast 4 October 2009.
15   S. Hopper in interview with the author, 19 October 2012.
16   *Ibid.*
17   M. Soule speaking at Nowanup, 2006.
18   S. Leighton interviewed by the author, 'Taking Down the Fences', *Encounter*, ABC Radio National, broadcast 4 October 2009.
19   *Ibid.*
20   A. Brandenburg interviewed by the author, 'Taking Down the Fences', *Encounter*, ABC Radio National, broadcast 4 October 2009.
21   Luscombe, 'Taking Down the Fences', broadcast 4 October 2009.
22   Hopper, interview, October 2012.
23   Bradby, interview, January 2012.
24   Leighton, 'Taking Down the Fences', broadcast 4 October 2009.
25   Bradby, interview, January 2012.
26   S. Smale interviewed by the author, 'Taking Down the Fences', *Encounter*, ABC Radio National, broadcast 4 October 2009.
27   Bradby, interview, January 2012.
28   Hopper, interview, October 2012.
29   D. Pannell in interview with the author, 14 December 2012.
30   Bradby, interview, January 2012.
31   *Ibid.*

32   *Ibid.*

33   *Ibid.*

34   S. Dennings interviewed by the author, 'Taking Down the Fences' *Encounter*, ABC Radio National, broadcast 4 October 2009.

35   *Ibid.*

36   K. Vaux, 1980. Quoted with permission of the author.

37   Dennings, in interview with the author, 16 January 2012.

38   *Ibid.*

39   *Ibid.*

40   *Ibid.*

41   *Ibid.*

42   Bradby, interview, 2012.

43   *Ibid.*

44   *A Report on the Fitzgerald River Reserve*, Environment Protection Council, EPA Library No. 502. 72EPC., pC6/A57, n.d., p. 11.

45   R. Erickson, *The Drummonds of Hawthornden*, Lamb Paterson, Perth, 1969, p. 116.

46   *Ibid.*

47   Canadian Biospheres Association website, viewed 7 March 2015, http:// biospherecanada.ca/en/.

48   FBG Fitzgerald Biosphere Group website, http://www.fbg.org.au/about. aspx.

49   A. Sanders in interview with the author, 21 December 2012.

50   *Ibid.*

51   George Seddon interview with Robyn Turner, *Country Hour*, ABC Rural, 14 March 1986. Copy in Fitzgerald Biosphere Project Archives F2.

52   Bradby, interview, January 2012.

53   *Ibid.*

54   E. Duyker and M. Duyker (eds. and trans.), *Bruny D'Entrecasteaux: Voyage to Australia and the Pacific 1791–1793*, Miegunyah/Melbourne University Press, Melbourne, 2001, p. 133.

55   Bradby, interview, January 2012.

56   *Ibid.*

57   K. Vaux interviewed by the author, 'Taking Down the Fences', *Encounter*, ABC Radio National, broadcast 4 October 2009.

58   *Ibid.*

59   *Ibid.*

60   *Ibid.*

61   Luscombe interview, 'Taking Down the Fences', broadcast October 2009.

62   S. Smale in interview with the author, 17 December 2012.

63   *Ibid.*

64   *Ibid.*

65   *Ibid.*

66   *Ibid.*

67   *Ibid.*

68   *Ibid.*

69   E. Eades interviewed by the author 'Taking Down the Fences', *Encounter*, ABC Radio National, broadcast 4 October 2009.

70   *Ibid.*

71   *Ibid.*

72   *Ibid.*

73   Smale, interview, December 2012.

74   Bradby, interview, January 2012.

75   Eades interview, 'Taking Down the Fences' broadcast October 2009.

76   Smale, interview, December 2012.

77   Hopper, interview, October 2012.

78   Pannell, interview, December 2012.

79   Bradby interviewed by the author, 'Taking Down the Fences', *Encounter*, ABC Radio National, broadcast 4 October 2009.

Notes to Chapter 4: Salinity – it's always been there

1   C. Beck in interview with the author, 26 February 2014.

2   M. Bignell, *First the Spring: A History of the Shire of Kojonup, Western Australia*, University of Western Australia Press, Nedlands, WA, for the Kojonup Shire Council, 1971, pp. 12–13.

3   Beck, interview, February 2014.

4   R. George in interview with the author, 7 March 2014.

5   L. Coleman in interview with the author, 25 March 2014.

6   B. Best, *Katanning 1840–1906*, thesis, Claremont Teachers College, Claremont, WA, 196? unpublished, accessed in the State Library of WA Q994.12KAT.

7   R. Teale, 'Hordern, Anthony (1842–1886)', *Australian Dictionary of Biography*, National Centre of Biography, Australian National University, vol. 4, MUP, 1972, viewed 3 January 2015, http://adb.anu.edu.au/biography/hordern-anthony-3915/text6009.

8   *The West Australian*, 4 July 1890, p. 3, viewed July 7, 2014, http://nla.gov.au/nla.news-article3135332.

9   George, interview, March 2014.

10   A. Richardson in interview with the author, 26 March 2014.

11   George, interview, March 2014.

12   V. Read, *Salinity in Western Australia: A Situation Statement, Resource Management Technical Report, No 8*, Department of Agriculture, Government of Western Australia, Perth, WA, 1988, p. 3.

13   D. Pannell in interview with the author, 14 December 2014.

14   Read, *Salinity in Western Australia*, p. 4.

15 J. Loneragan, 'Teakle, Laurence, John Hartley (1901–1979)', *Australian Dictionary of Biography*, National Centre of Biography, Australian National University, 2002, viewed 16 January 2015, http://adb.anu.edu.au/biography/teakle-laurence-john-hartley-11833.

16 Read, Salinity in Western Australia, p. 4.

17 G. C. Bolton, *Spoils and Spoilers: A History of Australians Shaping Their environment*, 2nd edition, Allen and Unwin, North Sydney, 1992, p. 138.

18 Read, *Salinity in Western Australia*, p. 4.

19 George, interview, March 2014.

20 P. Webse, *A History of the Katanning-Nyabing District*, typescript photocopy, State Library of WA, 1958, p. 23.

21 *Ibid.*, quoting letter from Mrs Foulds written to the author, 11 October 1958.

22 R. Anderson (ed.), *Katanning a Century of Stories: A Collection of Anecdotal Short Stories*, Katanning Shire Council, Katanning, WA, 1988, p. 374.

23 *Ibid.*, p. 376.

24 Beck, interview, February 2014.

25 J. Burdass in interview with the author, 26 February 2014.

26 *Ibid.*

27 M. Quartermaine in interview with the author, 25 March 2014.

28 S. Blyth in interview with the author, 25 March 2014.

29 *Ibid.*

30 *Ibid.*

31 *Ibid.*

32 *Ibid.*

33 George, interview, March 2014.

34 *Ibid.*

35 R. Ferdowsian in interview with the author, 7 March 2014.

36 Bligh, interview, March 2014.

37 L. Coleman, interview, March 2014.

38 *Ibid.*

39 *Ibid.*

40 J. Gardner in interview with the author, 24 March 2014.

41 A. Richardson, in interview with the author, 26 March 2014.

42 *Ibid.*

43 *Ibid.*

44 Beck, interview, February 2014.

45 *Ibid.*

46 Gardner, interview, March 2014.

47 A. Richardson, interview, March 2014.

48 *Ibid.*

49 J. Richardson in interview with the author, 26 March 2014.

50 A. Richardson, interview, March 2014.

51 L. Coleman, interview, March 2014.

52 A. Richardson, interview, March 2014.

53 *Ibid.*

54 Ferdowsian, interview, March 2014.

55 J. Richardson, interview, March 2014.

56 A. Richardson, interview, March 2014.

57 Blyth, interview, March 2014.

58 George, interview, March 2014.

59 Ferdowsian, interview, March 2014.

60 George, interview, March 2014.

61 Quartermaine, interview, March 2014.

62 George, interview, March 2014.

63 Blyth, interview, March 2014.

64 Beck, interview, March 2015.

65 Pannell, interview, December 2014.

66 A. Richardson, interview, March 2014.

67 J. Richardson, interview, March 2014.

68 Quartermaine, interview, March 2014.

69 George, interview, March 2014.

70 *Ibid.*

71 J. Richardson, interview, March 2014.

72 Gardner, interview, March 2014.

73 *Ibid.*

74 Quartermaine, interview, March 2014.

75 Blyth, interview, 2014.

76 *Ibid.*

77 M. Pridham in interview with the author, 29 April, 2014.

78 P. Blight in interview with the author, 29 April 2014.

79 Pridham, interview, April 2014.

80 G. C. Bolton, personal communication to the author, 28 March 2015.

81 Blight, interview, April 2014.

82 Pridham, interview, April 2014.

83 *Ibid.*

84 *Ibid.*

85 Blight, interview, April 2014.

86 *Ibid.*

87 Department of Agriculture and Food, *About the Rural Towns Program*, viewed 8 January 2015, http://archive.agric.wa.gov.au/PC_92372.html.

88 Pridham, interview, April 2014.

89 *Ibid.*

90 A. Hicks in interview with the author, 29 April 2014.

91 *Ibid.*

92 Pridham, interview, April 2014.

93   *Ibid.*

94   *Ibid.*

95   Hicks and Blight, interviews, April 2014.

96   P. Webster in interview with the author, 29 April 2014.

97   Pridham, interview, April 2014.

98   Hicks, interview, April 2014.

99   *Ibid.*

100 Blight, interview, April 2014.

Notes to Chapter 5: What are forests for?

1   B. Bunbury, *Reading Labels on Jam Tins*, Fremantle Arts Centre Press, South Fremantle, 1993, p. 212.

2   *Macquarie Concise Dictionary*, The Macquarie Library Pty Ltd, NSW, revised third edition, 2004.

3   *Forest Information, Forests in Australia*, Forest Learning Ltd, 2015, accessed 21 February 2015, http://forestlearning.edu.au/about/forest-information.html.

4   *Ibid.*

5   W. R. Wallace, 'Fire in the Jarrah Forest Environment', presidential address delivered 19 July 1965, *Journal of the Royal Society of Western Australia vol. 49*, 1966, pp. 34–5.

6   G. C. Bolton, *Spoils and Spoilers: A History of Australians Shaping Their Environment*. Allen & Unwin, North Sydney, 1992, p. 35.

7   G. C. Bolton in interview with the author, 8 February 2015.

8   *Ibid.*

9   W. R. Wallace, 'Fire in the Jarrah Forest', 1966, p. 33.

10   M. Calver in interview with the author, 28 July 2014.

11   *Ibid.*

12   *Ibid.*

13   *Ibid.*

14   H. Colebatch, *A Story of a Hundred Years: Western Australia 1829–1929*, Fred W. M. Simpson Government Printer, Perth, WA, 1929, p. 191.

15   *Ibid.* p. 188.

16   N. Burrows in interview with the author, 18 August 2014.

17   *Ibid.*

18   *Forests Act 1918* (WA), long title.

19   *Forests Act 1918* (WA) s. 19.

20   *Ibid.* s. 4, Interpretations.

21   J. Dargavel, *The Zealous Conservator: A Life of Charles Lane Poole*, University of Western Australia Press, Crawley, WA, 2008, p. 67.

22   L. T. Caron, 'Lane-Poole, Charles Edward (1885–1970)', *Australian Dictionary of Biography*, vol. 9, Melbourne University Press, 1983, http://adb.anu.edu.au/biography/lane-poole-charles-edward-7026.

23 M. Roe, 'Kessell, Stephen Lackey (Kim) (1897–1979)', *Australian Dictionary of Biography*, vol. 15, Melbourne University Press, 2000, http://adb.anu.edu. au/biography/kessell-stephen-lackey-kim-10731.

24 F. J. Bradshaw in interview with author, 16 January 2015.

25 *Ibid.*

26 R. Underwood in interview with the author, 28 January 2015.

27 *Ibid.*

28 J. Young in interview with the author, 2 February 2015.

29 G. C. Bolton, *Spoils and Spoilers*, 1992, p. 7.

30 B. Gammage in interview with the author, 6 January 2015.

31 *Ibid.*

32 *Ibid.*

33 *Ibid.*

34 *Ibid.*

35 N. Nannup in interview with the author, 28 January 2015.

36 B. Gammage, *The Biggest Estate on Earth: How Aborigines Made Australia*, Allen & Unwin, Crows Nest, NSW, 2012, p. 167 (originally cited by Gammage as Ward, 2000, n. 11. p. 191).

37 K. Cornwall in interview with the author, 2 February, 2015.

38 Gammage, interview, January 2015.

39 *Ibid.*

40 M. Quartermaine in interview with the author, 25 March 2014.

41 Gammage, interview, January 2015.

42 Calver, interview, July 2014.

43 Gammage, interview, February 2015.

44 E. O. G. Shann, *Cattle Chosen: The Story of the First Group Settlement in Western Australia, 1829 to 1841*, University of Western Australia Press, Nedlands, 1926 (facsimile edition 1978), pp. 51–3.

45 *Ibid.*

46 *Ibid.*

47 *Ibid.*

48 Underwood, interview, January 2015.

49 Burrows, interview, August 2014.

50 *Ibid.*

51 Underwood, interview, January 2015.

52 Burrows, interview, August 2014.

53 *Ibid.*

54 Bolton, interview, February 2015.

55 Calver, interview, July 2014.

56 *Conservation and Land Management Act 1984* (WA), long title.

57 Bolton, interview, February 2015.

58 *Ibid.*

59 Bradshaw, interview, January 2015.

60   *Ibid.*
61   Calver, interview, July 2014.
62   J. Young in interview with the author, 2 February 2015.
63   *Ibid.*
64   Bolton, interview, February 2015.
65   R. Underwood, note to the author, 11 February 2015.
66   *Ibid.*
67   D. Worth, *Reconciliation in the Forest: An Exploration of the Conflict over the Logging of Native Forests in Western Australia*, PhD thesis, Murdoch University, 2004.
68   Underwood, note to the author, 2 January 2015.
69   Bradshaw, interview, January 2015.
70   Young, interview, February 2015.
71   Bolton, interview, February 2015.
72   D. Worth in interview with the author, 29 July 2015.
73   Bolton, interview, February 2015.
74   G. Hardy in interview with the author, 17 February 2014.
75   *What is Phytophthora Dieback?* Dieback Working Group, website accessed 19 February 2015, https://www.dwg.org.au/what-is-phytophthora-dieback.
76   Hardy, interview, August 2014.
77   *Ibid.*
78   *Ibid.*
79   C. Marbus in interview with the author, 14 April 2014.
80   *Ibid.*
81   *Ibid.*
82   *Ibid.*
83   *Ibid.*
84   C. Marbus in note to the author, 19 January 2015.
85   Marbus, interview, April 2014.
86   K. Ruthrof in interview with the author, 15 September 2014.
87   Ruthrof, interview, September 2014.
88   Burrows, interview, August 2014.
89   Underwood, interview, January 2015.
90   *Ibid.*
91   Bradshaw, interview, January 2015.
92   Burrows, interview, August 2014.
93   D. Donnelly in interview with the author, 28 January 2014.
94   Bradshaw, interview, January 2015.
95   Ruthrof, interview, September 2014.
96   *Ibid.*
97   Fontaine, interview, September 2015.
98   Bradshaw, interview, January 2015.
99   Young, interview, February 2015.

100 *Ibid.*
101 Underwood, interview, January 2015.
102 N. Marchant in interview with the author, 4 February 2015.
103 Fontaine, interview, September 2014.
104 *Ibid.*
105 *Ibid.*
106 *Ibid.*
107 Marchant, interview, February 2004.
108 *Ibid.*
109 *Ibid.*
110 Donnelly, interview, August 2014.
111 Marchant, interview, February 2015.
112 S. Hallam *Fire And Hearth Karla Yoorda – A Study of Aboriginal Usage and European Usurpation in South-Western Australia*, University of Western Australia Publishing, Crawley, WA, republished 2014, p. 7.
113 D. Ward in interview with the author, 20 January 2015.
114 *Ibid.*
115 Ruthrof, interview, August 2014.

Notes to Chapter 6: When do we get it?

1 K. Cornwall in interview with the author, 2 February 2015.
2 *Ibid.*
3 *Ibid.*
4 F. Stanley in interview with the author, 28 July 2014.
5 C. Marbus in interview with the author, 14 April 2014.
6 C. Evans in interview with the author, 30 August 2014.
7 D. Postma in interview with the author, 7 March 2015.
8 P. Ciemitis in interview with the author, 12 November 2014.
9 *Ibid.*
10 *Ibid.*
11 *Ibid.*
12 *Ibid.*
13 *Ibid.*
14 *Ibid.*
15 *Ibid.*
16 *Ibid.*
17 D. Postma, interview, 7 March 2014.
18 D. Pannell in interview with the author, 2014.
19 V. Rodwell in interview with the author, 25 July 2014.
20 M. Quartermaine in interview with the author, 25 March 2014.
21 *Ibid.*
22 A. Wardell- Johnson, in interview with the author, 3 July 2014.

23   Evans, interview, 30 August 2014.
24   *Ibid.*
25   *Ibid.*
26   *Ibid.*
27   *Ibid.*
28   *Ibid.*
29   Australian farming and farmers, Australian Bureau of Statistics, 2012, http://www.abs.gov.au/AUSSTATS/abs@.nsf/Lookup/4102.0Main+Features10Dec+2012.
30   S. Smale in interview with the author, 17 December 2014.
31   Pannell, interview, 14 December 2014.
32   J. Richardson in interview with the author, 27 March 2014.
33   C. Beck in interview with the author, 26 February 2014.
34   K. Bradby in interview with the author, 26 November 2015.
35   *Ibid.*
36   *Ibid.*
37   M. Andrich in interview with the author, 17 December 2013.
38   *Ibid.*
39   K. Bradby, interview, November 2014.
40   J. Bradshaw in interview with the author, 16 January 2015.
41   *Ibid.*
42   *Ibid.*
43   N. Marchant in interview with the author, 4 February 2015.
44   J. Young in interview with the author, 2 February 2015.
45   N. Nannup in interview with the author, 28 January 2015.
46   Stanley, interview, July 2014.
47   D. Worth in interview with the author, 29 July 2014.
48   N. Burrows in interview with the author, 18 August 2014.
49   *Ibid.*
50   R. Olson, *Don't be Such a Scientist. Talking Substance in an Age of Style*, Island Press, Washington, DC, 2009.
51   R. Olson, *Flock of Dodos: The Evolution–Intelligent Design Circus*, documentary film, 2006.
52   M. Calver in interview with the author, 28 July 2014.
53   K. Bradby, interview, November 2014.
54   *Ibid.*
55   Walsham, interview, January 2015.
56   *Ibid.*
57   www.sustainabilitylinkonline.com.
58   S. Walsham, personal communication to the author, 17 March 2015.
59   K. Ruthrof in interview with author, 15 September 2014
60   J. Fontaine in interview with the author, 15 September 2014.
61   K. Lynch in interview with the author, 13 May 2014.

62 S. Smale in interview with the author, 17 December 2012.
63 Walsham, interview, January 2015.
64 *Ibid.*
65 Bradby, interview, November 2015.
66 *Ibid.*
67 *Ibid.*
68 Walsham, interview, January 2015.
69 Fontaine, interview, September 2014.
70 Marchant, interview, February 2015.
71 Cornwall, interview, February 2015.
72 Walsham, interview, 10 December 2014.

INTERVIEWS CONDUCTED BY THE AUTHOR, 1983–2015

Mark Andrich
Carl Beck
Philip Blight
Steve Blyth
Geoffrey Bolton
Keith Bradby
Jack Bradshaw
Annie Brandenburg
Joe Burdass
Neil Burrows
Michael Calver
Peter Casonato
Andy Chapman
Peter Ciemitis
Bill Coleman
Lynne Coleman
Fred Collard
Koodah Cornwall
Peggy Cross
Susanne Dennings
Des Donnelly
Eugene Eades
Chris Evans
Ruhi Ferdowsian
Joe Fontaine

Kathleen Ffoulkes
Bill Gammage
Jenny Gardner
Richard George
Giles Hardy
Justin Hardy
Allen Hicks
Richard Hobbs
Stephen Hopper
Bill Ipsen
Peter Lane
Sylvia Leighton
Peter Luscombe
Kath Lynch
Cielito Marbus
Neville Marchant
Craig McVee
Ron Meldrum
Kado Muir
Laura Mumford
Noel Nannup
Darren Orr
David Pannell
Allan Pastega
Damien Postma

Mark Pridham
Mike Quartermaine
Adrian Richardson
Jill Richardson
Jack Ricketts
Olive Robinson
Vic Rodwell
Katinka Ruthrof
Angela Sanders
Sid Slee
Simon Smale
Fiona Stanley
Coralie Tarbotton
Jack Thompson
Phil Thompson
Roger Underwood
Sam Walsham
David Ward
Angela Wardell-Johnson
Peter Webster
Shaun Whittaker
David Worth
Kingsley Vaux
Joanna Young

BIBLIOGRAPHY

Abbott, I. and Burrows, N. (eds), *Fire in Ecosystems of South-West Western Australia, Impacts and Management,* Backhuys Publishers, Leiden, Netherlands, 2003.

Anderson, R. (ed.), *Katanning A Century of Stories: A Collection of Anecdotal Short Stories,* Katanning Shire Council, Katanning, WA, 1988.

Australian cemeteries, *Echuca cemetery,* data provided by the Echuca Cemetery Trust, viewed 9 January 2015, http://www.australiancemeteries.com/vic/campaspe/echuca/echuca_p_data.htm.

Barrett-Leonard, E. G., George, R. G., Hamilton, G., Norman, H. C., and Masters, D. G., 'Multi-disciplinary approaches suggest profitable and sustainable farming system for valley floors at risk of salinity', *Australian Journal of Experimental Agriculture,* vol. 45, pp. 1415–24, 2005.

Best, B., *Katanning 1840–1906,* thesis, Claremont Teachers College, Claremont WA, 196?

Bignell, M., *First the Spring: A History of the Shire of Kojonup, Western Australia,* University of Western Australia Press for Kojonup Shire Council, Nedlands, WA, 1971 (1982 printing).

Bird, J., *West of the Arthur,* West Arthur Shire Council, Darkan, WA, 1990.

Blackwell, T., 'Streets as open space, in then, now, next' *Selected forum summaries from the Planning Institute of Australia (WA),* Urban Design Chapter, 2012–14.

Bolton, G. C., *A Fine Country to Starve In,* University of Western Australia Press, Nedlands, WA, 1972.

Bolton, G. C., *Spoils and Spoilers: A History of Australians Shaping their Environment,* Allen and Unwin, North Sydney, 2nd edn, 1992.

Bradby, K., 'A data bank is never enough: the local approach to Landcare', in Saunders, D. A. and Hobbs, R. J. (eds), *Nature Conservation 2: The Role of Corridors,* Surrey Beatty and Sons, Chipping Norton, 1991.

Bradby, K., 'Gondwana Link – ecological restoration at the scale this country needs', *Newsletter of the Land for Wildlife Scheme,* pp. 17–18, n. d.

Bradshaw, F. J., 'Trends in silvicultural practices in the native forests of Western Australia', *Australian Forestry*, vol. 62, no. 3 pp. 255–64, 1999.

—— 'Is there an ideal stand structure?', summary of presentation given to the workshop on un-evenaged management of native forests at the second research colloquium, ANU forestry, Canberra, 15–16 March 1999.

—— 'The changing face of forest management', an address given to the staff of the Sustainable Forest Management Division of the Department of Conservation and Land Management, Busselton, 2005.

—— 'The legacy of sustenance' in Calver, M. C., Bigler-Cole, H., Bolton, G., Dargavel, J., Gaynor, J., Horwitz, P., Mills, J., and Wardell-Johnson, G. (eds), *Proceedings of 6th National Conference of the Australian Forest History Society Conference*, CD-rom, Millpress Science Publishers, Rotterdam, 2005.

—— 'A century of forest management: management milestones; administrative milestones', papers provided by Jack Bradshaw to the author, January 2015.

Bradshaw, F. J and Rayner, M. E., 'Age structure of the karri forest: 1. Defining and mapping structural development stages', *Australian Forestry* 60 (3), pp. 178–87, 1997(a).

—— 'Age structure of the karri forest: 2. Projections of future forest structure and implications for management', *Australian Forestry* 60 (3), pp. 178–87, 1997(b).

Bunbury, B., *Reading Labels on Jam Tins*, Fremantle Arts Centre Press, South Fremantle WA, 1993.

—— *Unfinished Business: Reconciliation, the Republic and the Constitution*, ABC Books for the Australian Broadcasting Corporation, Sydney, NSW, 2001.

—— *Till the Stream Runs Dry: A History of Hydrography in Western Australia*, Department of Water, Government of Western Australia, Perth, WA, 2010.

Calver, M. and Wardell- Johnson, G., 'Sustained unsustainability: An evaluation of evidence for a history of overcutting in the jarrah forests of Western Australia and its consequences for fauna conservation', in *Conservation of Australia's Forest Fauna*, Lunney, D. (ed.), Royal Zoological Society of New South Wales, Mosman, NSW, 2004.

Carron, L. T., 'Lane Poole, Charles Edward (1885–1970)', *Australian Dictionary of Biography*, Australian Dictionary of Biography, Australian National University, 1983, viewed 10 August 2014, http://adb.anu.edu.au/biography/lane-poole-charles-edward-7026.

Carter, R., *Arresting Phytophthora Dieback: The Biological Bulldozer*, WWF and Dieback Consultative Council, Wembley, WA, 2004.

Colebatch, H. (ed.), *Story of a Hundred Years: Western Australia, 1829–1929*, Fred W. M. Simpson, Government Printer, Perth, 1929.

Copp, I., *Geology and Landforms of the South-West*, Department of Conservation and Land Management, Kensington, WA, 2001.

Crawford, P. and Crawford, I., *Contested Country: A History of the Northcliffe Area*, University of Western Australia Press, Nedlands, WA, 2003.

Dargavel, J., *The Zealous Conservator: A life of Charles Lane Poole*, University of Western Australia Press, Crawley, 2008.

Darwin, C., 'Journal of the Beagle', from *The Works of Charles Darwin*, Barnett, P. H. and Freeman, R. B. (eds), *Journal of Researches into the Countries visited during the Voyage*, part two, vol. 3 Pickering & Chatto, London, 1986.

Department of Agriculture and Food (DAFWA), *Have a Yarn: Talking Salt with Adrian Richardson*, SGSL (Sustainable Grazing on Saline Lands), DAFWA, South Perth, publication number 4, 2009.

Department of Agriculture and Food (DAFWA), *About the Rural Towns Program*, website viewed, 8 January 2015, http://archive.agric.wa.gov.au/ PC_92372.html.

Department of Conservation and Land Management (WA) and South Coast Natural Resource Management, *The Western Australian South Coast Macro Corridor Network: A Bioregional Strategy for Nature Conservation*, Department of Conservation and Land Management/South Coast NRM, Albany, 2006.

Department of Education, *Aboriginal Education, Noongar Towns and their Meaning*, Government of Western Australia, Perth, WA, viewed 14 July 2014, http:// www.det.wa.edu.au/aboriginaleducation/apac/detcms/aboriginaleducation/ apac/regions/albany/aboriginal-place-names.en?cat-id=9192388.

Department of the Environment, *Australia's 15 National Diversity Hotspots*, viewed 10 August 2014, http://www.environment.gov.au/ topics/biodiversity/biodiversity-conservation/biodiversity-hotspots/ national-biodiversity-hotspots#hotspot8.

Department of Water, *South West Regional Water Plan: Workshops Held with the Nyungar Community*, report prepared by Brad Goode and Associates, Department of Water, Government of Western Australia, Perth, WA, 2008.

Department of Water, *Vasse Wonnerup, Wetlands and Geographe Bay Water Quality Improvement Plan*, Government of Western Australia, Perth, WA, March 2010.

Devenish, B., *Sir James Mitchell, Premier and Governor of Western Australia*, Hesperian Press, Victoria Park, WA, 2014.

Donnelly, D., Address to Toodyay Wood Turners, unpublished, 2011.

—— Plantation Forestry in Western Australia, 1918–2013, unpublished, n.d.

—— Ludlow Forest Settlement, unpublished, n.d.

Duyker, E. and Duyker, M. (eds and trans.), *Bruny D'Entrecasteaux: Voyage to Australia and the Pacific 1791–1793*, Miegunyah/Melbourne University Press, Melbourne, 1998.

Environment Protection Council, *A Report on the Fitzgerald River Reserve*, EPA Library no. 502. 72EPC. pC6/A57/8, Environment Protection Council, Perth, WA, n.d.

Erickson, R., *The Drummonds of Hawthornden*, Lamb Paterson, Perth, 1969.

236

Erickson, R., *Rica's Stories*, L. Layman (ed.), Royal Australian Historical Society, Nedlands, WA, 2009.

Fernie, L. and Fernie, G., *In Praise of a National Park: The Origins and History of the Walpole-Nornalup National Park*, L. & G. Fernie, Walpole, WA, c. 1989.

Flannery, T., *The Future Eaters*, Reed Books, Kew, WA, 1994.

Flinders, M., *Terra Australis, Adventures in the Circumnavigation of Australia*; Flannery, T. (ed.), Text Publishing Melbourne, Australia, 2000.

Gammage, B., *The Biggest Estate on Earth: How Aborigines made Australia*, Allen and Unwin, Crows Nest, NSW, 2012.

George, R. J., Clarke, C. J. and Hatton, T., 'Computer-modelled groundwater response to recharge management for dryland salinity control in Western Australia', *Advances in Environmental Monitoring and Modelling* 2 (1), 2001, pp. 3–35.

George, R. J., Clarke, J. and English, P., 'Modern and palaeographic trends in the salinisation of the Western Australian wheatbelt: A review', *Australian Journal of Soil Research*, 46, CSIRO publishing, 2008, pp. 751–67.

Glover, R., *Plantagenet Rich and Beautiful: A History of The Shire*, University of Western Australia Press, Nedlands, WA, 1979.

Hallam, S., *Fire and Earth, a Study of Aboriginal Usage and European Usurpation in South-Western Australia*, revised edition, University of Western Australia Publishing, Crawley, 2014.

Hasluck, A., *Portrait with Background*, Oxford University Press, London, 1955.

Haila, Y., Saunders, D. A. and Hobbs, R. J., 'What do we presently understand about ecosystem fragmentation?', *Nature Conservation 3: Reconstruction of Fragmented Ecosystems: Global and Regional Perspectives*, Saunders, D. A, Hobbs, R. J. and Erlich, P. R. (eds), Surrey Beatty and Sons, Chipping Norton, NSW, 1993.

von Hugel, C. A. A., Clark, D. (ed.), *New Holland Journal 1833–1834 7th December 1833*, Miegunyah Press, Melbourne, in association with the State Library of NSW, 1994.

Ipsen, B., *Follow that Bell*, Bunbury, WA, 2000.

Jackson, S., *Aboriginal Cultural Values and Water Resources Management: A Case Study from the Northern Territory*, quoted in, *South West Regional Water Plan: Workshops Held with the Nyungar Community*, Department of Water, 2004.

Jennings, R., *Busselton: A Place to Remember 1850–1914*, Shire of Busselton, Busselton, WA, 1999, p. 87.

Landgate (WA), *History of Country Town Names*, viewed 26 November 2014, http://www.landgate.wa.gov.au/corporate.nsf/web/History+of+country+town+names.

Lane, J. A. K., Hardcastle, K. A., Tregonning, R. J. and Holtfreter, G. J., *Management of the Vasse-Wonnerup Wetland System in Relation to Sudden, Mass Fish Deaths*, technical report prepared on behalf of the Vasse Estuary Technical Working Group, (DPAW library), December, 1997.

Lewis, H.T., 'A parable of fire', *Traditional Ecological Knowledge: A Collection of Essays*, Johnnes, R. E. (ed.), World Conservation Union (ICUN), Gland, Switzerland, 1991.

Loneragan, J., 'Teakle, Laurence, John Hartley (1901–1979)', *Australian Dictionary of Biography*, National Centre of Biography, Australian National University, first published in hard copy 2002, viewed 16 January 2015, http://adb.anu.edu.au/biography/teakle-laurence-john-hartley-11833.

Lynch, K., Department of Water, CDs, *A Description of the Vasse Wonnerup Wetlands*.

—— *Vasse Wonnerup Wetlands and Geographe Bay WQIP*.

McDonald, E., Coldrick, B. and Villiers, L., *Study of Groundwater-Related Aboriginal Cultural Values on the Gnangara Mound Western Australia*, Department of Environment, Perth, WA, October 2005.

von Mueller, F., *Report on Forest Resources of Western Australia*, London, Reeve, 1879.

Mulvaney, J. and Green, N., *Commandant of Solitude, the Journals of Captain Collett Barker 1828–1831*, Miegunyah Press, Melbourne, 1992.

Obituaries Australia, 'Wallace, William Roy (1907–1981)', National Centre of Biography, Australian National University, viewed 22 February 2015, http://oa.anu.edu.au/obituary/wallace-william-roy-19014/text30617.

Ogle, N., *The Colony of Western Australia 1839: A Manual for Emigrants to that Settlement*, John Ferguson, in association with the Royal Historical Society, Sydney, 1977.

Phelan, T. A. D., *A Survey of the Busselton District Drainage Scheme and its Future*, 1968, viewed in the State Library of WA: Q627.54 PHE.

Poole, C. Lane, *Statement prepared for the 1920 British Empire Forestry Conference, London*, Forests Department, Government Printer, Perth, WA, 1920.

Radomiljac, P., *Those Karri Days, 90 Years Remembered*, Phillip Radomiljac, Bayswater, WA, 2007.

Read, V., *Salinity in Western Australia: A Situation Statement, Resource Management Technical Report, No 8*, Department of Agriculture, Government of Western Australia, Perth, 1988.

Reiner, M., *Cadillac Desert: The American West and its Disappearing Water*, Penguin Books, New York, 1993.

Richardson, A, 'Water Harvesting', conference paper, State Natural Resource Management Conference, Western Australian College of Agriculture, Denmark, WA, 2005.

Richter, D., 'Long-term soil experiments profoundly undervalued', ABC Rural, 23 March 2014, http://www.abc.net.au/news/rural/richter-dan/5332692.

Robertson, J. R., *Yelverton, Henry (1821–1880), Australian Dictionary of Biography*, National Centre of Biography, Australian National University, 1976, viewed 2 January 2015, http://adb.anu.edu.au/biography/yelverton-henry-4898.

Salt, B., 'The Big Picture: The Forces that Are Shaping Our Communities', Critical Horizons: Communities of the 21st Century conference, 14 May 2014, http://www.criticalhorizons.com.au/uploads/3/0/8/2/30820369/bernard_salt.pdf.

Sanders, A. (ed.), *Stories of the Pallinup River and Beaufort Inlet,* Water and Rivers Commission, Coastwest, Coastcare and National Heritage Trust, n.d.

Seddon, G., *Swan River Landscapes,* University of Western Australia Press, Nedlands, WA, 1970.

Shann, E. O. G., *Cattle Chosen, the Story of the First Group Settlement in Western Australia, 1829 to 1841,* University of Western Australia Press, Nedlands, facsimile edition 1978 (1926), pp. 51–3.

South Coast NRM, *Southern Prospects 2011–2016: The South Coast Regional Strategy for Natural Resource Management,* South Coast NRM, Albany, 2011.

Stanner, W. E. H., *After the Dreaming: Lecture 4 Confrontation,* The Boyer Lectures, 1968. Typescript provided by Australian Broadcasting Corporation Archives.

Taylor, J., *Australia's Southwest and our Future,* Kangaroo Press, Kenthurst, NSW, 1990.

Teale, R., 'Hordern, Anthony (1842–1886)', *Australian Dictionary of Biography,* National Centre of Biography, Australian National University vol. 4, 1972, viewed 3 January 2015, http://adb.anu.edu.au/biography/hordern-anthony-3915/text6009.

Underwood, R., *Foresters and the WA forest estate,* unpublished paper given at an international conference on conservation estates, Fremantle, WA. Paper provided by Dr Underwood to the author. January 2015.

—— *An old forester's perspective on forestry in WA: looking back and looking forward,* a presentation to the Centre for Excellence in Climate Change and Forest and Woodland Health, August 2011.

Wallace, W. R., 'Fire in the jarrah forest environment', *Journal of the Royal Society of Western Australia,* 49, 1966, pp. 33–44.

Ward, D. A., *Fire, flogging and measles, nineteenth century land use conflict in South Western Australia,* an essay on human ecology, Department of Conservation and Land Management, January 1998.

—— *The past and future of fire in the John Forrest National Park,* July 2001. Paper provided by David Ward to the author.

—— Time sequence of comments on bushfire by early visitors and settlers, present day farmers and Nyoongar Elders, 2010, Bushfire front, http://bushfirefront.com.au/historical-accounts/a-time-sequence retrieved 18 January 2015.

Ward, D. A., and Van Didden, G., *A Brief Partial History of Monadnocks Conservation Park, Western Australia, Based on Grass Tree Stem Data,* a report to the Department of Conservation and Land Management, February 2003.

—— *A Brief Fire History of the Coolgardie district of Western Australia, Based on Grass Tree Stem Data,* A report prepared for the Department Conservation and Land Management, March 2003.

—— Some notes on fire frequency in the jarrah forest, March 2012. Paper provided by Dr Ward to the author January 2015.

—— Bushfire truth in letters: seven official letters written in 1846. Draft provided by Dr ward to the author, January 2015.

Water Corporation, *Information for National Water Week, 2014,* Water Corporation, Perth, viewed 2 January 2015, http://www.watercorporation.com.au/about-us/in-the-community/events-and-activities/national-water-week-2014.

—— *Planning for the Future: Our Ten-Year Plan for Perth,* Water Corporation, Perth, viewed 2 January 2015, http://www.watercorporation.com.au/about-us/planning-for-the-future.

—— *Planning for the Future: Our Ten-Year Plan for Western Australia,* Water Corporation, Perth, viewed 2 January 2015, http://www.watercorporation.com.au/about-us/planning-for-the-future.

Webse, P., *A History of the Katanning-Nyabing District,* 1958. Typescript photocopy, viewed in State Library of WA.

Western Australian Planning Commission, *Busselton Wetlands Conservation Strategy, Final* WAPC, Perth, 2005.

Wollaston, J. R., *The Wollaston Journals Vol. 1 1840–1842,* Bolton, G. C. and Vose, H. with Jones, G. (eds), University of Western Australia Press, Nedlands, WA, 1991.

—— *The Wollaston Journals Vol. 2 1842–1844,* Bolton, G. C. and Vose, H. with Jones, G. (eds), University of Western Australia Press, Nedlands, WA, 1992.

Wooltorten, S. and Steels, F., *A Sense of Home: A Cultural Geography of the Leschenault Estuary District,* Edith Cowan University, Perth, 2013.

Worth, D. J., *Reconciliation in the Forest: An Exploration of the Conflict over the Logging of Native Forests in Western Australia,* PhD thesis, Murdoch University, 2004.

ACKNOWLEDGEMENTS

The first acknowledgement I want to make is to my wife, Jenny, without whose help this book would not have seen print and ink. Jenny transcribed many of the interviews, checked facts for accuracy, found helpful information sources and continually reviewed the material as I wrote each chapter.

There are many others who helped and you will meet them as you read, but I would like to thank all those who gave me their time and took me to places where we could see the problem and sometimes a solution. Their commitment to tackling environmental issues on their own patch was an inspiration. For a list of everyone I spoke to for this book, see the list of interviews on p. 233.

For background information and encouragement I am immensely indebted to professors Stephen Hopper, David Pannell, Michael Calver, Giles Hardy, Fiona Stanley and Richard Hobbs and, for helpful discussion en route, the late Geoffrey Bolton AO, who pioneered the writing of Australia's environmental history well ahead of me.

I'd also like to thank the following for specialist advice and interview material: Dan Carter, Richard George, Justin Hardy, Richard Hobbs and Mark Pridham for agricultural advice and comment; from the forest, Jack Bradshaw, Neville Marchant, Roger Underwood, David Ward and Joanna Young; and from plain, river and farm, Keith Bradby, Amanda Keesing, Peter Lane, Kath Lynch, Damien Postma, Simon Smale, Wayne Tingey and Angela Wardell-Johnson; and from an urban perspective, Peter Ciemitis and Leisha Jack.

Finally thanks to UWA Publishing, and in particular to Terri-ann White for her considerable help, encouragement and patience in awaiting the last word of Invisible Country.

PHOTOGRAPHIC SOURCES

Page	Source/owner
6	Amanda Keesing
11	Charlie Nicholson
19	Bill Bunbury
20	Jenny Bunbury
21	Bill Bunbury
22	Department of Parks and Wildlife, Forest collection
23	Bill Bunbury
26	Bill Bunbury
27	Photograph given to Bill Bunbury by Tom and Dawn Brittain, 1983
35	Bill Bunbury
39	Bill Bunbury
47	Bill Bunbury
51	Bill Bunbury
52	Bill Bunbury
54	Bill Bunbury
56	Bill Bunbury
57	Bill Bunbury
63	Bill Bunbury
67	Bill Bunbury
70	Airpics courtesy of Gondwana Link
76	Paula Deegan
78	Amanda Keesing
84	Rod Smith (provided by Susanne Dennings)
87	Airpics courtesy Gondwana Link

92	Amanda Keesing
95	Amanda Keesing
97	Bill Bunbury
98	Courtesy Eugene Eades
102	Amanda Keesing
115	Bill Bunbury
117	Jill Richardson
119	Bill Bunbury
120	Bill Bunbury
121	Bill Bunbury
122	Bill Bunbury
126	Lynne Colman
130	Bill Bunbury
135	Bill Bunbury
136	Bill Bunbury
137	Peter Webster
139	Bill Bunbury
142	Bill Bunbury
155	Phil Wyndham (photograph courtesy of Pickering Brook Heritage Group)
162	Bill Bunbury
168	Bill Bunbury
169	Bill Bunbury
172	Katinka Ruthrof
171	Bill Bunbury
175	Bill Bunbury
177	Joanna Young
181	Bill Bunbury
183	Bill Bunbury
188	Bill Bunbury
190	Peter Ciemitis
191	Peter Ciemitis
192	Peter Ciemitis
193	Bill Bunbury
198	Bill Bunbury
203	Airfix courtesy of Gondwana Link
209	Sam Walsham
215	Bill Bunbury

INDEX

www.ingramcontent.com/pod-product-compliance
Lightning Source LLC
Chambersburg PA
CBHW062208270326
41930CB00009B/1678